Thomas Pogge and His Critics

Thomas Pogge and His Critics

Edited by Alison M. Jaggar

polity

Individual chapters © their authors 2010; this collection © Polity Press 2010

First published in 2010 by Polity Press

Polity Press
65 Bridge Street
Cambridge CB2 1UR, UK

Polity Press
350 Main Street
Malden, MA 02148, USA

ISBN-13: 978-0-7456-4257-4
ISBN-13: 978-0-7456-4258-1(pb)

A catalogue record for this book is available from the British Library.

Typeset in 10.5 on 12 pt Times New Roman
by Toppan Best-set Premedia Limited
Printed and bound in Great Britain by MPG Books Group

The publisher has used its best endeavours to ensure that the URLs for external websites referred to in this book are correct and active at the time of going to press. However, the publisher has no responsibility for the websites and can make no guarantee that a site will remain live or that the content is or will remain appropriate.

Every effort has been made to trace all copyright holders, but if any have been inadvertently overlooked the publisher will be pleased to include any necessary credits in any subsequent reprint or edition.

For further information on Polity, visit our website: www.politybooks.com

Contents

List of Contributors

Neera Chandhoke is Professor of Political Science and Director of Developing Countries Research Centre, University of Delhi. She is the author of *The Conceits of Civil Society* (2003), *Beyond Secularism: The Rights of Religious Minorities* (1999), and *State and Civil Society: Explorations in Political Theory* (1995).

Jiwei Ci is Professor of Philosophy at the University of Hong Kong. He is the author of *Dialectic of the Chinese Revolution: From Utopianism to Hedonism* (1994) and *The Two Faces of Justice* (2006).

Joshua Cohen is Marta Sutton Weeks Professor of Ethics in Society, and Professor of Political Science, Philosophy, and Law, at Stanford University. Editor of *Boston Review* since 1991, Cohen is author of *Philosophy, Politics, Democracy* (2009); *Rousseau: A Free Community of Equals* (2010); and *The Arc of the Moral Universe and Other Essays* (2010).

Alison M. Jaggar is Professor of Distinction at the University of Colorado and Research Coordinator at Oslo's Center for the Study of Mind in Nature. Her latest books are: *Just Methods* and *Abortion: Three Perspectives* (co-authored). She recently edited an issue of *Philosophical Topics* on global gender justice and is co-authoring a book on moral justification in circumstances of diversity and inequality.

Erin Kelly is Associate Professor of Philosophy at Tufts University. She works broadly in moral and political philosophy. Her publications include "Criminal Justice without Retribution," *Journal of Philosophy*, and "Doing without Desert," *Pacific Philosophical Quarterly*. She is editor of John Rawls, *Justice as Fairness: A Restatement*. Her recent work criticizes retributive justice and emphasizes collective responsibility.

Lionel K. McPherson is Associate Professor of Philosophy at Tufts University. His publications, which range from ethics to political and social philosophy, include "Normativity and the Rejection of Rationalism," *Journal of Philosophy*, and "Is Terrorism Distinctively Wrong?," *Ethics*. He is writing a book about racial/ethnic identity, solidarity, and progress in an officially post-racial era.

Charles W. Mills is the John Evans Professor of Moral and Intellectual Philosophy at Northwestern University. He works in the general area of oppositional political theory, and is the author of over sixty journal articles and book chapters, and five books. His most recent book is *Radical Theory, Caribbean Reality: Race, Class and Social Domination* (2010).

Thomas Pogge received his PhD in philosophy from Harvard and has published widely on Kant and in moral and political philosophy, most recently *Politics as Usual*. Holding positions at Yale and the ANU, he currently leads a team effort toward developing a complement to the pharmaceutical patent regime that would improve access to advanced medicines for the poor worldwide (www.healthimpactfund.org).

Kok-Chor Tan is Associate Professor, Philosophy, at the University of Pennsylvania. He works in social and political philosophy, with special interests in the topic of global justice. His publications include *Justice Without Borders* (2004), and *Toleration, Diversity, and Global Justice* (2000). He is currently completing a book entitled *Luck, Institutions, and Justice*.

Leif Wenar has degrees from Stanford and Harvard, and is currently Chair of Ethics at King's College, London. His work on international trade in natural resources can be found under the "Clean Trade" heading at wenar.info.

Acknowledgments

I would like to offer my deep appreciation to all those individuals and institutions whose support made this book possible. The project was obviously inspired by Thomas Pogge's groundbreaking work and I am enormously grateful to all the critics who examined this work so closely and who raised so many interesting and important questions about it. I also appreciate Thomas's exceptionally thorough responses. Everyone involved in the project responded extremely graciously to my requests to revise and to meet deadlines and, to those who were asked to hurry up only then to be asked to wait, I apologize for the unavoidable delays. I hope you will all think that the finished volume is worth your efforts.

I'd like to thank the departments of Philosophy and of Women and Gender Studies at the University of Colorado at Boulder for their support. In addition, I'm very grateful to the Center for the Study of Mind in Nature at the University of Oslo, which provided me with a marvelous environment for working on this book. I also greatly appreciate the help provided by the people at Polity, including Louise Knight, David Winters, and Neil de Cort.

Finally, I'd like to thank my family, especially my perennially supportive partner, David.

Alison M. Jaggar

List of Abbreviations

EITI	Extractive Industries Transparency Initiative
FAO	Food and Agriculture Organization
GDP	gross domestic product
GNI	gross national income
GRD	Global Resources Dividend
IMF	International Monetary Fund
IPL	international poverty line
MAA	minimally adequate arrangement
MCA	Millennium Challenge Account
NGO	nongovernmental organization
OECD	Organization for Economic Cooperation and Development
PPP	purchasing power parity
TRIPS	Trade-Related Aspects of Intellectual Property Rights
UN	United Nations
UDHR	Universal Declaration of Human Rights
UNDP	United Nations Development Program
UNCTAD	United Nations Conference on Trade and Development
UNESCO	United Nations Educational, Scientific and Cultural Organization
US	United States
WHO	World Health Organization
WIEGO	Women in Informal Employment: Globalizing and Organizing
WTO	World Trade Organization

Introduction

Alison M. Jaggar

Thomas Pogge is one of the world's most influential philosophers of global justice. His best-known book to date is *World Poverty and Human Rights: Cosmopolitan Responsibilities and Reforms* (*WPHR*). Published by Polity Press in 2002, the book became an instant classic and a reference point by which other global justice theorists situated their work. In 2008, a second edition appeared which included new proposals for pharmaceutical patent reform. The publication of the second edition of Pogge's landmark book provides an excellent opportunity for reexamining and reassessing his ideas.

The authors of the present volume are leading political philosophers from a range of geographical locations and philosophical points of view. They do not undertake their project in the spirit of a *Festschrift*, which looks backward to celebrate an author's achievements; instead, their aim is as much critical as appreciative. In undertaking a reevaluation of Pogge's ideas, their larger purpose is to broaden and deepen the debate over global justice and moral responsibility.

1 A central line of thinking in Pogge's work

WPHR transformed the terms of Western philosophical debate about global justice, especially debate over how the citizens of affluent countries should respond morally to profound and widespread poverty occurring simultaneously with unprecedented affluence. Much of the earlier philosophical debate viewed the existence of global poverty as an unfortunate circumstance either to be regarded as a "cosmic injustice," occurring independently of human action, or to be explained in terms of mismanagement on the part of poor countries. Starting from the assumption that global poverty was a highly regrettable misfortune involving people far away, Western philosophers typically focused on whether or how much the citizens of affluent countries were morally obliged to assist "distant strangers." When the problem was framed in this way, obligations to assist the global poor were typically conceived as "positive" humanitarian duties rather than as the "negative" duties required by justice. Such duties of assistance were often thought to have limited moral weight, since most Western moral thought regards humanitarian obligations as having lower moral priority than obligations of justice. *WPHR* challenges this widely accepted way of framing the issues both of global poverty and of the responsibilities of citizens in affluent countries, offering alternative moral diagnoses both of the situation and of the responsibility for addressing it.

1.1 Global poverty as unjust

Pogge is morally outraged by the occurrence and persistence of global poverty which, he reports, causes one third of all human deaths every year. In other words, he asserts, more than 18 million human beings die annually from preventable causes such as hunger and disease. Of course, many people are outraged by this state of affairs but Pogge's indignation stems not only or even primarily from the scale and enormity of the human suffering involved. Instead, it stems from his view that most global poverty is an injustice whose causes cannot be attributed only to random misfortune, the "backwardness" of poor countries, or the corruption of their leaders. Although Pogge acknowledges that such factors play a role, he argues that their effects are vastly aggravated by the operation of international institutions and policies which interact with national institutions and policies to create a global order that systematically disadvantages poor countries and predictably deprives their citizens of secure access to the objects of their human rights. The rights that remain underfulfilled include but are not limited to the most basic rights of access to the world's natural resource base.

Pogge regards the global order as unjust on several levels. Most obviously, many trade treaties, tariffs, antidumping laws, agricultural subsidies, and intellectual property rights unfairly provide special advantages to wealthy and powerful countries which are already reaping unjust benefits from their violent role in a world history characterized by conquest, colonization, exploitation, and genocide. Even though poor countries typically agree to participate in the present system, Pogge argues that they are often so weak that they have no feasible alternative other than formal assent; moreover, the consent of poor countries' rulers often fails to express the consent of their populations. In this sense, the global institutional order is imposed coercively by precisely those wealthy, powerful countries that benefit most from it. Pogge contends that this institutional order causes direct and severe harm to the citizens of poor countries because it foreseeably results in massive violations of their human rights and indeed makes the full realization of their rights impossible.

In Pogge's view, the harms inflicted by the global order are not only foreseeable; they could also be avoided without a high moral cost. Pogge argues that it would not be difficult to devise alternative institutional arrangements that would be more just and makes several recommendations as to how this might be accomplished.

1.2 Moral responsibility for global poverty

Who is morally responsible for the massive underfulfillment of human rights that occurs in many poor countries? For Pogge as for Rawls, justice and injustice are primarily matters of institutional design. Pogge contends that responsibility for injustice always falls on all and only those who participate in the institutions that constitute an unjust social system. "It is their responsibility, collectively, to structure this system so that all its participants have secure access to the objects of their human rights" (2/e:72). In the world as it presently exists, national societies are the paradigm examples of such systems, and so responsibility for establishing institutional arrangements capable of securing people's human rights falls in the first instance on their governments and compatriots. From this, it seems to follow that the underfulfillment of people's human rights in poor countries should be attributed to moral or practical failure on the part of the political leaders, government officials, and citizens of those countries. At first sight, such an attribution of moral responsibility is plausible, especially since democratic institutions are often weak in poor countries and their governing elites are sometimes autocratic, brutal, and corrupt. However, although Pogge acknowledges that these states of affairs often obtain, he contends that they do not result exclusively from factors internal to the poor countries in question. Instead, he argues that civil strife, authoritarianism, corruption, and poverty are produced systematically in many poor countries, especially countries with substantial natural resources, by several key features of the global institutional order.

The first of these features is what Pogge calls the international resource privilege, according to which any group that exercises de facto power within a country is recognized internationally as that country's legitimate government and the owner of its natural resources. The international resource privilege provides powerful incentives toward *coups d'état* and civil wars in resource-rich countries. Additional incentives are provided by the international borrowing privilege, which puts a country's full credit at the disposal of its rulers, enabling those rulers to borrow money cheaply to maintain themselves in power even against widespread popular opposition. Moreover, at a background level, Pogge argues, the global order contributes to the persistence of poverty in poor countries by increasing their dependence on international trade, so exacerbating their economies' vulnerability to the vicissitudes of the global market.

Pogge's analysis emphasizes the causal significance of the present international institutional order in generating and maintaining global poverty. From his analysis, it follows that those agents who bear the greatest moral responsibility for global poverty are the citizens and governments of the wealthy and powerful countries that lead the way in imposing this unjust order. Their (for Westerners, "our") moral responsibility is not grounded solely in the duty of humanitarian assistance, a duty that may be regarded as supererogatory or going beyond minimal moral requirements, nor does it stem solely from our enjoyment of undeserved benefits produced by an unjust social order. It does not even rest mainly on the fact that the citizens and governments of powerful countries are in the best position to make reforms in the global order. Pogge does not deny the moral force of any of these arguments but he regards the most compelling reason why we bear the moral responsibility for global poverty as being, in the final analysis, that we have culpably colluded in compelling poor countries to accept a global order that systematically and predictably results in the underfulfillment of their citizens' human rights. Thus, Pogge argues that the citizens and governments of wealthy powerful countries have violated the uncontroversial and morally fundamental requirement not to cause severe harm to innocent people for minor gains. It is this culpability that constitutes the basic and incontrovertible ground of our responsibility to address global poverty.

The harms for which we are culpable are not minor and the tone that Pogge adopts in diagnosing them is strongly condemnatory. He notes that "we" have installed many of the most oppressive rulers in poor countries, bribed them, and sold weapons to them. We have also allowed them to sell their country's natural resources and borrow money in its name. While the tyrannical rulers certainly are not innocent, our own leaders' culpability is greater because they have established and maintain the international system that systematically rewards coups and corruption in poor countries. The harms done by this international system are predictable and sometimes even deliberate. Moreover, the ordinary citizens of wealthy powerful countries are also gravely at fault because we have either authorized our leaders to establish the unjust global order or at least passively acquiesced in its establishment. Arguably, we are all accomplices in a monumental crime against humanity.

1.3 Discharging our moral responsibility for global poverty

On Pogge's view, as we have seen, responsibility for global poverty belongs to all those who participate in the unjust order that predictably generates such poverty, though not to all of them equally. It is conceivable that individuals might escape this responsibility by withdrawing from that order, emigrating, or becoming hermits, but in the real world these possibilities are feasible for few people, if any. Pogge argues that the best way of alleviating our culpability for global poverty is to diminish the injustice of the international institutions that regulate all of our lives.

Pogge argues that global poverty can be substantially reduced through three independent institutional reforms that he calls minor. He refers to them as the three Ps: Protectionism, Privileges, and Pharmaceuticals. First, Pogge calls for an end to the protectionist measures by which wealthy countries protect their markets against cheap imports of goods and services from poor countries. Second, he calls for abolishing the international resource and borrowing privileges that the global system confers upon rulers who manage to bring a country under their control. And third, he calls for redesigning the global pharmaceutical-patent regime, so that the development of important new drugs can be rewarded in proportion to the health impact of those drugs rather than through the monopoly rents established by the international system of

Alison M. Jaggar

patent protections. Instituting these reforms, in Pogge's view, is to be justified not in terms of assisting the global poor but rather in terms of protecting them from the injustice of global rules that we have established and from which we benefit.

1.4 Is Pogge's a radical moral view?

The idea that the ordinary citizens of affluent countries, specifically Western countries, are to blame for most global poverty runs quite counter to the unreflective moral thinking of the majority of these citizens. In this sense, it appears to be a profoundly radical conclusion. However, Pogge denies that his view is morally radical; to the contrary, he insists, his view is quite modest. First, he contends that his conclusion follows logically from relatively minimal moral premises that few such citizens would deny. Specifically, he says, it follows from the uncontroversial moral claim that it is wrong to cause severe and foreseeable harm to innocent people for minor gains. Second, Pogge insists, his view is not radical in the sense that discharging our responsibility for global poverty would require superhuman sacrifices that could be made, if at all, only by saints. On the contrary, he asserts, most global poverty can be alleviated through some institutional reforms that would not cost a great deal to the wealthy.

1.5 The complexity of Pogge's argument

Whether or not one accepts Pogge's assertion that his moral view is not at all radical, his philosophical argument is undeniably innovative. Pogge entirely reframes the question of responsibility for global poverty and the systematic underfulfillment of human rights. Although his argument may appear simple at first sight, this appearance is deceptive. The argument includes a controversial philosophical diagnosis of why global poverty is morally wrong, an equally controversial philosophical account of moral responsibility for this wrong, and specific recommendations about how particular agents should discharge their alleged responsibility. Like most political philosophy, the argument relies on an assortment of conceptual, normative, and empirical components, which are sometimes difficult if not impossible to separate from each other. The conceptual elements include analyses of justice, harm, causation, moral responsibility, and feasibility, and implicit or explicit in these analyses are moral judgments regarding such questions as injustice, well-being, complicity, the relevance of intention to fault, and the salience of social location and community membership. In addition, Pogge's argument depends on a range of disputable social scientific claims regarding causality, predictability, and the possibility of alternative institutional arrangements. Many of the conceptual, normative, and empirical aspects of Pogge's thought have become foci of investigation for his critics.

2 The critics examine Pogge's thinking

2.1 Joshua Cohen

Cohen recognizes, with Pogge, that global poverty is a human disaster and he also acknowledges that this disaster is not the inevitable result of resource scarcity. However, Cohen disputes what he calls Pogge's Strong Thesis. This is the claim that most of the problem of extreme global poverty could be eliminated through minor modifications in some global economic rules and that the changes would result in only slight reductions in the incomes of the affluent. Cohen accepts that some global poverty could be eliminated by changes in global rules that would not themselves result in serious moral injuries but he considers this claim to be uncontroversial and refers to it as the Conventional Thesis. However, he contends that Pogge's Strong Thesis is entirely unsupported by available evidence and argument.

Cohen challenges three ways in which Pogge defends the Strong Thesis. First, he notes that some countries with very large numbers of poor people have succeeded in growing rapidly even under existing global rules. This fact, Cohen observes, suggests that the main cause of poverty in the remaining poor countries likely does not lie in unjust global trade rules, as Pogge contends, but is rather attributable to the countries' failure to adopt successful policies. Cohen rejects as unpersuasive two ways in which Pogge attempts to dismiss the successful performance of some poor countries as irrelevant to the Strong Thesis.

Second, Cohen considers Pogge's contention that those responsible for imposing global rules bear moral responsibility for most poverty, even if responsibility for that same poverty can also be attributed to corrupt and incompetent political elites in poor countries. The double assignment of responsibility would make sense if the same effects could be produced by different causal pathways or were remediable by two different strategies; for instance, it is conceivable that global poverty could be eliminated either by domestic rule changes, holding global rules constant, or by global rule changes, holding domestic rules constant. As noted earlier, Cohen thinks it is indisputable that global rules make at least some causal contribution to global poverty so that the claim that global elites bear some moral responsibility for it is uncontroversial but this acknowledgment does not go beyond the Conventional Thesis. The claim that the governments and citizens of wealthy countries bear the main responsibility for global poverty depends on the truth of the Strong Thesis, that changes in global rules would eliminate most global poverty even if domestic institutions and regimes were held fixed, and Cohen regards the Strong Thesis as highly implausible.

Cohen last challenges Pogge's principal argument for the Strong Thesis. This is the argument that the existence of corrupt institutions in poor countries can be substantially or fully explained in terms of global institutional factors. Cohen grants that global rules provide one causal element for explaining the shape of domestic institutions but he offers three reasons for skepticism regarding the claim that changing those rules, for example by imposing sanctions on unaccountable regimes, would have much impact on extreme global poverty. First, Cohen argues, many unaccountable regimes would simply not respond to sanctions. Second, he thinks that many poor countries have sufficient accountability to escape sanctions. And third, he speculates that countries could make minimal changes sufficient to avoid sanctions without those changes having much substantive effect on poverty.

Much of Cohen's discussion concerns empirical probabilities but it is framed by his conception of the central task of political philosophy. In Cohen's view, this task is the exploration of "realistic utopias," possible alternative ways of organizing our social world that are objects of reasonable hope. Such philosophical exploration is subject to demanding normative and empirical constraints. Despite Pogge's concern that political philosophy should investigate feasible solutions to real-world moral problems (a concern highlighted in Charles Mills's contribution to this volume), Cohen argues that Pogge's central empirical claim (the Strong Thesis) is unsupported by available social scientific evidence. The improbability of the Strong Thesis undermines both Pogge's arguments for the global elite's culpability for harming the global poor and his practical proposals for eliminating global poverty. Indeed, Cohen contends, Pogge's nearly exclusive focus on the harm caused by global institutions distracts philosophical attention from other important moral reasons for condemning wealthy countries' inaction in the face of global poverty and from less sweeping and more feasible proposals for addressing this poverty. Following Rawls, Cohen suggests that the reasons may include wealthy countries' failure to meet their positive obligations and the proposals may include establishing just or at least decent domestic institutions and policies in poor countries.

2.2 Kok-Chor Tan

Tan is also concerned with Pogge's attribution of the main moral responsibility for global poverty but he approaches this issue through a critical examination of Pogge's institutional account of justice. Pogge follows Rawls in regarding the principles of justice as being concerned primarily with the design of social institutions but he departs from Rawls by taking the existence of some institutional structure to be a precondition for any duties of justice existing at all. Against this move, Tan argues that Pogge's more stringent institutional conception of human rights is unjustifiably limited in its scope. In addition, he questions whether Pogge's supposedly minimal moral assumptions, which emphasize only negative duties, are strong enough to support Pogge's claim that rich and powerful countries actually harm the global poor when they impose unjust global institutions.

Tan identifies two further aspects of Pogge's institutional conception of human rights. First, this conception regards human rights violations as wrongs that are attributable primarily to the state and its agents. While people may be harmed by private individuals, their rights are violated only if the state fails systematically to protect them from such harm. A second aspect of Pogge's conception is that it allows claims that human rights be protected to be made only against people who participate in a common institutional scheme; such claims are demands that other people work to ensure that their rights are protected in this scheme.

Tan challenges the latter aspect of Pogge's institutional conception by contending that Pogge is mistaken in restricting human rights claims to those who share an institutional order. On the contrary, Tan argues, human rights are intended to articulate the basic moral claims that human beings can make against each other. Requiring that such claims be contingent on social membership opens the possibility that the most vulnerable human beings may be deprived of rights by being declared to be nonmembers. Tan recalls that in practice this rationale has routinely been used to justify the denial of rights to outcast groups.

Tan's second challenge to Pogge is to justify the assertion that rich countries wrongfully harm the global poor when they impose an institutional order that is disadvantageous to the poor. Given Pogge's supposedly minimal moral assumptions, which commit him to the existence only of negative duties, how can he defend the assertion that the rich are morally required to offer more advantageous terms to the poor? Libertarians, who believe only in negative rights, do not have available the moral resources necessary to argue that existing institutional arrangements should be assessed by comparison with feasible alternatives that would be more advantageous to the poor. Such a claim can be justified by theorists committed to other moral positions, such as utilitarianism or positive rights, but Tan does not see how the claim can be supported by drawing only on a minimal commitment to negative rights.

Tan concludes that problematic philosophical issues, not simply factual ones, are at stake in Pogge's claim that global elites harm the global poor when they impose an institutional order that is disadvantageous to them. He is doubtful that the global egalitarian commitments that Pogge supported in earlier work can be built from the minimal moral materials to which Pogge now proposes to limit himself. Tan, like Cohen, thinks that Pogge may well be mistaken in restricting his moral commitments to negative duties.

2.3 Neera Chandhoke

Chandhoke welcomes Pogge's recognition that the citizens of affluent countries share responsibility for global poverty and the massive underfulfillment of human rights. However, she raises several concerns about Pogge's assertion that such citizens bear the main burden of this responsibility.

First, Chandhoke shares Cohen's skepticism that the causes of global poverty can be attributed primarily to global institutions. She appreciates Pogge's identification of the causal link between the agricultural policies of the World Trade Organization, on the one hand, and, on the other hand, the suicides of many farmers in those Indian states that are the most integrated into the global economy. Nevertheless, Chandhoke points out that complex states of affairs typically result from a multitude of factors and that extensive discretion is available in deciding which factors are the most causally significant. Attributions of causality are inherently disputable and someone else could plausibly argue that local factors are more important than Pogge acknowledges in causing poverty and routine human rights deficits in many poor countries. As we have seen, Joshua Cohen makes precisely such an argument.

Second, Chandhoke wishes to expand Pogge's analysis of the moral basis of responsibility for redressing injustice and the underfulfillment of human rights. Like Cohen and Tan, Chandhoke contends that human rights violations are of universal concern and create a moral claim on all. She believes that Pogge's argument for responsibility based on culpability for causing avoidable harm must be supplemented by recognizing the universality of the duty to address human suffering and violations of human rights. In Chandhoke's view, it is safe to assume that many of the activists and NGO members who confront powerful states and powerful global institutions act because they feel that universal human rights impose universal obligations on relevant agents.

Finally, Chandhoke worries that Pogge's argument focuses too exclusively on the responsibilities of Westerners. The governments and civil societies of poor countries also bear responsibility for challenging the poverty, injustice, and human rights deficits that exist in their countries and indeed the responsibility falls in the first instance on them. Chandhoke agrees that the citizens of wealthy countries share in the responsibility for remedying these states of affairs but she notes that in practice their activism to end poverty and human rights deficits tends to be motivated by a more general humanitarian concern for alleviating suffering than by any acknowledgment that they are culpable of contributing to injustice.

2.4 Jiwei Ci

Ci's essay complements Chandhoke's reflections on Pogge's insistence that Westerners are mainly responsible for global poverty. Whereas Chandhoke is concerned that Pogge may overlook the agency and responsibility of the governments and citizens of poor countries, Ci is persuaded by Pogge's analysis of Westerners' culpability. However, he doubts that Pogge's moral position is as modest as he claims it to be, contending that general acceptance of Pogge's analysis would require a profound transformation in Westerners' moral psychology. Specifically, it would require that Westerners become as sensitive to institutional as to interactional wrongs.

We have seen already that Pogge justifies his charge of Western culpability for global poverty in terms of the negative duty to refrain from predictably and avoidably harming innocent people in order to achieve minor gains. As Ci notes, this duty certainly appears to be modest, minimal, and uncontroversial but underlying it is an approach to morality that departs radically from ordinary Western moral thinking. The departure occurs when participating in imposing unjust institutions is construed as directly harming the people whose lives are regulated by those institutions.

Ordinary moral thinking is interactional, focusing on the moral assessment of individual behavior and taking for granted the justice of background institutions. In daily life, Ci observes, it is much easier for most Western citizens to respond appropriately to familiar interpersonal vices such as cruelty than to respond appropriately to injustices perpetrated by one's government on a global scale. Indeed, moral common sense regards failing to fulfill positive duties to other known individuals as a larger fault than failing to fulfill negative duties to countless unknown people. To recognize the latter as a significant moral lapse requires extensive moral reflection as well as interpersonal empathy. In order to reeducate ordinary citizens' moral sensibility, unreflectiveness will have to be recognized as a fault equal to cruelty.

Ci believes that much of what the West regards as its own moral progress in fact has been severely compromised, perhaps even made possible, by a shift of injustice from the domestic to the international arena. Thus Ci is doubtful that what has been marketed as moral progress provides much hope for achieving what he calls "net" improvement in global justice. Precisely for this reason, however, Ci finds great value in Pogge's rare combination of moral universalism with the institutional perspective, which Ci regards as a powerful philosophical antidote to the tendency to shift injustice from one immediate locus or direct perpetrator to another, especially across the boundaries of strong and weak nations. Ci views Pogge's work as a rare exemplar of genuine as opposed to self-serving moral universalism and observes that such universalism stands in opposition both to nationalism, which advocates stronger standards of justice for nation-states than for global institutions, and to the selective universalism that focuses exclusively on political systems while ignoring economic rights.

2.5 Erin I. Kelly and Lionel K. McPherson

Along with several other authors, Erin Kelly and Lionel McPherson question the compatibility of Pogge's earlier commitment to cosmopolitan egalitarianism with his present emphasis on minimal negative duties. Even though the later Pogge distances himself overtly from controversial egalitarian commitments, emphasizing instead the duty to refrain from engaging in harm that is both predictable and avoidable, Kelly and McPherson are doubtful. They contend that he is still tacitly committed to cosmopolitan egalitarianism, the view that justice requires egalitarian principles of economic distribution to be instituted on a global scale insofar as he continues to have a philosophically distinctive position. Their essay challenges this moral vision of global economic justice. They argue that it is a mistake to construe global economic justice in egalitarian terms, because to construe it in this way is to give insufficient moral weight to the values of autonomy, toleration, and respect across societies, and the wrong kind of moral weight to equality. In place of cosmopolitan egalitarianism, Kelly and McPherson recommend a model of global justice that they call cosmopolitan cooperationism. This model requires economic reciprocity among nations but, unlike cosmopolitan egalitarianism, it denies that justice demands symmetry between principles of national and global justice.

Kelly and McPherson begin by considering Pogge's criticism that Rawls is unfair and inconsistent when he recommends that the difference principle should guide economic justice at the national but not at the global level. Against what they take to be Pogge's underlying egalitarian vision, they argue that it would be wrong to advocate symmetry between principles of economic justice at the national and global levels respectively. They point out that the members of a global society of peoples are not equivalent to persons in a liberal domestic society, even though both have overlapping interests. They argue that the cosmopolitan egalitarian notion of fair economic arrangements that they take Pogge to favor is not supported by any of the considerations that he advances. Specifically, it is not supported by appeals to the negative duty not to harm, to a minimal default view of fairness, or the abstract principle of moral universalism.

The last part of Kelly and McPherson's essay develops a normative model of global economic justice which they present as a model preferable to the cosmopolitan egalitarianism that they attribute to Pogge. Cosmopolitan cooperationism accepts a straightforward humanitarian duty of assistance and supplements this with a duty of just engagement for reciprocal economic benefit. The duty of just engagement does not involve a commitment to luck egalitarianism, the requirement that people should be compensated for any disadvantages beyond their control, but it does not allow some highly inegalitarian economic arrangements to which poor societies might conceivably agree out of desperation. Kelly and McPherson spell out how they envision a minimum threshold of fair agreements being specified. In addition to the duties of assistance and just engagement, cosmopolitan coopera-tionism also includes a duty of reparations to some of the worst-off people in burdened societies. The reparations would be justified on grounds of corrective justice but would not be construed as compensa-tion for actual damages or as promoting corrective justice in a com-prehensive sense. Instead, they would be seen as one strategy for helping lift burdened societies out of poverty. Kelly and McPherson challenge Pogge to explain why their cosmopolitan cooperationism, with its duties of assistance, just engagement, and reparations, is an inadequate account of global economic justice.

2.6 Leif Wenar

Leif Wenar accepts much of Pogge's causal explanation for the so-called resource curse, namely, the frequent correlation between the possession of natural resources, on the one hand, and, on the other, the occurrence of such social pathologies as authoritarianism, civil conflict, and lower rates of economic growth. Like Pogge, Wenar believes that a major causal link is the global rule that Pogge calls the "resource privilege," the international legal convention that accords to any group sufficiently powerful to maintain control over a territory's population the legal right to sell off that territory's natural resources. The convention creates a powerful motivation for coups and tyranny in countries that possess abundant natural resources. Wenar shares Pogge's concern to eliminate the resource privilege but he disagrees with Pogge's practical proposal for accomplishing this.

Pogge proposes to add an amendment to the constitutions of resource-rich developing countries, declaring that only its constitu-tionally democratic governments may effect legally valid transfers of ownership rights in public property and forbidding any of its govern-ments to recognize ownership rights in property acquired from a pre-ceding government that lacked such constitutional power. To determine whether or not the resource-rich country remains democratic, Pogge recommends that an international "Democracy Panel" be established. This would be composed of reputable, independent jurists living abroad who are sufficiently well informed about the country to judge whether a particular group's acquisition and exercise of political power is or is not constitutionally legitimate.

Wenar sees several problems with the feasibility of Pogge's proposal. One major problem, in his view, is that the proposal is grounded on the moral value of democracy, which Wenar considers to be a value that is too contestable to receive universal assent. In Wenar's view, requiring democracy would also set the bar of legitimate ownership too high because it would prevent even relatively decent governments from selling their country's assets. Wenar proposes to replace Pogge's idea of a constitutional amendment supplemented by a Democracy Panel with alternative institutional arrangements designed to embody the legal principle that a country's citizens are ultimately the legitimate owners of that country's resources.

Wenar regards this principle as intuitive, uncontroversial, and embodied already in much national and international law. However, two problems must be solved in order to institutionalize it adequately. The first is the criterial problem of identifying the minimal conditions that must exist in a country for it to be possible that a people may authorize a regime to sell off its resources. The second is the enforcement problem of discouraging buyers from purchasing resources that, in effect, are stolen from a people.

Wenar addresses the first problem by drawing on the notion of valid consent to derive minimum conditions for a people to authorize the sale of its resources. He argues that these conditions include minimal freedom of the press, the possibility of exchanging information about resource sales, and some effective political mechanisms through which people can express their unhappiness about resource sales. Wenar suggests that the nongovernmental organization Freedom House, based in the United States, be accepted as an authoritative source for rating countries on their civil liberties and political rights. If a country receives only the lowest rating on the Freedom House scale, then its regime lacks the legitimate authority to sell that country's resources.

Wenar thinks that this minimal standard for determining whether a regime is authorized to sell a country's resources could be enforced through several different strategies of civil and criminal litigation. He further proposes that a Clean Hands Trust, funded through a duty-and-trust mechanism, should be established to compensate a people whose resources have been stolen through illegitimate sales. The existence of such a trust would reduce the incentive to buy resources from illegitimate regimes and limit illegitimate rulers' ability to enrich themselves by looting their country. Wenar regards this set of proposals as solving the problems he finds in Pogge's proposed remedies for the resource curse and as offering a more feasible means of reducing global poverty.

2.7 Charles Mills

Mills's essay provides perhaps the most fundamental challenge to Pogge's work, though Mills is also a sympathetic critic. Mills entirely approves of the main direction of Pogge's argument, which he sees as correctly locating the main causes of global poverty in the structure of the world political and economic order. He also applauds Pogge's criticisms of the method of "ideal theory." However, he argues that Pogge fails to develop his own insights about the seriousness of this methodological mistake. Specifically, Mills asserts, Pogge fails to recognize the special historical, causal, and moral significance of race and gender in the history of the real world.

Mills has been a leading critic of the ideal-theoretic approach to political philosophy made popular in the last few decades by the work of John Rawls. Pogge too has repeatedly criticized this approach, in part because it requires envisioning and assessing social worlds that are quite remote from our own, while neglecting important questions regarding the design of feasible alternatives to existing social arrangements. Mills summarizes the criticisms of ideal theory that are becoming increasingly familiar in political philosophy but he advances them by insisting that the orientation toward ideal theory is a fundamental mistake. In Mills's view, the social ontology of liberal ideal theory presupposes that the metaphysics of a racialized and gendered world have already been successfully dismantled, even though the same theory's epistemology obscures the obstacles to such dismantlement. Mills contends that political philosophy should focus on non-ideal theory in the form of rectificatory racial and gender justice, because only through such a normative project can the ideal even be glimpsed.

Although Pogge makes many comments which recognize the need for political philosophy to begin by addressing injustice rather than starting with a philosophical fantasy of a just world, Mills contends that Pogge still does not push far enough beyond Rawls. He argues that Pogge's work would be strengthened by making racial and gender exploitation more central and by recognizing explicitly that race and gender are social constructions in the strong sense that they would not exist in a world that had not already been racialized and gendered. Specifically, Mills advises Pogge to acknowledge race itself as an international institution via European colonialism and as a fundamental feature of the global basic structure. The explanatory nationalism that Pogge condemns should be recognized as simply a contemporary sanitized version of explanatory continentalism.

Mills concludes by recommending that Pogge should expand and deepen the critique of liberalism that his work has already begun. Pogge should formally move from ideal to non-ideal theory, reject existing liberalism's misleading portrayal of itself as abstract and universalist, and make explicit its complicity with gender injustice, racial imperialism, and the domination of the majority of the world's population. Such a reconstitution of social memory is indispensable to developing a non-ideal political philosophy that has the resources to address the most pressing issues of global rectificatory justice.

3 Interwoven strands of criticism

This collection of critical essays presents a formidable set of challenges to Pogge's work. Most of the challenges address a few distinct themes. One of the themes is whether or not Pogge's normative vision is convincing and what that vision's relationship with ordinary morality is. Is Pogge's institutional conception of global justice and human rights compatible with libertarian or other minimal moral beliefs? Does it demand too much or too little? A second theme concerns the moral responsibility borne by the citizens of affluent countries for a global order marked by conspicuous inequality, poverty, and the underfulfillment of human rights. How can the weight of various causal factors be determined and who, if anyone, is culpable for establishing these factors or allowing them to continue? What is the normative basis of duties to redress poverty and the underfulfillment of rights? Do the duties depend on culpability for contributing to a system that produces these problems, on participation in the system, on shared nationality, or on membership in the human species? A third theme addressed by several essays suggests alternatives to Pogge's analysis and practical proposals. Even some authors who are very sympathetic to the spirit of Pogge's work contend that his proposals are unworkable or that his analysis does not go far enough. Although the critics often disagree substantively with each other as well as with Pogge, their common focus on these themes means that the essays not only contrast with but also complement each other. Together, they constitute a major contribution to the debate over global justice and moral responsibility.

1

Philosophy, Social Science, Global Poverty

Joshua Cohen*

> Every Night & every Morn
> Some to Misery are Born.
> Every Morn & every Night
> Some are Born to sweet Delight.
> Some are Born to sweet Delight,
> Some are born to Endless Night.
> (William Blake, "Auguries of Innocence")

> This was a tremendous idea – that to find something out, it is better to conduct some careful experiments than to carry on deep philosophical arguments.
> (Richard Feynman, *Lectures on Physics*, 7.1)[1]

1 A Strong Thesis

Global poverty is a human disaster. It brings great misery, ruins vast human potential, and is visited on a billion people who were born to it. Moreover, the problem – focusing here on extreme poverty, people living on less than a dollar a day (an arbitrary line, of course) – is not resource scarcity, but an awful mismatch between available resources and human needs. To be sure, the conjunction of continued population growth and the global income growth needed to address extreme (and severe, but less extreme) poverty will make genuine resource scarcity a large concern, requiring technological innovation and not simply institutional renovation or better distribution. But the mismatch of resources and human needs is and, absent concerted efforts at remedy, will likely remain a pressing concern.

Less clear, however, are the sources of extreme poverty and the range of remedies that might combine to alleviate it. Thomas Pogge apparently disagrees. In *World Poverty and Human Rights*,[2] and several subsequent essays, he asserts that there is considerable clarity on sources and especially on remedies, at least to this extent: suitable changes in some global economic rules – in fact, *"minor modifications* in the global order that would entail *at most slight reductions* in the incomes of the affluent"* (SPH30) – would eliminate most of the problem of extreme global poverty. I will call this claim about the impact of appropriate global rule changes the Strong Thesis:

> *Strong Thesis*: Most of the global poverty problem could be eliminated through minor modifications in the global order that would entail at most slight reductions in the incomes of the affluent.

I do not see a case for this striking assertion. Before explaining why I want to make three points of clarification.

1 Though "minor modifications" and "global order" leave much room for interpretation, the thrust of the Strong Thesis seems clear enough, and I am not going to say anything about *most, minor*, or *slight*. As for "global order," it comprises treaty- and convention-based rules about security, trade, property rights, human rights, and environment: rules that govern global rule makers, the norms and standards associated with territorial sovereignty, policies adopted by global rule-making bodies (say, TRIPS or the decisions of the World Trade Organization's Appellate Body), and the security and assistance policies of the world's most powerful states. To be sure, the global order is not a well-defined system. Consider, for example, labor standards. There are now some 10,000 "private voluntary codes" adopted by firms as codes for their suppliers.[3] Are these rules themselves part of the global order? Should we count (non)compliance by suppliers and subcontractors as part of that order? How much does it matter in answering these questions that firms could do more to foster compliance, that national labor ministries could do more (especially if they cooperate with firms), that labor standards could be incorporated into trade rules?[4] I am not sure these questions, matters of classification that may not track morally relevant distinctions, are

worth asking. But because of the uncertainties about the answers, I will try to make the argument independent of the precise characterization of that order.

2 Pogge presents his Strong Thesis as part of a more general normative outlook. The core of the outlook is that the global order harms the global poor, harms them by treating them unjustly, unjustly treating them by violating their human rights, violating those rights by enforcing rules that could be changed in ways that would relieve *most of the world's extreme poverty*. More pointedly – de-reifying and personalizing – *we* harm the global poor, we citizens of rich countries, by imposing (at least through culpable complicity) current global rules, and by not making the poverty-alleviating rule changes that would address most of the problem. My focus is the Strong Thesis itself, not the normative ideas about harm, rights, and justice that surround it.

3 The Strong Thesis is not that changes in global rules are the *only* way to reduce extreme poverty. With fixed global rules, countries could (consistent with the Strong Thesis) succeed in moving large numbers out of poverty, as has happened in truly remarkable numbers over the past three decades in China (of course, most countries do not have more than a billion people in their internal markets, but a number of other countries achieved "fast, sustained growth" in the post-World War II period, including Botswana, Brazil, Hong Kong, Indonesia, Japan, the Republic of Korea, Malaysia, Malta, Oman, Singapore, Taiwan, and Thailand).[5] The Strong Thesis says that changes in global rules would suffice to eliminate "most severe poverty" (SPV77), and we would not now be seeing these effects if the global order had been designed differently. According to the Strong Thesis, "radical inequality and the continuous misery and death toll it engenders are foreseeably reproduced under the present global institutional order as we have shaped it. And *most of it could be avoided* [emphasis added] . . . if this global order had been, or were to be, designed differently" (SPV55).

It seems to me indisputable that there is much that wealthy countries and global rule makers could and ought to do, and that citizens of those countries share responsibility for extreme poverty and its alleviation. The Strong Thesis is, however, entirely speculative, unwarranted by available evidence and argument. I see no reason to accept the claim that changes in global rules would suffice to lift most of the terrible poverty that so many people suffer from. In particular, I see no case for the claim that such changes will suffice while holding domestic institutions fixed, and no reason to think that they will suffice by changing incentives and opportunities in ways that induce poverty-alleviating alterations in domestic institutions. I will also suggest along the way that, for much of the interesting action about poverty allevia-tion and economic development, the question "domestic or global?" – as in the labor codes example mentioned earlier – is not very helpful and probably misleading.[6]

Two larger points frame my discussion of the Strong Thesis and the shortfall between argument and assertion. First, on political philoso-phy and social science: explorations of human possibility – especially the attractive possibilities that John Rawls called "realistic utopias" – are the central and irreplaceable work of political philosophy.[7] Done right, such explorations are not (as in a common caricature) wish lists or fanciful inventions, but are subject to demanding intellectual constraints, including the constraints on showing that an ideal is a realistic possibility for human beings, an object of reasonable hope, compatible with our nature, realizable under the conditions of social life as they might be, and perhaps accessible from where we now are. The demands of that enterprise are very different, however, from the comparably serious intellectual constraints on the social scientist's efforts to show what is actually the case, identify causes, estimate the magnitude of their effects, and understand what benefits might be achieved with available social levers, and at what costs. Abstractly stated, these points are obvious: while political philosophy draws on social science, it is not social science. But they too often suffer neglect. They are neglected by social scientists who, conflating fact and norm, endorse the caricature of political philosophy as fanciful invention. And they are neglected by philosophers who, conflating norm and fact, give insufficient attention to the distinction between exploring a hopeful possibility, a way the world might be, and showing what is the case.

Second, on theory and practice: extreme global poverty is of com-manding moral importance, and we should not be distracted in efforts to address it by unwarranted confidence in particular diagnoses and strategies. At any level of resolution that bears on practice, it is mis-guided to say that we know what needs to be done, and that the problem is simply to muster the will to do it. Uncertainty is no reason for paralysis. But it does recommend humility,[8] provide a case for diversifying efforts in the hope of learning something, and suggest that we should think about development and poverty alleviation as arenas for evaluation, organized learning, and attention to local knowledge and circumstance rather than as arenas for implementing sweeping preconceptions.

2 Possible and actual

Before getting to the details of Pogge's view, I want to illustrate my general concern about philosophy and social science – and introduce some distinctions that I will draw on later – by discussing a striking example of the shortfall between argument and assertion. In *World Poverty and Human Rights*, just before a discussion of "The Causal Role of Global Institutions in the Persistence of Severe Poverty," we find the following remarks:

> Social scientists [provide for the most part] "nationalist" explanations which trace flaws in a country's political and economic institutions and the corruption and incompetence of its ruling elite back to this country's history, culture, or natural environment. Because there are substantial differences in how countries, and the incidence of poverty within them, develop over time, it is clear that . . . nationalist explanations must play a role in explaining national trajectories and international differentials. *From this it does not follow, however, that the global order does not also play a substantial causal role* [emphasis added] by shaping how the culture of each poor country evolves and by influencing how a country's history, culture, and natural environment affect the development of its domestic institutional order, ruling elite, economic growth, and income distribution. In these ways global institutional factors might contribute substantially to the persistence of severe poverty in particular countries and in the world at large. (*WP*112)

The italicized logical point about the consistency of national and global explanations is right. Suppose a country suffers from severe poverty because of its institutions – say, absence of an effective rule of law or arrangements for official accountability or decently functioning markets. It does not "follow" that the global order is relieved of responsibility.

To see how, let us first put aside a familiar kind of story – call it *Combined Effects* – about the joint role of national and global factors in explaining extreme poverty. The familiar story might be expressed in a time series model of intertemporal variations in country-level poverty. The model includes, let's say, a bunch of independent variables, and we want to test for both domestic and global factors: variables for rule of law, regime type, per capita income, resource dependence, global trade-openness (measured some way or other), global aid commitments, and stringency of global norms on debt repayment. We start, say, with a specification that is confined to the domestic variables, and find substantively and statistically significant estimates for the coefficients. But of course it does not follow from the fact that domestic factors matter that global factors do not matter as well. When we add the global variables, we may account for more of the variance, and conclude that both domestic and global factors matter. So far, so familiar.

Pogge's point about national and global is entirely different from Combined Effects. He imagines someone asserting what he calls the Purely Domestic Poverty Thesis (PDPT), that extreme poverty is *fully* explained by internal factors (history, geography, culture), a view that strikes me as pretty obviously wrong:[9]

> *Purely Domestic Poverty Thesis*: "The persistence of severe poverty is due solely to domestic causes" (AGP265).

Even if variations in poverty are *fully* explained by domestic factors, he argues, global factors might also be important causes and remedies of extreme poverty. Logically speaking, there are two ways this might be true.

First, *Independent Effects*. Both domestic conditions and global rules may be independently and fully responsible for cross-national or intertemporal variation in poverty rates, meaning that a change in either would have been (and would now be) sufficient to alleviate the extreme poverty in a country (SPV63). Consider a highly stylized hypothetical. Suppose extreme poverty in a country would be relieved by easy access to iron pills that would cure widespread anemia and thus increase work effort.[10] Universal access to the iron pills could be financed either by a price change – say, a change in global patent policy that would significantly reduce the price – or by a domestically financed subsidy – say, increased taxes on a wealthy domestic elite, with the revenues used to pay for the pills at existing prices. Either price change or subsidy suffices for addressing the extreme poverty. Domestic elites could keep their extravagance if patent policy changed prices; pharmaceuticals could keep their extravagance if domestic elites used their resources more decently. An explanation of poverty that emphasizes the domestic roots of resource (mis)allocation in a corrupt elite culture, does not, then, undermine a case for global responsibility, which says that poverty is a product of global rules that limit availability of medicine. Each remedy (in this wildly stylized example), working separately, would fully address the problem.

The second reconciliation of global and national I will call *Endogenous Institutions*. Here, the idea is not that the extreme poverty could be lifted even with bad institutions held constant, but that bad institutions are substantially explained by global rules. So changes in global rules would alleviate extreme poverty not by operating independently of domestic factors but by shifting domestic political incentives and opportunities in ways that transform domestic institutions and policies.[11]

To illustrate: consider the argument that bad institutions (inducing low growth and high poverty) are the legacy left by colonial powers looking to extract natural resources from places where natives of the colonial country did not want to live (say, because the environment is unhealthy for them), a legacy sustained by a powerful inertia of extractive colonial institutions.[12] Suppose now that someone says that bad domestic institutions – with poorly defined property rights, an absence of any limits on or accountability of officials, limited capacity to resolve conflict, and sharp restrictions on social mobility – explain extreme poverty. They have not excluded a global rule-based explanation, because global factors may in turn explain the bad institutions.

Although this example shows the compatibility of domestic and global explanations, it imperfectly illustrates Pogge's story about global rules in three essential ways. First, the imposition of extractive colonial institutions operated several hundred years ago, whereas Pogge emphasizes global rules since 1980 (SPV55). Second, if there is significant institutional inertia, there is no obvious implication about what to do now to remedy the long-standing national-level effects. And third, the case (as described) works though external imposition, not by enforcing global rules that create domestic incentives and opportunities.

Consider, then, a second illustration, drawn from discussions of rules on repudiating odious debt (a topic I return to later).[13] Suppose that international law includes an exceptionless rule of repayment, requiring governments to repay debt incurred by a previous regime, regardless of its repressiveness and of how it squandered the money. Those rules arguably increase the benefits of controlling the state, encourage more ruthless elites to aim for power by increasing expected returns on control of it (getting control of the government vastly increases your borrowing power), and enable those elites to buy weapons to maintain their power by killing the opposition. In short, global credit market rules establish incentives and opportunities that encourage bad domestic institutions. Alternative rules on debt repayment might establish exceptions to the rules of repayment, say, requiring an *ex ante* announcement of which borrowers you should not lend to, except on certain well-specified and monitored conditions about the use of the credit. This change might help to reduce poverty by reducing the economic returns on autocratic rule, thus fostering different institutions. It is essential to the story that the institutions have not only, as an historical matter, been shaped by the rules, but that they are highly responsive to changes in the global rules, and the incentives and opportunities created by those rules.

It is difficult to rest much confidence in such arguments. Generally speaking, arguments from changing rules to changing outcomes are complicated, and much depends on details. I will return to these issues later. My aim here is simply to illustrate the logical point that domestic explanations need not undermine explanations in terms of global rules.

The logical point is, however, of limited substantive relevance. Global rules *might* explain the bad institutions, but then again, they might not. We want to know if they *do*. Aware of this limited substantive relevance, Pogge adds that "global institutional factors" *do* "contribute substantially to the persistence of severe poverty in particular countries and in the world at large," proposes to "show that this is indeed the case" (*WP*112), and then, in a few pages, claims to "have *shown* how two aspects of the global economic order [the resource and borrowing privilege, to be discussed later] contribute substantially to the persistence of severe poverty" (*WP*115, emphasis added).

The idea, in essence, is that returns on autocratic rule are very sensitive to global rules on resource ownership and access to finance, that political competition in a country is very sensitive to these rates of return, that current global rules induce *very* high returns on autocracy, and that autocracy accounts for much of the world's extreme poverty. I will explore these issues later. My point here is about what has been *shown*. An argument of this brevity is insufficient for any empirical thesis worth exploring. It falls well short of what is needed for an ambitious claim about the impact of one part of a complex social-economic order on another part, an argument that depends in particular on highly contested claims about behavioral and institutional responsiveness in a country to shifting external rules – themselves established and enforced by a range of competing external actors – with uncertain influence of the rates of return on political activity. There is a large gap between *might explain* and *does explain*: between noting that a global rule-based explanation of most extreme poverty can coexist with explanations focused on domestic conditions and showing that current global rules do contribute substantially to variations in domestic poverty. That gap simply cannot be filled in a few pages. Social science is not that easy.[14]

3 Clarifying the Strong Thesis

To sharpen the terms of discussion, I want to locate the Strong Thesis in a space of claims about global rules and extreme poverty, and then explain why I focus on the Strong Thesis.

3.1 Most or some?

Pogge says that the current global order has caused and continues to cause most of the world's severe poverty. That order comprises rules that are enforced, and which could be different; moreover, were the rules changed in the right ways, we would eliminate most extreme global poverty (see, for example, SPH30). Thus,

> *Strong Thesis*: Most of the global poverty problem could be eliminated through minor modifications in the global order that would entail at most slight reductions in the incomes of the affluent.

Elsewhere, Pogge mentions the weaker thesis that "most" of the current "radical inequality and the continuous misery and death toll it engenders . . . could be avoided . . . if [the present global institutional order] had been, or were to be, designed differently." This thesis is weaker because it does not say that the relevant changes in global rules are "minor" or that the income reductions required of the affluent are "at most slight." But it preserves the essential claim about the magnitude of the effects:

> *Strong Thesis B*: Most of the global poverty problem could be eliminated through modifications in the global order that would not result in any injury to those who are now better off that is in any way comparable to the injury now suffered by the world's poor.

Because of their claims about the magnitude of the effects, both the Strong Thesis and Strong Thesis B are considerably stronger than the Conventional Thesis, which says that some changes in global rules would alleviate some extreme poverty:

> *Conventional Thesis*: *Some* global poverty could be eliminated by changes in global rules that would not themselves result in serious moral injuries.

This claim (associated with what I earlier referred to as Combined Effects) is essentially a rejection of the Purely Domestic Poverty Thesis, that extreme poverty is due "solely to domestic causes." Though relatively uncontroversial, the Conventional Thesis is, morally and practically speaking, of extraordinary importance, and provides sufficient reason for concerted action. But it is widely accepted and vastly less ambitious than the Strong Thesis.

Consider, for example, Paul Collier's observation that "everyone knows" that OECD trade policy has "indefensible aspects." Agricultural protection probably is near the top of everyone's list.

> When US and European Union trade negotiators jointly proposed that instead of the OECD lowering these production subsidies poor countries might shift to other activities, I personally felt they had crossed the line beyond which the normal diplomatic act of lying for your country becomes too shaming to accept. The US South really does have alternatives to cotton . . . . But cotton growers in Chad?[15]

But we should be cautious about inferring the nature and magnitude of the effects of a policy change from the magnitude of the shamelessness. According to a World Bank estimate, a complete elimination of all trade barriers in agriculture and manufactures would produce a $22 billion gain for developing countries.[16] The resulting dent in extreme poverty would likely be pretty small because most of the direct benefit would not be captured by the extremely poor, or even by the poorest countries, but, for example, by Brazilian cotton exporters and Argentine beef exporters. That is no reason for hesitation about the changes, but it is a reason for resisting exaggeration of their poverty-reducing effects.

3.2 Why focus on the Strong Thesis?

It is easy to be distracted from the striking assertions in the two Strong Theses by some philosophical issues about global justice and responsibility.[17] For example, Pogge says that the global order *harms* the poor. We might wonder whether to count the enforcement of current rules and corresponding failure to alleviate mass destitution by modifying the global order as *harming* the poor, rather than as a (culpable) failure to alleviate poverty. Moreover, Pogge has said that his claims about the global order harming the poor depend only on the relatively weak normative idea that we ought not to make people worse off, as distinct from the more demanding idea that we ought to provide help, or to ensure full justice. In response, we may wonder whether Pogge's claim about harm presents a morally demanding idea in morally minimal mufti: that while he says that he is not relying on morally demanding ideas, he really thinks that we make people worse off, thus harm them, when we impose rules that make them less well off than they would be under fair or "more evenhanded institution[s]" (SPH41). He responds that his argument about harm relies only on the idea that we harm people when we violate their human rights and that that is a morally minimal standard. But the critic may think that he makes use of a more demanding idea of human rights than many classical liberals or libertarians would ever accept.[18]

These concerns, however interesting, may distract attention from the most striking elements of Pogge's view, though the distraction is understandable in light of Pogge's chosen strategy of argument. Instead of arguing that changes in institutions or rules or policies could alleviate significant global poverty, and that such alleviation has great moral urgency, Pogge has argued that the globally rich and powerful are harming the poor. The underlying thought is that the injunction to do no harm is more compelling to more people than the moral injunction to alleviate remediable suffering or ensure full justice.

These injunctions are distinct, and in some contexts the distinctions would be very much worth attending to. But in the setting in question, I wonder about their importance. It is as if, in response to the observation that someone is drowning and could be saved at very little cost, we worried most about responding to the person who says "I did not do it, I did not push her in." And replied to this person: "OK, you may not have pushed her, but you are harming all the same because you supported the property tax cuts that led to the cuts in the municipal budget for the parks department that hires the lifeguards." To which the response will be: "Of course I supported the cuts, because the parks department would have spent the money on landscaping, oak desks, office parties, not lifeguards." Why not say: "Who cares whether you pushed? When someone is dying who could, without much effort, be saved, you are responsible for helping to save, and are complicit in the death if you do not."

Philosophical issues about global justice and responsibility are of great interest, but the Strong Thesis makes them seem less essential, at least as a practical matter. If the Strong Thesis is true, then the failure to modify global rules is barbaric. Whether the barbaric conduct should be registered as causing harm (by enforcing rules that have the predictable consequence of avoidable extreme poverty) or failing to assist, and the debate about whether harm is a matter of making people worse off than they were, or leaving them less well off than they are entitled to be under some allegedly minimal understanding of justice, are theological distractions from a moral disgrace.

To see the point, imagine a world in which the Strong Thesis is more or less true, by construction. We have one rich and very powerful lord and a group of other lords, all legally independent and all ruling over separate territories. The rich and powerful lord rules over a relatively wealthy and healthy population. Some lesser lords rule with a comparably velvet glove over relatively wealthy territories. Others are cruel despots, ruling ruthlessly over desperately poor subjects, whose desperate poverty results in part from their political subjection. Assume now that the states ruled by the lords are interdependent. The rich and powerful lord, as well as the equally decent lesser lords, buy relatively cheap minerals and raw materials from the cruel autocrats and also lend them money. The autocrats use the money for palaces and to buy weapons to coercively control their populations. By ending the purchases and lending, the wealthy lords would curtail the ability of cruel autocrats to sell and borrow, thus undermine their power, thus disable them from continuing to impoverish their subjects, and thus eliminate the incentives of others with comparably ruthless aims to grab power (see Endogenous Institutions). Cruel lords and associated poverty are a response to incentives and opportunities created by the rules made and enforced by rich lords. By changing the background rules, the rich lords would lift the blight of extreme poverty.

But none of this happens. Unwilling to require even small "sacrifices" from their populations (say, higher prices for minerals), and not subjected by those populations to pressure to do better, and despite the relative transparency of the necessary changes, the wealthy lords actively oppose (or at least fail to actively support) such rule changes.

Moreover, as a further twist, assume that the cruel lords are poisoning parts of their populations, and that the wealthy lords have a cheap antidote that could easily be ministered *even with the cruel lordly dictator in place*. But they withhold it and store it all as insurance against an improbable domestic emergency (Independent Effects).

Imagine now that the wealthy lords each say:

> I am not harming anyone. I am not harming the desperately poor and politically repressed people in the surrounding communities run by cruel lords. I am not the cause of their bad situation, even of their poisoning. After all, *some* places are doing very well, and the places that are not doing well could do better if they had better rulers/rules; and in addition, while it is true that I have an antidote that could cure the poisoned population, I would not need to lift a finger and minister the antidote

if the cruel autocrats were not poisoning the population. And in any case, it is one thing to accuse me of harming them – I agree I should not – and quite another to say that I am not helping them.

If the facts are as stipulated, then the right response to the wealthy lords is not a philosophical debate about causation and responsibility, harming and helping, and the role of a negative/positive responsibility distinction in this setting. The right response is moral condemnation, and practical insistence on changes of policy.

In the world of the parable, the Strong Thesis is true, both because of Independent Effects and Endogenous Institutions. How we think about global issues will depend a great deal on whether we think the Parable of the Bad Lords provides an illuminating informal model of our world. We know that it is a world with some cruel autocrats, considerable desperate poverty, and large amounts of innocent suffering, in which some of the desperate poverty is in autocracies, and in which the policies of rich countries (and the rules they endorse) are often squalid. But is it true – as in the world of the Bad Lords – that with minor modifications in global rules (which would result in at most a slight income decline), we could avoid most current global poverty?

4 Assessing the case for the Strong Thesis

I have said that the Strong Thesis is vastly stronger than anything that Pogge has plausibly defended. I want now to explain why.[19]

One point to preface these remarks: much contemporary discussion of global justice and global poverty gives insufficient inattention to the political geography of global poverty. By "political geography," I simply mean the location of extremely poor people in very different places with different developmental trajectories (past and projected growth rates) and varying institutional capacities for addressing domestic poverty. Thus in 2002, 30% of the one billion people living on less than a dollar a day were in sub-Saharan Africa, where the numbers had increased by roughly 90% since 1981, during a sustained period of general economic (and political) disaster throughout much of the continent.[20] In East Asia, in contrast, the numbers fell by nearly 600 million people over the same period, the most extraordinary anti-poverty thrust in human history, while numbers in South Asia fell by less than 10%.

More to the point, roughly half the extreme poverty in the world is now still in India and China, despite their extraordinary growth performance (vastly much more extraordinary over a longer period of time in China than India of course). Another (nearly) 100 million are in Nigeria, and some 70 million are in Pakistan and Bangladesh. Generalizations about "global rules" and the "global poor" that abstract from these contextual differences – including differences in expected growth rates – may obscure these important differences in circumstances and associated differences in possible remedies and actual prospects.

With these observations as background, I will discuss three lines of defense that Pogge suggests for the Strong Thesis (in the section of *WP* discussed earlier, and elsewhere).

1 While the Strong Thesis is about the sufficiency of global rule changes in alleviating poverty, the force of the thesis might be attenuated if we thought that all countries could have succeeded under existing rules by changing their own institutions and policies. And we might be tempted to infer the possibility of universal success from the success of some. Pogge's first point is to expose the error in that inference: maybe existing global rules only allowed the success of some.

2 Suppose all *could have* succeeded by changing institutions and policies. Still, the Strong Thesis may be true because of Independent Effects: all would *also* have succeeded with no domestic changes had there been suitable changes in global rules.

3 Even if success in alleviating extreme poverty required domestic changes, those changes would have been the result of changes in global rules: thus Endogenous Institutions.

The thread that runs throughout my comments is that we are given no reason for endorsing the Strong Thesis as distinct from the Conventional Thesis. It would be *very* surprising if massive poverty alleviation could proceed through changes in global rules that had no impact on domestic institutions and policies. And it would also be very surprising if domestic institutions and policies were as shaped by and responsive to global rule changes as Pogge's invocation of Endogenous Institutions requires. (A very strong version of that idea played a role in versions of dependency theory and world-systems theory that explained domestic social and political arrangements in terms of a country's position – say, as raw material supplier, or manufacturing

center, or commercial headquarters – in a global division of labor.[21])
There is a very large space between the Purely Domestic Poverty Thesis
and the Strong Thesis. A large space, and the right space to occupy
with projects that coordinate domestic and global efforts.

4.1 Rise of all the rest?

One concern about the force of the Strong Thesis begins with the
observation that some countries with large numbers of poor – China,
the Asian tigers, India, Botswana – have grown very rapidly under
existing global rules (typically by playing against the conventional
wisdom). Call it "the rise of the rest." If they managed, why not others?

In response to this objection, Pogge observes that the success of
some countries does not show that all others could have done as well.
Those who point to this evidence of differential success may be com-
mitting a "some–all fallacy" (SPH44), arguing that "some have succeeded; therefore all could have been as successful." They say that the
success of some (say, with export-led growth) shows that the deficien-
cies are not in the global rules, which do not need reform, but in the
failures of others to adopt those successful policies.

Some observers may be fairly accused of this fallacy. But the logical
point seems misguided as a response to empirical arguments about the
relevance of national experiences in addressing domestic poverty.

First, as I mentioned, half the world's extreme poverty remains in
China and India, countries with successful growth performance (China
doubling every nine years since 1978). The distinction between successful and unsuccessful economic performers is not entirely pertinent to
the issue of alleviating most global poverty. Even if every economy
had performed as well as China and India, most world poverty would
still remain. To make the case for the Strong Thesis – that much of
current extreme poverty would have been avoided with the right global
rules – we need a case not simply that others could have performed as
well in terms of growth and poverty alleviation as the best performers,
but that the large numbers of poor in China and India, despite their
relative economic success, are a product of global rules. That is possible (most things are). In particular, it is *possible* that the distribution
of income in China and India would have been different under alternative global rules, but that case needs to be made.

The task of making the case is rendered that much more difficult by
Pogge's assertion, already noted, that his case about harm to the global
poor depends only on what has happened in the world since 1980

(SPV55). Over that period, under the actual global rules, extreme poverty in China and India declined by hundreds of millions. Under what alternative rules and policies would it have declined further? Perhaps there is a good answer. But concerns about logically fallacious some–all inferences are simply beside the point because most extreme poverty would have remained even if all countries had been as successful as China and India.

Second, staying at the level of national economic performance, appealing to the success of some countries provides some evidence for the thesis that others could have succeeded. It shows that a certain claim – that global rules are designed to keep everyone in place, thus simply preserving a rich–poor status quo – is misguided. To be sure, improved national performance under existing rules by some poor countries is not a proof that all countries could have succeeded. But we need to understand why the evidence *is* irrelevant, not simply to be reminded that it might be.

Pogge suggests two lines of argument for such irrelevance. First, that if less successful countries had adopted the export-led strategy of the successful developers, that strategy would have delivered much less benefit to the successful countries because the market for their low-end consumer goods would have been flooded. The less successful countries might have done better, but at some cost in success for those that were more successful. Perhaps, though the market for consumer goods is not fixed, the development strategies of successful countries were not all the same, and the successful performers did not grow exclusively by exporting cheap consumer goods: there was also steel and ships.

But suppose that the strategy would have been less advantageous to the successful performers. Still, some countries were stagnant between 1975 and 2000, in particular in sub-Saharan Africa, where extreme poverty grew significantly worse: if they had grown 3 percent annually, their per capita income would have doubled during that period, instead of shrinking. The aggregate results for extreme poverty are uncertain and depend, of course, on how the gains from growth would have been distributed in the poorest countries, but it might well be less pressing now in the places where it has grown so much worse.

The second claim is that markets were limited by protectionism in affluent countries, and this protectionism – an alterable feature of the global order – precluded any generalization of the success stories. Perhaps. But first, while protectionism in affluent countries may have limited growth possibilities for some developing countries, it is also true that trade protections have decreased significantly, and that the persistence of protectionism can hardly explain the extraordinary

differences between successful and unsuccessful economic performance
in developing countries. Second, consider sub-Saharan Africa: between
1975 and 2000, per capita income fell 15%, though there was also
considerable variation in performance, with Botswana and Mauritius
on the high end. If growth rates had been 3% – nothing like the very
strong performance in Botswana – income would have doubled instead
of falling disastrously. The fact that all could not, in the present global
order, have achieved 8% growth rates for 30 years – let's simply stipu-
late this – is not especially relevant to the economic disasters of the
past generation. Moreover, I am not sure how, under some alternative
global rules there might have been a generalization of South Korean
or Chinese growth rates. (Dropping agricultural protections in affluent
countries? Probably a small effect. Free movement of people across
borders? Hard to know: the effects could be *very* large because of wage
differences, but would depend on how the politics works out.)

4.2 Symmetry of global and national?

Suppose we assume now that poor countries could all have developed
at decent rates without any change in the global rules. Pogge argues
that this assumption does not absolve the global rules "of responsibility for any excess poverty that would have been avoided if the political
elites in the poor countries were less corrupt and less incompetent"
(SPH45). Of course not. It would be absurd to deny that some changes
in global rules would be more favorable to the extreme poor. That is
what the Conventional Thesis says. But what about the Strong Thesis?
    In its defense, Pogge makes two symmetrical assertions:

S1 Most severe poverty in the world could be avoided through changes
in political arrangements and policies in poor countries, even if the
current global order were not changed;[22] and

S2 Most severe poverty would be avoided, despite the corrupt and
oppressive regimes holding sway in so many poor countries, if the global
institutional order were designed to achieve this purpose. (SPH46)

S1 seems pretty implausible, but it is not immediately relevant. Let's
focus on S2, which expresses the idea I earlier called Independent
Effects. According to S2, mass poverty in, say, the Congo, Zimbabwe,
Sierra Leone, Bangladesh, Pakistan, Nigeria, or India could be avoided
(and could have been avoided) by changes in (or historically different)

global rules, *even if domestic institutions and regimes were held fixed.* I know of no evidence at all for this extraordinary claim. I am not sure how trade policies, or new patent rules, or more generous development assistance, or alternative rules on debt repayment would have a large impact in any of these countries, given current regimes, institutions, and policies. While the alleged symmetry *might* hold, this assertion of Independent Effects is extremely implausible, as an empirical matter, given the importance of local conditions in mediating the effects of global factors. Consider, for example, health, education, and employment creation: it is difficult to see a case for large, sustainable poverty-reducing effects through changes in global rules operating completely independently of changes in domestic regimes.

A temptation to endorse the symmetry might come from the case of development assistance, but the evidence suggests that we should resist the temptation. The (often polemical) debate about its benefits continues unresolved. Aid skeptics remind us that China has set the record for growth and poverty reduction with no development assistance, argue that assistance is often a destructive substitute for domestic investment and can sever the relationship between spending and popular support, and observe that assistance in sub-Saharan Africa fell over the course of the mid and late 1990s, leading up to the current phase of renewed growth there, which began around 2000.[23] Aid optimists remind us that a pathetically small amount of aid has been given over the past 50 years, particularly when we exclude Cold War-motivated assistance. There does seem to be a good (though not entirely uncontroversial) case for the proposition that assistance is particularly helpful in addressing extreme poverty when institutions are decent, but that of course is no support for Symmetry.[24] It is much harder to make the case that aid does much to relieve severe poverty regardless of the domestic institutional and policy setting.[25]

4.3 Domestic institutions and global rules: background

But Pogge's principal argument is about Endogenous Institutions, not Independent Effects. A few words of background first.

Much work on economic development over the past generation has emphasized the importance of domestic institutions – including institutions that establish a rule of law, secure property rights, political accountability, risk regulation, and macroeconomic stability – in explaining economic performance.[26] To illustrate the point about institutions, consider just one striking finding. A vast amount has been written about the so-called resource curse. The idea is that natural resources may be harmful to a country's economic performance, as the evidence indicates for Nigeria or Sierra Leone. But of course for every Nigeria or Sierra Leone there is a Norway or a Mexico (where oil was not very damaging) or, for that matter, the United States, which in 1913 was the leading producer of nearly every industrial mineral. Are natural resources good or bad for economic development? Can anything general be said?

Take the sample of resource-rich countries, measured by resource exports as a percentage of GDP, and divide it into countries with good and bad institutions. What you find is that countries with good institutions are not resource-cursed. Indeed, $r^2 = 0$ when you regress growth on resource dependency. But you also see a strong resource curse in the places with bad institutions.[27]

So institutions seem important, but I am not suggesting that it follows that they are all that matters. Consider the Extractive Industries Transparency Initiative (EITI), a recent, voluntary effort, with support from some affluent countries (among others, Canada, Spain, Norway, Netherlands, Belgium, France, the United Kingdom, and the United States), NGOs (including Transparency International, Oxfam, and Global Witness), international organizations, and companies. EITI aims to encourage resource-rich (understood operationally as a high degree of fiscal- or export-dependence on hydrocarbons or minerals), poorer countries and the companies operating there to ensure transparency on revenues paid by companies to governments: "Regular publication of all material oil, gas and mining payments by companies to governments ('payments') and all material revenues received by governments from oil, gas and mining companies ('revenues') to a wide audience in a publicly accessible, comprehensive and comprehensible manner."[28] The idea is that such transparency in the extractives sector will help to combat the resource curse by enabling all players, including domestic groups in poor countries, to know what is happening with their resources, thus reducing incentives and opportunities for corruption and unaccountable use of national resources.

I mention EITI not because it has been a great success. It is very early in the game, and it is not likely to be a great success without, *inter alia*, standards beyond simple transparency (power is not exclusively information).[29] Still, it illustrates how global actors – including governments of affluent countries, private firms, international organizations (World Bank and African Development Bank), and NGOs – can *both* acknowledge the importance of domestic institutions in imposing the resource curse *and also* acknowledge their own role. The idea behind the EITI is that outside actors – including governments, companies, and international organizations – have a responsibility to change global rules in ways that encourage domestic actors to reshape their conduct and fashion institutions that help to diminish the resource curse in places where it has done real damage. The thought behind the transparency initiative is that access to information is at least necessary if citizens are to hold governments accountable. EITI thus requires that domestic "stakeholders" be part of the transparency initiatives. Ensuring their presence and their access to good information about flows of revenues will shift at least in small ways – anyway, this is the theory – the balance of domestic power.

EITI illustrates an animating idea behind Endogenous Institutions: domestic institutions need to be explained, and global rules are one element in the explanation. Two features of EITI, however, bear emphasis. First, an essential feature of EITI is that it does *not propose simply to change external rules* in the expectation that domestic actors will suitably adjust their conduct while threatening sanctions for failure. Instead, it requires – for better or worse – domestic government cooperation as an initial threshold condition for participation in the initiative. A second and related point is that EITI does not depend on the very strong version of Endogenous Institutions that I stated earlier, according to which institutions are very substantially or fully explained by global rules. As EITI suggests, you can accept that global rule changes may constructively change incentives and opportunities that animate domestic political conflicts (by, for example, reducing the returns on predatory rule) without accepting the view, reminiscent of dependency theory, about domestic-institutional and political dependence on global structure.

4.4 Do global rules explain domestic institutions?

This idea about the importance of the global background of domestic political economy animates Pogge's view. In defense of the Strong Thesis, he says that bad domestic arrangements are a result of global rules, and explores the role of two features of the global order – the *resource privilege* and *borrowing privilege* – in generating bad domestic arrangements.[30]

The idea of a resource privilege is that current global rules assign *full* control of a country's natural resources – land, minerals and oil – to whomever rules the country, regardless of the viciousness of their rule. This rule encourages bad institutions: it increases the returns on

autocracy and predation, provides no economic incentives for rulers
to be decent, decreases the benefits of shared control of the state (the
global rules make domestic power independent of sharing the resource
rents), and may attract ruthless people into political life. If power
holders in a country could be acknowledged by outsiders as owners of
resources only if they met certain conditions – rule of law, basic popular
accountability – then domestic institutions would improve because the
value of controlling the resources would be contingent on meeting the
conditions. Changing global rules would reduce the benefits of autocratic power, attract fewer ruthless people, and thus improve political
conduct.

For example, consider a recent suggestion about how changes in
current global rules on resource ownership might mitigate the resource
curse.[31] Leif Wenar argues that oil and other extractive companies may
be seen as trafficking in stolen property, and consumers purchasing
stolen property, when they extract or purchase resources from countries in which governments are entirely unaccountable to the governed.
The underlying idea is that the governed are themselves the owners of
the country's natural wealth. Lack of accountability amounts, then, to
stealing from the people of the country (the owners). Conventional
legal rules against the possession and sale of stolen property could then
be used to prevent imports from such countries, which would provide
incentives to make the governments accountable according to some
agreed minimal standards of political accountability, including both
political and civil liberties.

To operationalize the proposal, Wenar uses Freedom House scores.
A "not free" score of 7 on either political or civil liberties categorizes
natural resources sold by the regime as stolen. Under this proposal,
regimes in 20 countries (according to 2008 classifications) would be
treated as stealing natural resources, and companies trading in those
resources would be treated as trading in stolen goods. Among the
countries are China, Vietnam, Saudi Arabia, and Cuba, as well as
Myanmar, North Korea, Somalia, Sudan, and Zimbabwe.[32]

Putting many important questions about the proposal aside, I want
to underscore that this proposal is unlikely to do much about extreme
global poverty. (Wenar does not suggest otherwise. I use his proposal
simply to illustrate my concerns about global rule changes alleviating
domestic poverty.) First, there is the problem of useless sanction
(useless in terms of alleviating extreme poverty). A number of the
countries that might be subject to sanction because of their unaccountable regimes are places (Saudi Arabia, Syria, Belarus, Tunisia, and
Cuba) with very little extreme poverty. Others are places – like China

and Vietnam – with very high growth rates, in which it is hard to see how the proposal would help on the poverty issue, and – while acknowledging the difficulties of estimating general equilibrium effects – might well make things worse.

Second, much extreme poverty is in countries – India, Nigeria, and Bangladesh – that are well within the accountability conditions required for valid contracts, and would thus face no troubles.

Third, there are concerns about the antipoverty impact of induced reforms. Whatever the operational standards for ownership are, it may be possible for countries to game them, doing just enough to satisfy the basic conditions of accountability, which is unlikely to have much substantive effect. Moreover, even if an opposition emboldened by the new global rules conscientiously pursued it, a shift from below the accountability line to just above the line is unlikely to have much substantive effect. Consider a country below the accountability line, with widespread repression of association, no rule of law, no meaningful elections, sharp limits on free expression, and where the political opposition lacks sufficient organized strength to change the political terms, but the change comes about because of a shift in global rules. The development of new domestic forms of accountability and rule of law will likely proceed slowly, with very uncertain impact on growth rates and poverty reduction.[33]

There are other, more political strategies for restricting the resource privilege than Wenar's property-rights approach. For example, extensions of the EITI (like the World Bank's new EITI++, see note 29) aim to build transparency and accountability without relying so heavily on legal instruments, and in ways that aim more directly to promote improved domestic politics, though they also depend, as I said earlier, on engagement by the countries themselves. But I do not see a story that would make domestic institutions and poverty strongly endogenous to global rules, and thus no empirically plausible way to embed the explanatory importance of domestic institutions in a larger story about the explanatory sufficiency of global rules. To make that case we would need to know, *inter alia*, how responsive autocrats are to the expected returns on the control of natural resources, how much that expected rate of return varies with changes in global rules, and how dependent the growth rate and poverty rate are to meeting whatever conditions are stipulated.

Consider, more briefly, the borrowing privilege. Here again, the idea is that troubles arise because of the very large returns that flow from political rule, given the current rules on borrowing and repayment. Essentially, rulers who hold de facto power have sovereign borrowing privileges and can use loans to pay for the weapons they use to ruin the lives of people through war and crush their opposition, and then lenders can require a successor government to pay off the debt of the despot.

One way to address this problem would be to modify the current understanding and treatment of odious debts in international law by establishing a global body (or empowering a range of existing global and regional bodies) with the power to make *ex ante* declarations that some regimes are "odious debt prone."[34] The consequence of such declaration (publicly known), on this Due Diligence Model, would be that lenders – now given due notice – would be required to specify legitimate public purposes for loans and monitoring plans to ensure compliance with those purposes. Successor governments could only permissibly repudiate loans when the funds were diverted from the approved purpose and the lender failed to implement the announced borrowing plan. This would mean reduced incentives to lending to brutal regimes, reduced incentives to being a brutal regime because of the difficulty in borrowing, reduced capacity to be a brutal regime because of the difficulty in sovereign borrowing, and stronger incentives for challengers because they would not be saddled with large odious debts.[35] The *ex ante* announcement would create greater certainty in financial markets than more standard legal strategies for declaring debt odious, while the due diligence condition would permit beneficial lending, and thus help protect the population from the harmful results of economic sanctions.

There is much to be said for this strategy for dealing with the odious debt problem. It is hideous to see a successor regime, thus the citizens of a country, saddled with paying off debt incurred to feed some predator's taste for blood diamonds. But for all the reasons I have already discussed, the relationship between a sensible odious debt doctrine that appropriately limits subsequent burdens and claims about alleviating extreme poverty is tenuous, both because so much extreme poverty is untouched by issues about borrowing privileges, and because the implications for poverty alleviation of changing those rules is so uncertain.

5 Conclusion

A large number of people now live on the edge, excluded from the benefits of the extraordinary global growth of the past 30 years. They are excluded not because of some wrong they have committed but despite their innocence. The fact that so many are living so badly is a moral disaster, not least because the problem of extreme poverty is not beyond remedy. Building a world without extreme poverty – a reasonable ideal – will require a range of efforts, depending on location (keeping in mind the differences between, say, China, India, Nigeria, Bangladesh, Sudan, Somalia, and Sierra Leone). Building it in a sustainable way will depend (*inter alia*) on decent domestic arrangements as well as global rules (and on larger doses of global coordination to address growing pressures on resources and climate). And wealthier countries have significant responsibility in building that world. Philosophy, too, has a role to play, in clarifying the bases of that responsibility, exposing excuses for not discharging it, and explaining how a world without extreme poverty is one part of a reasonable ideal.

But in figuring out what to do, we should learn something from recent history. The Washington Consensus – now consigned to history's crowded dustbin – said that countries needed to stabilize, liberalize, and privatize. Lots of places followed that advice and did badly; lots of other places did well during the period of the Washington Consensus, especially places that broke the Consensus rules.[36] What we need now is not a replacement recipe – "get the global rules right," instead of "get the prices right" or "get the institutions right" – and least of all a recipe, backed by speculations about possibilities, presented as social science. Instead, the circumstances call for a mix of moral conviction about the importance of addressing the issue of extreme poverty, an open-minded, empirical, and experimental spirit about how best to deal with it, and institutions, both domestic and global, organized to foster such learning.

Notes

*I am grateful for comments on earlier drafts to Pranab Bardhan, Charles Beitz, Helena DeBres, Judith Goldstein, Alison Jaggar, Eszter Kollar, Stephen Krasner, Pietro Maffettone, Sebastiano Maffettone, Edward Miguel, Rajan Menon, Helen Milner, Avia Pasternak, Matthias Risse, Ingrid Salvatore, Debra Satz, Seana Shiffrin, Robert van der Veen, and Leif Wenar.

1 Richard Feynman, Ralph Leighton, and Matthew Sands, *The Feynman Lectures on Physics* (San Francisco: Pearson, 2006).
 2 1st edn: (Cambridge Polity, 2002), hereafter *WP*. See also "'Assisting' the Global Poor," in *The Ethics of Assistance: Morality and the Distant Needy*, ed. Deen K. Chatterjee (Cambridge: Cambridge University Press, 2004), pp. 26–88, hereafter AGP; "Severe Poverty as a Violation of Negative

Duties," *Ethics and International Affairs* 19(1) (2005), pp. 55–83, hereafter SPV; and "Severe Poverty as a Human Rights Violation," in *Freedom From Poverty as a Human Right*, ed. Thomas Pogge (Oxford: Oxford University Press, 2007), pp. 11–53, hereafter SPH.

3 The figure of 10,000 comes from Dan Henkle, Gap's Senior Vice President for Social Responsibility (private communication). The precise magnitude does not matter: the point is there are lots, and they now play a role in a (not very effective system of) system of global labor regulation.

4 For discussion, see Gay Seidman, *Beyond the Boycott* (New York: Russell Sage, 2007); Richard Locke, Fei Qin, and Alberto Brause, "Does Monitoring Improve Labor Standards? Lessons from Nike," *Industrial and Labor Relations Review* 61(1) (October 2007): 3–31; Sanjay Reddy and Christian Barry, *International Trade and Labor Standards: A Proposal for Linkage* (New York: Columbia University Press, 2008).

5 The list comes from a recent report from the World Bank Commission on Growth and Development, *The Growth Report: Strategies for Sustained Growth and Inclusive Development, Conference Edition* (Washington, DC: World Bank, 2008), p. 20.

6 For background on this assertion, see Joshua Cohen and Charles Sabel, "Extra Rempublicam Nulla Justitia?," *Philosophy and Public Affairs* 34(2) (2006): 147–75; and *idem*, "Global Democracy?" *New York University Journal of International Law and Policy* 37(4) (2006): 763–97.

7 John Rawls, *The Law of Peoples* (Cambridge, MA: Harvard University Press, 1999), pp. 11–13.

8 See the forceful statement in Dani Rodrik, *One Economics, Many Recipes: Globalization, Institutions, and Economic Growth* (Princeton: Princeton University Press, 2007), pp. 5–6. Abhijit Banerjee expresses a broadly similar attitude in *Making Aid Work* (Cambridge, MA: MIT Press, 2007). See also William Easterly (ed.), *Reinventing Foreign Aid* (Cambridge, MA: MIT Press, 2008), especially the summary contributions from John McMillan and Nancy Birdsall.

9 Pogge says that PDPT is "widely held" in the developed countries. My impression is that this is not true, but I would welcome evidence one way or the other. Pogge associates PDPT with John Rawls's *Law of Peoples* (AGP261–64). I think the association is misguided, but explaining why would take me too far afield.

10 The example is suggested by Duncan Thomas et al., "Causal Effect of Health on Labor Market Outcomes: Experimental Evidence," California Center for Population Research, On-Line Working Paper Series (University of California, Los Angeles), http://repositories.cdlib.org/ccpr/olwp/CCPR-070-06.

11 The idea in the text is one variant of a more generic claim about endogenizing institutions. A more familiar story says that geography explains institutional quality, and that variations in institutional quality in turn account for variations in performance. See for example Stanley L.

Engerman and Kenneth L. Sokoloff, "Colonialism, Inequality, and Long-Run Paths of Development," in *Understanding Poverty*, ed. Abhijit Vinayak Banerjee, Roland Benabou, and Dilip Mookherjee (Oxford: Oxford University Press, 2006), pp. 37–61, esp. p. 39.

12 See Daron Acemoglu, Simon Johnson, and James A. Robinson, "Reversal of Fortune: Geography and Institutions in the Making of Modern World Income Distribution," *Quarterly Journal of Economics* 117 (November 2002): 1231–94. For instructive doubts about the argument, see Rodrik, *One Economics*, p. 186.

13 See Jeff A. King, "Odious Debt: The Terms of the Debate," *North Carolina Journal of International Law and Commercial Regulation* 32(4) (2007): 605–68, and Lee C. Buchheit, G. Mitu Gulati, and Robert B. Thompson, "The Dilemma of Odious Debts," *Duke Law Journal* 56(5) (March 2007): 1201–62.

14 The discussion in *World Poverty and Human Rights* is not a condensed version of more expansive arguments elsewhere: SPH44–51 and AGP263–64 are comparably concise.

15 *The Bottom Billion* (Oxford: Oxford University Press, 2007), pp. 159–60.

16 I take the estimate from a March 2006 presentation by Dani Rodrik, "Making Globalization More Development-Friendly." For related discussion see Rodrik, *One Economics*, p. 222.

17 See the interesting criticisms of *World Poverty and Human Rights* in essays by Matthias Risse, Debra Satz, Alan Patten, Rowan Cruft, and Norbert Anwander, in *Ethics and International Affairs* 19(1) (2005). Satz's criticisms at pp. 48–50 are closest to my own. But for the reasons mentioned in the text, I put my principal emphasis elsewhere.

18 My sketch of Pogge's views in this section draws particularly on SPV, pp. 55–6, 59–61, 74–8.

19 The discussion in this section applies, I believe, with equal force to the Strong Thesis and Strong Thesis B.

20 On more recent (improved) performance, see Edward Miguel, "Is It Africa's Turn?" *Boston Review* 33(3) (May–June 2008).

21 See Andre Gunder Frank, *Capitalism and Underdevelopment in Latin America* (New York: Penguin, 1971); Fernando Henrique Cardoso and Enzo Falletto, *Dependency and Development in Latin America*, trans. Marjorie Mattingly Urquidi (Berkeley: University of California Press, 1979), esp. pp. 26–7; Immanuel Wallerstein, *The Modern World-System I: Capitalist Agriculture and the Origins of the European World-Economy in the Sixteenth Century* (New York: Academic Press, 1980). Though the emphasis in dependency theory is on the global system, the essential idea is not that domestic rates of return depend on global political-economic rules, but that natural resources and a surplus extracted from the periphery fuel growth in the core of the world economy.

22 As was suggested in the third point of clarification in the opening section.

23 On the recent upswing in African growth rates, see Miguel, "Is It Africa's Turn?" Though not an aid skeptic, Miguel expresses doubts about the role of assistance in helping the upturn.

24 Steven Radelet, Michael Clemens, and Rikhil Bhavnani, "Aid and Growth," *Finance and Development* 42(3) (September 2005): imf.org/external/pubs/ft/fandd/2005/09/radelet.htm. For critical discussion, see William Easterly, *The White Man's Burden: Why the West's Efforts to Aid the Rest Have Done So Much Ill and So Little Good* (Oxford: Oxford University Press, 2007), pp. 42–3.

25 For a discussion of ideas about assistance that is not so completely stylized, see the essays in William Easterly (ed.), *Reinventing Foreign Aid* (Cambridge, MA: MIT, 2008).

26 See Douglass C. North and Robert Thomas, *The Rise of the Western World: A New Economic History* (Cambridge: Cambridge University Press, 1976); Acemoglu, Johnson, and Robinson, "Reversal of Fortune"; Elhanan Helpman, *The Mystery of Economic Growth* (Cambridge, MA: Harvard University Press, 2004), ch. 7, for a synthesis. For a quick introduction, see Daron Acemoglu, "Root Causes" and Jeffrey Sachs, "Institutions Matter, But Not for Everything," both in *Finance and Development*, June 2003.

27 See Halvor Mehlum, Karl Moene, and Ragnar Torvik, "Institutions and the Resource Curse," *The Economic Journal* 116 (January 2006), 1–20; James A. Robinson, Ragnar Torvik, and Thierry Verdier, "Political Foundations of the Resource Curse," *Journal of Development Economics* 79 (2006): 447–68; Halvor Mehlum, Karl Moene, and Ragnar Torvik, "Cursed by Resources or Institutions?," *The World Economy* (2006): 1117–31. For a more skeptical view, see Stephen Haber and Victor Menaldo, "Do Natural Resources Fuel Authoritarianism? A Reappraisal of the Resource Curse," unpublished (on file with the author).

28 See www.eitransparency.org/principlesandcriteria.htm, August 14, 2005.

29 On the virtues and limits of EITI, see Paul Collier and Michael Spence, "Help Poor States to Seize the Fruits of the Boom," *Financial Times*, 10 April 2008. The World Bank's recently announced Extractive Industries Transparency Initiative Plus Plus (EITI++) is an ambitious effort to build on EITI, moving past transparency on the flow of funds from companies to governments to transparency on expenditures of those revenues and capacity-building efforts that will better enable states to manage resource-based revenues and use them for constructive purposes.

30 Although I am focusing on bad effects of global rules on current institutions, not all the current effects are bad, as Pranab Bardhan has reminded me in discussion.

31 Leif Wenar, "Property Rights and the Resource Curse," *Philosophy and Public Affairs* 36(1) (2008): 2–32. Wenar notes the connection with Pogge's resource privilege at p. 13, n. 29.

32 *Freedom in the World 2008: Selected Data from Freedom House's Annual Global Survey of Political Rights and Civil Liberties* (Freedom House,

2008). The results would be somewhat different if we used Polity IV scores, and set the cutoff at autocracy (= −6). In 2006, Zimbabwe, Sudan, Tunisia were at −4, and Chad at −2, and thus would have been sufficiently accountable, though all had at least one score of 7 on Freedom House. See www. systemicpeace.org/polity/polity06.htm.

33 The evidence on democracy and poverty reduction is mixed. See, for example, Michael Ross, "Is Democracy Good for the Poor?" *American Journal of Political Science* 50(4) (October 2006): 860–74; Masayuki Kudamatsu, "Has Democratization Reduced Infant Mortality in Sub-Saharan Africa? Evidence from Micro Data" (December 2006, unpublished).

34 On the Due Diligence Model, see Seema Jayachandran and Michael Kremer, "Odious Debt," *American Economic Review* 96 (March 2006): 82–92. I am grateful to Jayachandran, Kremer, and other members of the Working Group on Odious Debt for discussion of these issues.

35 If debt repayment is substantially driven by reputational concerns, then the extent of reduced saddling is not so clear. See, in general, Michael Tomz, *Reputation and International Cooperation: Sovereign Debt across Three Centuries* (Princeton: Princeton University Press, 2007).

36 See Rodrik, *One Economics*, pp. 18–21, 239.

2
Rights, Harm, and Institutions
Kok-Chor Tan*

1 Pogge's institutional approach

In *World Poverty and Human Rights*, Thomas Pogge advances a distinctive approach to the problem of world poverty.[1] Instead of presenting the case to assist the global poor as a duty grounded on some fundamental principle of humanitarian assistance requiring positive steps to assist or rescue persons in severe need, Pogge takes the duty of the global affluent to assist the poor to be logically a form of recompense for the affluent's past and prevailing harming of the poor. As Pogge puts it, he wants to approach the problem of alleviating world poverty not "in terms of helping the poor" but in terms of "protecting them from the effects of global rules whose injustice benefits us and is our responsibility" (p. 23). The rich have this duty to protect the global poor from the harmful effects of the global order because they are causally responsible for imposing this order on the poor. We don't need to endorse the idea that the poor have some independent and antecedent *basic* rights to *positive* assistance from the rich to counter their suffering. On Pogge's view, all we need to recognize, quite uncontroversially he believes, is that the poor, like anyone else, have the right not to be subject to a social order that is harmful towards them. The affluent have the duty of justice not to do harm, but the problem is, Pogge argues, that they are failing in this basic duty. The affluent therefore have *the duty of justice* to make amends for the injustice they are inflicting on the poor. Thus Pogge's preference is to speak of the duty towards the global poor in terms of protecting the poor, that is, as a duty to protect them from the harms that we are inflicting on them, rather than in terms of assistance as such.[2]

Having a derivative duty of justice to make amends for an injustice that one is responsible for causing can entail a combination of different responses. In the case of institutionally generated injustices, for example, the culpable agents can be expected to do a number of things to make good the institutional injustice. They can eliminate the specific features of the institutional setup that are unjustly harming people. That is, they should cease harming as a first step. They can also establish new institutional mechanisms and safeguards to counteract or mitigate the harms that existing features of the institutional order could inflict (when eliminating these features is not an option for some reason); and they can be expected to provide assistance to persons who are already or are being harmed. These steps require positive actions and, because they are steps to correct injustices, they are duties of justice. Yet they derive fundamentally from the uncontroversial moral principle that persons have the duty of justice not to inflict harm on another.

According to Pogge, this way of conceptualizing the problem of world poverty has a distinct advantage over traditional approaches. Beginning from the negative duty not to do harm, the "libertarian tenet" as he calls it, Pogge sidesteps the philosophical debate over whether there are also positive duties of justice beyond negative duties. The challenge that Pogge has set for himself is not the philosophical one of establishing that the global poor have a positive human right to be assisted, but the "factual" one of showing how the global rich are in fact harming the poor, that is, how they are violating their basic negative duty (and therefore have the consequent moral duty to take steps to make amends) (pp. 13–14, 25). The factual challenge is, however, by no means trivial, and it is to Pogge's credit that he is able perceptively to identify and illustrate the various ways in which the global institutional order is systematically disadvantaging the poor and how the global rich and powerful are in several ways causally responsible for sustaining this order. Because the key analysis for Pogge is the way the global affluent are supporting and sustaining a global *institutional order* that is *harming* the global poor, he refers to his approach frequently as an *institutional approach*.

In this critical commentary, I will apply pressure to two related aspects of Pogge's institutional approach. One concerns specifically Pogge's account of human rights within this institutional framework;

the other concerns Pogge's notion of harm in his claim that the global order harms the poor. On the issue of human rights, I will argue that Pogge presents an account of human rights that is indefensibly limited in its scope. It limits the claimants of human rights to only those who share some social order with us. Yet given that one of the basic aims of a notion of human right is to protect the disenfranchised, the disposed, and the outcasts, any conception of human rights that is contingent on social membership is fatally compromised. On the second point, I will suggest that it is not clear how the global order is in fact *wrongly* harming the poor, given Pogge's own starting assumption that there are only negative duties. None of my comments is meant as an outright refutation of Pogge's distinctive and influential approach to global justice and world poverty. The first point on human rights is an invitation to Pogge to clarify the scope of human rights on his account; the second is an invitation to clarify the notion of harm so crucial to his thesis.

2 Human rights and institutions

Pogge's institutional approach to human rights conceives human rights *institutionally* in two distinct senses. One is that human rights violations are institutional violations, that is, they are violations against persons that are carried out by the institutions of the state and its agents. Pogge refers to this as "official disrespect" (p. 59). Thus, a person may suffer physical harm from a random street mugger *in a society that meets reasonable standards of security and safety*, or be similarly injured by a systemically corrupt police force while the state either does nothing or, worse yet, permits and encourages such official beatings.[3] Only the latter counts as a human rights violation because of its institutional character. This institutional feature of human rights thus specifies the kinds of violation that count as a violation of human rights. It aptly captures the idea that human rights are the responsibility of states, and rights violations are violations by the state and its agents.

The second way Pogge's account of human rights is institutional concerns not the type of harm that is pertinently an offense against human rights, but the relevant subjects and agents of human rights. On Pogge's institutional approach, human rights demands are demands that persons who are subject to a common institutional order can make against each other. The scope of human rights is defined institutionally in that the claimants and agents of human rights are just those persons participating in a common institutional scheme. It is this second sense of being institutional that I want to focus on.

First, recall Pogge's strategic motivation for the institutional approach. He feels that the discourse on human rights and poverty is often entangled over the issue of whether there are positive duties in addition to negative duties of restraint. His institutional approach to human rights "allows us to transcend the terms of this debate," he notes (p. 64). The institutional approach "emphasizes negative duties across the board," and thus "narrows the philosophical gap" between those who hold that there are only negative duties of human rights and those who hold that there are also positive duties of human rights (p. 70). Human rights on this approach are defined negatively; they are reduced basically to the (negative) right not to be exposed to a social arrangement that coercively deprives one of access to the goods necessary for a flourishing human life (p. 65). Pogge's point is that because the rich are subjecting the poor to a harmful social order, namely a social order in which their access to basic goods is compromised severely, they are violating the human rights of the poor, and therefore have the derivative duty of justice to take different steps to make good their injustice against the poor.

I will turn to the problem of the sense in which the global order is unjustly harming the poor in the next section. Here what is of relevance is that on this account of human rights, only those who are subject to a social order can make human rights demands against only those with whom they share this social order.[4] As Pogge writes: "Responsibility for a person's human rights falls on all and only those *who participate* with this person in the same social system" (p. 66, my emphasis). Another remark puts the negative side of the claim more plainly: human rights are "*claims not against all other human beings,* but specially against those who impose a coercive institutional order upon you" (p. 67, my emphasis). Persons outside our social system are in no position to make human rights-based demands against us; only persons belonging to a common social order belong to a human rights community.[5]

But this confining of human rights to only those with whom one shares a common social system seems to limit the scope of human rights implausibly. Indeed, any conception of human rights that restricts the scope of human rights in this way is fatally flawed, it would seem. After all, human rights are meant to provide protection not just for members of a social order but also, importantly, for nonmembers. We want the concept of human rights to protect the most vulnerable and defenseless of humanity, "to provide some minimal protection

against utter helplessness to those too weak to protect themselves," as
Henry Shue has noted.[6] The defenseless and vulnerable can include
members of a social order obviously, for example minorities or disenfranchised persons within a state. But the most defenseless and vulnerable also include persons classified as nonmembers. Indeed historically,
the most remarkable atrocities were committed by states against
persons regarded to be unfit for membership, that is, against persons
who are seen not as members of the common social order. When a
regime carries out genocide, it seeks not to impose a social order on
the targeted people, but to eliminate it from membership in any social
order. On other occasions, as in colonialism, atrocities were indeed
committed against persons who fell outside the colonizers' social order.
To the extent that violations against persons are facilitated by first
rendering the targets of abuse as social outcasts or explicitly as outsiders or aliens, limiting human rights protection to only fellow members
removes protection from the most vulnerable. Generally, we want a
conception of human rights to be able to say that rights are demands
that members of humanity can make against the rest of humanity, and
not merely demands that only co-members of a given social order can
make against each other. For human rights to do the work that they
are meant to do, the scope of human rights must be understood pre-
institutionally rather than institutionally. That is, human rights ought
not to be limited by contingencies like membership in any particular
social order.

To illustrate, suppose a group of people (that is, human beings and
so potentially subjects of human rights) were suddenly to be discovered
on the far side of Venus (to borrow Pogge's own example on p. 198).
On Pogge's account, it would seem that these inhabitants, because by
hypothesis they just happened to be there and they don't share a
common social order with us currently or in the past, are in no position
to make human rights demands against us on earth. It seems to imply
then that we earthlings can do anything we wish to them – to colonize
them, to exploit their natural resources, subject them to biological
experiments without consent, and so on – and the alien humans would
have no grounds for complaint. Certainly they can't object on human
rights grounds. Surely if we want the language and authority of human
rights to do anything, it is to protect those who are perceived to be
outside of our social group from egregious abuses by others. Indeed,
on a strict reading of Pogge's claim that only those belonging to the
same social order can make human rights demands against each other,
it would seem that a people who is in the process of being colonized
cannot claim that the human rights of its members are being violated

for the colonizing is being carried out precisely to bring them, by coercion no doubt, within the same social world. But until that goal is achieved, until they are actually colonized and hence subjects to the same social arrangement, the victims of the colonizing process can't claim that their human rights are being denied. But this would be perverse of course: it says to the members of a society who are being colonized that while the colonization process is taking place they can't complain that their human rights are being violated by the colonizers because they don't yet stand in human rights relations vis-à-vis their aggressors. Only when the colonization process is successfully completed and they have been successfully subjugated within the social order of the colonials are human rights demands triggered.

So on Pogge's institutional conception of human rights, indigenous peoples in the Americas would not be able to invoke the language of human rights against their European invaders during the period of colonization. I don't mean of course that concept was historically available to them (it wasn't and they could not have made such claims). My point is that we would want as a minimal test of the plausibility of a conception of human rights that it can say that the human rights of indigenous Americans were being violated during the process of colonization. More generally, we would want minimally for a conception of human rights that it applies to all human beings, including those perceived to not belong to one's social world for these are often also the most vulnerable persons. European colonization of Asia, America, and Africa was commonly rationalized as a civilizing mission – to bring heathens into the Europeans' Christian social order. Indeed a literal reading of Pogge's definition presents this moral hazard: if human rights are really important and yet they apply only to those who belong to your social world, then one may feel compelled and morally justified to annex outsiders into your arrangements, by force if need be, so that they can become rightful subjects of human rights in relation to you.[7]

The above objection assumes that human rights refer to the basic moral rights that individuals have *qua* human beings, and so to limit the scope of human rights to only fellow members of a social order implies that outsiders have no moral standing whatsoever, and that we may do anything to them. Now one might object that my criticism confuses basic morality with human rights, claiming instead that someone who has no human rights standing vis-à-vis us is still entitled to some minimal moral respect from us, in particular the *moral right* not to do harm. Indeed Pogge generally writes as if the duty not to do harm is a basic duty of justice that applies among all persons independently of whether or not they share a social order. For example, he writes more generally that "it is wrong severely to harm innocent people for minor gains" (p. 25). Therefore, while Pogge's conception of human rights limits its application to co-members of a given social order, one might attempt to say, in defense of Pogge against the above objection, that it does not follow that nonmembers have no moral standing whatsoever – it is a severe moral wrong to harm any person for some gain to oneself. It is open to Pogge's theory that outsiders still have the moral right not to be harmed even though this right is not properly speaking a human right, thus cushioning the worry canvassed above that Pogge's account of human rights is too restrictive in scope.

But if this is indeed Pogge's position (he is not explicit on this), why not call this basic right not to be harmed a basic *human* right, therefore rejecting (the aspect of) the institutional approach that ties human rights to membership of a social order? After all, we use the language of human rights to refer to the most fundamental moral claims that human beings *qua* human beings have against each other; so if there is indeed a fundamental right not to be harmed by another that is independent of agents' membership of a social order, then why not refer to this as a human right? Not much is served by introducing a more basic level of morality distinct from human rights if human rights are meant to speak to the most important and basic of human's justifiable moral claims and demands. Ontologically speaking, the positing of a distinct category of moral claims when these claims can be covered by the ideal of human rights is uneconomical. Normatively speaking much is lost, for the concept of human rights loses much of its force and its purpose if it is not conceived to take account of the most fundamental and pressing of human moral demands.

My objection to Pogge's restriction of the scope of human rights to persons who share a social order does not reject the other sense in which human rights are institutional, namely that human rights are meant to protect persons against official (institutional) violations. This sense of being institutional is independent of the second sense criticized above, that human rights apply among persons sharing a social order. The first provides an institutional account of what kinds of wrongs and violations human rights are meant to address; the second addresses the question of what the appropriate subjects of human rights are. One can agree with Pogge that human rights are meant to address institutional injustices without also accepting that human rights apply only among persons sharing a common social order. Institutional injustices can and have been inflicted upon nonmembers. That is, one need not be a member of a given social arrangement in order to suffer systemic and institutionally sanctioned violations against oneself. When a state commits war crimes against the citizens of another state, it commits an institutional violence against them (this is an offense that is institutionally executed after all), even though they aren't being subject to the aggressors' social order. A defensible account of human rights should not be barred from identifying such offenses as human rights offenses.

To be sure, Pogge's central thesis, that there is effectively a common global social system in which virtually all persons participate, guarantees that all of humanity belongs to a common social order, and so in practice in the real-world human rights are in effect demands that any member of humanity can make against the rest of humanity. But my objection is a conceptual one about how we should understand the scope of human rights, or membership in the human rights community. The world could contingently not be the way Pogge describes it. Or new societies of humanity not part of our given social order could be discovered. More poignantly, history tells us that it is a common strategy for tyrants to declare their specially targeted victims as social outcasts or nonmembers to justify their mistreatment. An account of human rights that limits its scope to just members cannot respond to such maneuvers. It seems to take the force out of human rights just when they are most needed, that is, when they are needed to offer protection to those whom society has cast out. So I believe that Pogge's institutional account of human rights can be strengthened by explicitly rejecting the notion that the scope of human rights is defined by membership in or subjection to a common social order. My comments here are meant as an invitation to Pogge to clarify his account of who can stand in a human rights relation to others, whether or not we should really conceive of human rights as demands that fellow participants in a social order can make against each other, instead of more broadly and standardly (and attractively to my mind) as claims that all of humanity can make against the rest of humanity.

3 Only "negative rights across the board"?

There is another aspect of Pogge's theory of human rights worth digressing a little to remark on briefly. This concerns not the question of scope but the question of the content of human rights, or more precisely the categories of duties of human rights. Pogge's account of human rights that begins with only "negative rights across the board" may transcend, as is his hope, some difficult debates about the content of human rights duties, and may sidestep the libertarian critique against social and economic rights, but it escapes confrontation with the libertarian only to come into confrontation with mainstream defenders of human rights. Consider Pogge's own fictional example: "Suppose we discovered people on Venus who are very badly off, and suppose we could help them at little cost to ourselves. If we did nothing, we would surely violate a positive duty of beneficence. But we would not be violating a negative duty of justice because we would not be contributing to the perpetuation of their misery" (p. 198). On Pogge's account, there is no obligation based on human rights to assist these imperiled persons on Venus even if we could (at little cost). Even if it is true that we have the negative duty not to harm these aliens (regardless of whether we want to call it a human rights duty or not), Pogge is clear that we don't have any positive duty to assist them.[8]

Of course this is a consequence that Pogge accepts for his theory. But it has to be pointed out that this runs against the grain of contemporary human rights thinking. As the idea of human rights progressed, it has become more accepted that it applies and can apply positively (in the sense that it can generate duties on the part of others to provide subjects with basic needs) to human beings as such. To present an account of human rights that says, for instance, absent some past or ongoing social interaction with you, we don't owe others anything *positively* runs against the tide of the human rights revolution. Pogge's theory of human rights to be sure is inspired by the wish to avoid the libertarian critique; but it results in an account of human rights that is severely weakened.[9] Again, I acknowledge that this is precisely Pogge's mission – to provide what he thinks is a noncontroversial (i.e., morally modest) conception of human rights that grounds only negative duties. But, so it seems to me, it is a mistake to think that this morally modest account of human rights is uncontroversial. The claim that we have no positive duties of any kind towards persons who are not part of our social order is no less counterintuitive than the libertarian claim that we have only negative duties is intuitive. So Pogge's approach may placate the libertarian, but it will alienate most typical defenders of human rights. Pogge may successfully escape battle with the libertarians over the content of rights-duties; but he is forced into battle with proponents of human rights, ironically the party on his side in the world poverty debate. In making his concession to the libertarians and offering a theory of human rights that emphasizes only negative duties, he is able to preach to, and perhaps even reach, the unconverted in the human rights debate, but this will be at the price of offending and losing the already converted. He is trading one philo-sophical contention for another. Given that Pogge's main opponent is the libertarian who denies that there are positive rights, it is under-standable why Pogge would make the trade. But it is also important to note what is being traded away.

To sum up my comments so far: Pogge takes human rights to be contingent on social membership by beginning with the presumption that human rights are fundamentally negative (that of not subjecting another to a harmful social order). I have suggested to the contrary that an attractive theory of human rights has to be able to *support positive duties* to those deprived of urgent needs independently of injustices done to them; and a minimally defensible theory of human rights *should not limit membership* in the community of human rights to just those who are members of a common social order.

4 Does the global order unjustly harm the poor when it disadvantages them?

As mentioned, Pogge sees his key task to be the factual one of showing how the global order is harming the poor and how the global affluent are responsible for imposing this order on them. He powerfully docu-ments, just to take some examples, the coercive WTO regimes that rich countries are imposing on poor countries; the unfavorable trade terms and agreements the poor are forced to accept; the norms and principles of international law, such as those pertaining to sovereignty, territorial integrity, resource control and borrowing privileges, and intellectual property rights.[10] All of these are features of a global order that is on the whole to the advantage of the rich but severely detrimental to the poor. And yet this order is sustained, because it is advantageous to the rich, through the choices of the rich, via the efforts of their govern-ments who represent their interests in international forums, their own consumption habits, and their indifference and so on (e.g., chapter 1).

It is hard not to be persuaded by Pogge's powerful arguments and examples that the global order has features that are disadvantageous to the poor while beneficial to the rich. But my use of "disadvantageous" here rather than "harm" is deliberate for we need to know whether this disadvantaging in fact constitutes a harm, or more precisely an unjust harm.[11] We have to ask whether this disadvantaging counts as a harm on the assumption that persons have only the negative duty of forbearance at the outset. This last point is significant because, while it would be easy for a utilitarian, say Singer, to say that the rich are really harming the poor by not redistributing resources to them when they can do so at little cost, or Shue's claim that there are positive duties of basic human rights to assist those deprived of urgent needs, Pogge's concession to the libertarian tenet, that there are only negative duties, disallows him from making a claim along either of these lines. Pogge will need a different way of showing why, just because the global order deprives the poor of certain goods, the global order is *unjustly harming* the poor. As I will argue, it is not clear how Pogge can conclusively say that the global order is harming the poor if we begin with the idea that we owe to each other only negative duties at the outset.[12]

So how is the present global order, which no doubt is disadvantageous to the poor, indeed harmful to the poor? As Pogge himself notes, harm is a comparative notion – someone is being harmed if he or she is made worse off compared to how he or she would fare under some other state of affairs. But what is the appropriate comparative baseline? It will be useful to work through some alternative baselines to see why Pogge is moved to endorse the one he does, and then to see whether he is indeed entitled to the endorsed comparative baseline.

One option is to say that a person is harmed if he or she is made worse off compared to how that person was at some earlier moment in time. But this "diachronic" approach is unsatisfactory, as Pogge points out (pp. 15–16). The current global economic order may be disadvantageous to the global poor, but if a case could be made that, even though the poor don't fare as well as the rich under the present arrangement, they are nonetheless doing better under this arrangement than they were under a previous one, then the present global order is really not harming them at all (but is in fact promoting their interests). The diachronic approach to harm suggests the implausible claim that, just because I am beating you up less frequently now than I was previously, I am not harming you even though I am still continuing to beat you. So the global poor may indeed do better under the present WTO regime, where patent-laws and intellectual property rights regulations are highly against their interests, where more powerful countries are able to claim exemptions from WTO requirements contrary to free trade to the detriment of poorer countries (by imposing tariffs, providing subsidies for domestic sectors, etc.), than they did prior to any trade agreement. But it does not follow that just because there is an improvement in their present situation they aren't being harmed. It is possible that, even though the pre-WTO era was more harmful to the poor than the present era, the latter is still severely harmful to them.

So the diachronic approach is unacceptable in Pogge's view, and rightly so. As an alternative, Pogge contemplates the possibility that the poor would be much better off under a global state of nature than they are under the present order. He notes that "one cannot even say with confidence that poverty would be worse in a global Lockean state of nature in which all human beings have access to a proportional share of the world's natural resources" (pp. 16, 138–9). Perhaps then, the state of nature can be taken as the default position against which all other arrangements can be compared.

But Pogge rightly notes that invoking a hypothetical state of nature is just too speculative for the purpose of establishing an appropriate comparative baseline (p. 16). It is virtually impossible to hypothesize reasonably the conditions of an imagined global state of nature and how persons would fare under such a state in terms of their access to the basic goods essential to human flourishing. Indeed, the concept of human flourishing would be radically different under any imagined state of nature. How are we to determine what counts as a flourishing human life in a state of nature, to begin with, and then identify with reasonable accuracy persons' access to basic goods that are essential for this flourishing? Furthermore, the comparative baseline provided by a state of nature can be radically different depending on whether we imagine the state of nature in Lockean or Hobbesian terms. Consequently, while it is at least imaginable for one to conclude that, compared to a Lockean state of nature, persons are faring worse under the present regime than they would naturally, one would be forced to say that the present arrangement is preferable to any natural condition if one understands the state of nature as Hobbes does, as a condition under which human life is "solitary, poor, nasty, brutish, and short."

Thus an imaginary global state of nature does not provide a satisfactory comparative baseline for determining whether the present global order is harmful to the poor. Pogge's own proposal is this: The present global order is not just disadvantageous to the poor but is in fact harming them because they are worse off under this arrangement than they would be under some other feasible and easily attainable alternative arrangement (p. 67).

In other words, even though the poor are arguably doing better under the present social order than the previous one, they are still being harmed because they are prevented from establishing an alternative arrangement in which their access to basic goods is even less restricted than the rich have opted not to support and bring about. To illustrate: suppose a person needs X units of goods (say 3,000 calories/day) to lead a minimally decent human life. That he now, thanks to a new social arrangement, has access to X minus n units (say 2,000 calories/day) when before he had only X minus 2n units (say 1,000 calories/

day) does not mean that he is no longer being harmed (as the dia-chronic approach would say) if there is an easily attainable and feasible alternative arrangement under which he can get the full X units he needs. His negative right to basic goods is still being violated, even though his access to them has improved, according to Pogge. Thus, the full range of alternative social arrangements that could be effec-tively put into place to ensure that persons are able to sufficiently meet basic needs is Pogge's comparative baseline. That is, we are to compare a given social arrangement against all possible feasible alternatives and, if there is an alternative in which persons would have adequate access to basic goods, then the present arrangement in which access to basic goods of some people is limited is harmful to those whose access it limits. They are being unjustly harmed by the rich because it is the choice of the rich not to bring into effect the social arrangement that would be kinder to the poor.

First notice what Pogge is not committed to. Pogge does not say that under an arrangement in which all persons receive at least X units that anyone is being harmed just because an alternative is available under which all can do better by getting 2X units. Pogge's concern is with securing the social order in which persons have adequate access to the basic goods necessary for a minimally flourishing human life, not with maximizing on persons' access to goods. Call this the commitment to "minimally adequate access." Minimally adequate access is clearly unlike Rawls's difference principle: it does not say that we have to pick the arrangement under which the least advantaged does best; it just says modestly that we pick at least the arrangement under which no one is deprived of the minimal amount of basic goods necessary for a flourishing human life (however that is to be defined). Pogge's chief concern in *World Poverty* is with world poverty, absolute deprivation of a severe kind, and not with egalitarian distribution.[13]

But a question remains: is Pogge entitled to say that the poor are being harmed when they are deprived of a feasible arrangement under which they can have adequate access to basic goods? A utilitarian like Singer could make this claim, if the better arrangement could be put in place without significant costs to those footing the bill; indeed for Singer, this can be ratcheted up to the point when the next available arrangement is going to result in overall decrease in utility because of the marginal utility of the more affluent.[14] Or a defender of positive basic rights like Shue can say that the poor are indeed being wronged if an available alternative arrangement is not given to them in which their basic rights to subsistence could be more fully met.[15] But Singer and Shue are able to say this – that the present arrangement in fact harms the poor – because of their theoretical commitments: Singer in virtue of his utilitarian maximizing commitment, and Shue because of his commitment to securing basic subsistence rights. On either account, it can be said that members of the advantaged class have a *positive duty* of justice to bring about the better arrangement. The rich wrong the poor if they do not attempt to bring about this friendlier alternative. It is hard, however, to see how Pogge can say that the affluent owe it to the poor to bring on this minimally adequate arrangement (or MAA for short). MAA may be the order under which the poor now have no restricted adequate access to basic goods. But how are they being wronged when the rich do not give them this arrangement? They can't claim that the rich owe them this arrangement on the grounds that the rich have a positive duty to help or rescue them. On Pogge's own stipulation, the rich only have the negative duty not to harm and so long as they are not harming the poor, they have no other duty, including the duty to provide MAA. So either Pogge abandons his libertarian starting point in favor of a more demanding first-order principle, or he accepts that the duty of the rich vis-à-vis the poor need not offer the current global poor much.[16]

Pogge could say in reply that the harm is that of the rich *forcing* a particular arrangement on the poor. There is no option on the poor's part of refusing the present global arrangement that is so disadvantageous to them. So as a basic duty the rich ought to get out of the way, and allow the poor real freedom to pursue their ends. But this response presupposes that the poor would be better off in some global state of nature, or at the minimum they would be better off if they were to be simply left alone. But as discussed above, there is no real basis for thinking this. It is open to argument that the poor are doing better by joining this present global order rather than none (if opting out were even possible), or that they are doing at least better now than under the preceding (pre-WTO) order, arguments that Pogge himself has noted. The problem of global poverty is not that of the rich getting in the way but that of the rich refusing to cooperate with the poor in certain ways. The poor need better trade terms, revisions in how we conceive certain basic principles of international law (such as those pertaining to sovereignty and state legitimacy and resource ownership), some reconceptualization of intellectual property rights, and so on. These are to be achieved with the cooperation and participation of the influential and powerful countries of the world rather than their disengagement from the poor. It is thus not clear if the poor would opt to be left alone, and the fact is that the poor of the world aren't asking to be left alone but are instead calling for better terms of cooperation with the rest of the world. But, as argued above, we can morally demand this of the rich only if the rich have a standing duty of justice to put in place institutions of a certain kind. Absent this antecedent positive duty of justice, it is not clear how the rich are letting the poor down by not imposing on the poor one particular arrangement over another. The rich are entitled to ask, if we endorse the libertarian tenet, "Why should we cooperate?" While the libertarian premise (that no harm be done to another) can plausibly demand that the rich not get in the way of the poor, it cannot demand that the rich cooperate with them on certain terms.

In sum, even if the present global order is *disadvantaging* the global poor, it remains to be shown that it is *unjustly harming* them. One may be disadvantaged under a given arrangement but it does not follow that one is being dealt with unjustly. To demonstrate an injustice in the form of a wrongful harm, it must be shown that there is a duty on the part of some agent or the collective to support an alternative arrangement wherein no one is so disadvantaged. But this would require some antecedent notion of what duties of justice people have, what duties, for example, they have to bring about certain kinds of social arrangement, and this would entail an abandonment of the libertarian tenet that there are only negative duties in favor of the more robust principle that persons have the positive duty to support certain kinds of institutions. Put another way, what counts as an unjust harm, an injustice, is determined by reference to the duties of justice people owe to each other.

It seems then that, in spite of Pogge's claim that his central task is mainly factual (p. 13), that is, that of revealing and demonstrating how the global order is harming the poor, what counts as harm is not just a factual question but also a philosophical one, and hence what it means for the global order to harm the poor, whether it is indeed harming the poor, is also conceptual rather than simply factual. It is unclear if Pogge may help himself to the notion of harm he needs (in order to show that the global order is in fact harming the poor) if he wants to grant at the outset the libertarian tenet that there are only negative duties across the board. In other words, whether or not we are unjustly harming another relies on some understanding of the duties we owe to each other; and because Pogge limits at the outset the duties we owe to each other to the negative duty of nonintervention, the notion of harm that he can really get at is correspondingly limited and not robust enough for him to support his "factual" thesis that the global order is harming the poor when the global rich choose not to support an alternative global social order. If this is right, then either Pogge accepts that he can't get the conclusions he wants with his libertarian starting point (which would defeat the point of his whole project), or he accepts that he must reject the libertarian premise (which will mean giving up on the distinctiveness of his approach). My claim is not that there isn't any possible conception of harm that can be invoked to show that the global order harms the poor when it disadvantages them. The claim is that it is not clear that the comparative baseline Pogge needs for establishing that the global order is in fact harming the poor is available to him, *given his own starting concessions to the libertarian premise* that there are only negative duties of justice. A complete defense of Pogge's distinctive approach has to clarify why the rich are indeed unjustly harming the poor when the former opt not to support an alternative arrangement that is more advantageous to the poor when the only duty there is at the outset is the negative duty of forbearance.

In his reply to earlier criticisms of *World Poverty and Human Rights*, Pogge notes that his goal was to present a diversity of ways in which the present global order is unjustly harming the global poor.[17] His approach, he clarifies in his reply, is ecumenical and therefore is obliged to provide different accounts of what counts as harm. But my objection here is not that there is a perceived inconsistency in his different accounts of harm, but that it is not clear how he can convince the libertarian, his key interlocutor, that the present global order is unjustly harming the global poor. The necessary comparative baseline against which we can say that the present order is unjustly hurting the poor – namely, the existence of feasible alternatives – is not available once we grant the libertarian premise that the only moral duty we owe to each other at the outset is the negative duty of forbearance.

I should stress that I agree with Pogge's conclusion that the present global order is *unjustly harming* the poor. But this is because I believe that there is a natural positive duty of justice to support social institutions of certain kinds (in particular social institutions under which the worst-off benefit most in the general Rawlsian spirit), and where we fail to do so, we are unjustly harming those who are most disadvantaged under the present arrangement. *World Poverty and Human Rights* is to be commended and recommended for the powerful fashion in which it uncovers and explicates the several ways the present global order is to the severe disadvantage of the neediest of the world. The issue I am raising is however a conceptual and theoretical one: is Pogge entitled to say that the global order is unjustly harming the poor if he grants the libertarian premise that moral duties at the outset are only negative. My worry is that this concession to the libertarian gives up more than Pogge suspects or should like.

5 Conclusion

It is useful to briefly contrast Pogge's approach to poverty and global justice with Henry Shue's well-known position. Shue takes on the philosophical question that Pogge seeks to avoid, namely the question of whether there are positive duties of human rights, and defends the idea that there are positive duties to assist those deprived of basic needs.[18] Pogge feels that it is easier to factually demonstrate that the global rich are harming the global poor – thereby violating a basic negative duty and correspondingly having a duty to take steps to make amends – than it is to show that there are positive duties off the bat. But as I have tried to suggest, the factual task is not necessarily easier; indeed, it is not simply factual and nonphilosophical because it relies on how we understand the concept of harm. I have tried to argue that if we begin with the libertarian tenet, then it becomes quite difficult to show how the current global order is harming the poor. The problem of world poverty may require us to face rather than avoid, as Shue recognizes, the philosophical problem of convincing the libertarian that there are positive duties, as a matter of basic morality, to assist persons deprived of basic needs.

Even if Pogge's institutional approach succeeds, it is important to note a certain limitation by design (so the following is a question rather than a criticism). What it aims to do is to provide reasons why the global rich have the duty of justice to take steps to protect the global poor (a duty that derives on Pogge's view straightforwardly from the failure of the rich to meet the basic duty not to do harm). That is, its problem is the problem of global poverty. But does global justice also include a distributive egalitarian commitment? That is, do the global well-off have a duty of justice to engage in some global distributive arrangement for the sake of regulating inequalities between them and the less well-off? Pogge's approach, focusing on harm and the responsibility to repair harms done or being done, does not seem to have the resources to support global egalitarianism. One way it could attempt to do this might be to try to argue that the only way of not harming the global poor is to put in place an egalitarian global order, say a global order regulated by Rawls's difference principle. But as suggested above, it is not clear how something like this could be demanded as a matter of duty of justice if we begin from the assumption that people owe to each other only negative duties. To the extent that global justice requires an egalitarian distributive component, as some would argue, Pogge's distinctive approach, even if defensible on its own terms, appears to fall short. It is also worth noting that Pogge himself in other contexts has argued for global egalitarianism.[19] It is thus of interest to see how his minimalist approach to world poverty in *World Poverty and Human Rights* can be reconciled with his defense of global egalitarianism elsewhere. Are these two distinct projects or does Pogge see them as unified in some way? Particularly of interest is this: does he think his minimalistic approach can also account for global egalitarianism? Can global egalitarians sign on to Pogge's institutional approach to global justice? These are questions for another time.

Notes

*I thank Alison Jaggar for very helpful comments and criticisms.

1 References to this work are to the first edition and will be noted in parentheses in the text.

2 See Alison Jaggar's "Introduction" for a fuller exposition.

3 It is important to note that, if society does not provide reasonably adequate security and police protection for its citizens against ordinary crime or other forms of injuries and offenses, this counts as an institutional failure and in relevant contexts can count as a human rights violation. The distinction between acts carried out by persons as such and those carried out by official representatives presupposes that, in the former circumstance, due protection is being provided by the state (hence the italicized part of the preceding sentence in the text). Thus, Pogge's institutional account can say that human rights offenses are taking place in a society in which personal attacks against women occur frequently while the state does nothing to discourage such abuses. Or when a state fails to protect its minorities from persistent racist attacks by others, Pogge can say too that this is an institutional failure that amounts to official disrespect, and can count as a human rights violation (see pp. 60–1).

4 The focus on official actions is not rescinded here: ordinary citizens can be implicated in human rights violations if they support a state that systemically violates human rights. And to "support" can mean more than just giving assent. Ordinary citizens who, say, enjoy the benefits of their country's global exploits can be said to "support" the state's activity even if they did not expressly give consent. Indeed, Pogge will say that many of us in the developed world are implicated in the violations against the global poor in this and other indirect ways (pp. 20–4).

5 It will be useful to contrast what Pogge has to say about human rights with Thomas Nagel's view of global justice and human rights as presented

in Thomas Nagel, "The Problem of Global Justice," *Philosophy and Public Affairs* 33(2) (2005): 113–47. For Nagel, membership in a particular kind of social order is necessary for generating *distributive egalitarian* commitments among persons. That is, it is only as members of a collectively authorized coercive social political order that we see ourselves as having the obligation to regulate and limit inequalities among ourselves. Nagel's limiting of distributive justice to membership in a shared political order can be challenged, I believe. But what is relevant here is that Nagel nonetheless accepts that there are certain basic human rights that are prepolitical, that is, rights that apply to persons independently of political membership. These include the human rights to basic security and subsistence, and these for Nagel are rights that are claimable by persons against others, regardless of membership in any political society. Importantly, these rights also generate positive duties on the part of others. In contrast, Pogge's institutional account of human rights seems to reject human rights as prepolitical altogether, taking all human rights to be institutionally derived. That is, while Nagel accepts that certain basic human rights are pre-institutional even though distributive justice commitments are institutionally defined, Pogge takes human rights across the board to be institutionally derived as well as only fundamentally negative.

6 Shue, *Basic Rights* (Princeton: Princeton University Press, 1996 [2nd edn]), p. 18.

7 One might point out that in cases where colonization stems from a state's official policy, the victims are subject to an institutional harm and hence are victims of human rights violation. But human rights violations are official disrespect or offenses conducted by one party against another *who first stands in a human rights relation to the other*. If a victim of abuse doesn't stand in the right relationship, that is, is not a rightful subject of human rights vis-à-vis the attacker, then, by definition, his or her human rights cannot be violated by an attacker even if the offense against the victim is officially sanctioned. On a literal reading of Pogge's account of who may make demands of human rights, victims of colonization fall outside the social order of their colonizers and therefore can't make human rights demands against their invaders. The fact that the colonization process is part of the colonizing country's official policy is immaterial as regards whether the action counts as a human rights offense.

8 Pogge, to be sure, goes on immediately to say that this "point could be further disputed" but grants it for purpose of discussion. But it is not hard to see that on Pogge's own concession of negative rights across the board, he must endorse this conclusion as a matter of consistency with what he claims he is granting.

9 Consider, for example, John Rawls's notion of human rights, which can generate positive duties as well as negative ones (*The Law of Peoples*, Cambridge, MA: Harvard University Press, 2001). If Rawls's theory is already commonly criticized by some commentators as too weak, Pogge's account that stresses only negative rights is even weaker. For one criticism

of Rawls's theory of human rights as too thin, see Allen Buchanan, "Taking the Human out of Human Rights," in Rex Martin and David Reidy (eds), *Rawls's Law of Peoples: A Realistic Utopia?* (Malden, MA: Blackwell, 2006), pp. 150–68.

10 See Alison Jaggar's "Introduction."

11 Recall the earlier note that it is not just harms that matter but harms that *are unjust*. I presume unjust harms henceforth unless otherwise qualified.

12 By harming Pogge means harming *unjustly*. A person is harmed by a tornado – but not unjustly so. To put it more perspicuously, the person is not wronged. But a person, when harmed by another moral agent deliberately, is being unjustly harmed. He or she is wronged and not just harmed. I follow Pogge in using the term "harm" to mean unjust harm unless otherwise qualified. For discussion on harming versus wronging, see Rahul Kumar, "Who Can Be Wronged?," *Philosophy and Public Affairs* 31(2) (2003): 99–118.

13 Contrast Pogge's defense of global Rawlsian egalitarianism in *Realizing Rawls* (Ithaca, NY: Cornell University Press, 1989), part III. Here he attempts to globalize the difference principle.

14 Peter Singer, "Famine, Affluence and Morality," *Philosophy and Public Affairs* 1(1) (1972): 229–43.

15 Shue, *Basic Rights*, p. 52.

16 This line of argument has also been made by Alan Patten, "Should We Stop Thinking About Poverty in Terms of Helping the Poor?," *Ethics & International Affairs* 19 (2005): 19–27.

17 Pogge, "A Cosmopolitan Perspective on the Global Economic Order", in Gillian Brock and Harry Brighouse (eds), *The Political Philosophy of Cosmopolitanism* (Cambridge: Cambridge University Press, 2005).

18 Shue's argumentative strategy is that of urging consistency in light of given commitments: if we are prepared to accept the notion of basic rights to security, then we have also to accept the idea of basic rights to subsistence; and the duties associated with basic security that we accept include both positive and negative duties; Shue, *Basic Rights*, chs 1 and 2.

19 See, for example, *Realizing Rawls*, part III.

3

"How Much Is Enough, Mr Thomas? How Much Will Ever Be Enough?"

Neera Chandhoke*

1 Introduction

In his 1995 film *White Man's Burden*, Desmond Nakano imagines an alternative America in which poor whites inhabit inner-city ghettos, and African Americans dominate society in precisely the sort of way the whites do now. The defining moment of the film arrives when Louis Pinnock (John Travolta), a poor working-class white man, is fired by his African American boss Thaddeus Thomas (Harry Belafonte) for an incident that belongs purely to happenstance. The sacking propels a series of catastrophes involving a kidnapping, marital discord, and intensification of police brutality on poor whites. Towards the end of the film, Marsha Pinnock refuses Thaddeus Thomas's offer of monetary compensation for harm done. "What, isn't it enough?" asks Thomas. "How much is enough, Mr Thomas?" asks Marsha. "How much will ever be enough?"

Thomas Pogge's *World Poverty and Human Rights* evokes roughly the same sort of question in my mind. Pogge's moral indictment of an unequal and unjust global order that wreaks havoc on the lives of people living in the developing world, his indignation that citizens of affluent countries who benefit from this global order are supremely indifferent to the plight of the global poor, and his sophisticated philosophical arguments on global justice are more than compelling. Though he insists that he offers an innovative (institutional) theory of human rights that occupies the middle ground between the moral maximalism of utilitarianism and the moral minimalism of libertarianism, I think Pogge's contribution lies much more in his conceptualization of shared responsibility for harm done by an unjust global institutional order. His theory of negative duties that follows recognition of shared responsibility is intricately and rigorously worked out. This part of his theory constitutes the strength of his work. It possibly constitutes one of its major weaknesses as well. What two of these weaknesses are is the focus of this essay. The first weakness, Pogge's notion of *why* the affluent West owes the global poor, is substantive. The second weakness might well be unintended; the construction of a "we" versus "they" that underlies his theory. This dimension of his argument can be, I suppose, interpreted as nitpicking. But an entire concept of equal moral status, which *should* form the linchpin of a theory of *global* justice, rests on this construction. At the end of the essay the logic of the title should be evident: How much will *ever* be enough? Even if it is not so evident, the title surely speaks for itself. There is much more to global poverty than Pogge acknowledges, and consequently more to the duties that humanity has towards the global poor.

2 Global poverty, shared responsibility, and negative duties

Let me begin by citing a case from agrarian India. According to one research study, a hundred and fifty thousand farmers committed suicide in India between 1997 and 2005, mainly by consuming pesticide.[1] The study estimated that two thirds of these suicides occurred in the four highly globalized states of the Indian Union: Maharashtra, Andhra Pradesh, Karnataka, and Madhya Pradesh.[2] Agriculture in these states is dominated by the production of cash crops, and is, therefore, exceedingly commercialized. In the past the Indian government had cushioned Indian farmers against the problems endemic to Indian agriculture, such as lack of irrigation and degraded land. Today, under the direction of global institutions, public investment in agriculture has dried up, and bank credit has been curtailed. The tightening grip of large multinational corporations over inputs has led to a steep escalation of prices. As a result, cultivation costs in these high input zones have shot up, Indian farmers have been rendered even more vulnerable to a market increasingly shaped by the policies of global institutions, and indebtedness has increased considerably.

In addition, following the dictates of global regulatory institutions, the government has scrapped quantitative restrictions on various agricultural products, and has reduced tariffs on many items. Therefore, all kinds of agricultural products from fruit, to wheat, to vegetables have flooded the market. In other words, agricultural surpluses in Western countries have driven down the price of agricultural commodities in India, particularly in the case of cotton. The influx of cheaper imports, and the consequent slowing down of domestic demands for crops like oil seeds, have hugely impoverished farmers. Indian farmers, already hit by the reduction of public investment and the steep rise in the prices of inputs, are simply not in a position to compete with highly subsidized agricultural commodities produced in the US and in Western Europe. In sum, as the study points out, at a time when subsidies for corporate farmers in the West rose, "we cut our few, very minimal life supports and subsidies to our own farmers. The collapse of investment in agriculture also meant it was and is most difficult to get out of this [debt] trap."[3]

The close causal connection between the policies of global regulatory institutions and farmers' suicides cannot be more obvious. In 2005, more than 50,000 farmers participating in a huge protest rally in Mumbai demanded that agriculture be taken out of the WTO, that import duty on agricultural commodities should be increased, that quantitative restrictions should be reinstated to protect farmers and farming, and that the surge of agricultural commodities that have been dumped in the country by the developed world be brought to an end.[4] Agrarian distress and farmers' suicides in times of globalization are not unique to India. At the WTO's Fifth Ministerial Conference in Cancun Mexico in 2003, Lee Kyung Hae, the leader of the Korean Federation of Advanced Farmers, stabbed himself in the chest. He was wearing a sandwich board that read: "The WTO kills Farmers."

Agrarian distress marks most of the developing world, and the future of this sector remains bleak. According to the 2003 *Human Development Report*, even *if* governments of developing countries adopt appropriate national policies, and even *if* donor financing is increased, the Millennium Development Goals will *not* be achieved *if* nontraditional exports of these countries continue to be blocked, or if they lose value in the world markets because of rich country protectionism.[5] As a former Indian Minister of Commerce, often castigated by the international media as stubborn and obstructionist during his tenure, was to protest often enough: "You just can't be talking about free trade, you've got to talk about *fair* trade." The American journalist who had interviewed the minister concurred. The United States and the countries of the European Union hand over billions of dollars in trade-distorting subsidies to their agricultural industries, and it is expected that more than half a billion Indian subsistence farmers deprived of aid can still compete with rich agri-businesses. More significantly, as the (former) minister pointed out, when the WTO was established in 1995, the developing countries had neither the wherewithal nor the technical expertise to understand the content or implications of the agreement.

> They were afraid of being isolated and they had too much at stake. If they refused to participate they might risk their standing with the World Bank and the IMF, two institutions which have imposed draconian reforms on borrower countries in the past and forced them to open their markets, all too often with terrible results. So they signed and hoped it would work.[6]

In *World Poverty and Human Rights*, Thomas Pogge constructs a complex philosophical argument on global justice on precisely this sort of reasoning. One, in an increasingly interdependent world, any decision taken by global institutions necessarily affects the lives of people, wherever they might live. Two, since global institutions are dominated by rich Western countries, this naturally works to the advantage of the advanced capitalist world. "We," rues Pogge (speaking of and to the West), are harming the global poor through participation in an unjust global order in which protectionist policies for agriculture, and anti-dumping measures in sectors in which the developing world is best able to compete such as agriculture, clothing, and textiles, lead to global poverty.[7] Three, most countries in the developing world have been historically weakened by colonialism. They therefore are not in a position to bargain either on equal terms or for better terms. These countries simply have no "voice" in decisions that systemically disadvantage them and the better-off enjoy significant advantages in appropriating wealth from the planet, such as crude oil. At the same time the worse-off are largely, and without compensation, excluded from the gains of these appropriations.[8] Pogge concludes that an unjust global institutional order produces and reproduces deep poverty in the developing world.

This is not the first time in the history of ideas that the Western-dominated global order has been held responsible for the creation and the recreation of poverty in the developing world. The intellectual stage for theories of imperialist exploitation was set early in the twentieth century by Rosa Luxemburg and Lenin. Their theories were rediscovered and reinvented in the 1970s when scholars belonging to the dependency school took on the modernization theorists.[9] The dependency theorists alleged that countries of the developing world, because of their shared experience of colonialism, could neither replicate the path taken by the West nor compete with the advanced capitalist world. Though formal colonialism ended by the 1960s, it cast a long shadow. South America, sub-Saharan Africa, and South Asia had been so thoroughly impoverished that they were fated to infinite dependence on the advanced capitalist world. As Andre Gunder Frank was to put it memorably, what we see and will continue to see in the indefinite future is the "development of underdevelopment" in the former colonies. Development and underdevelopment are, he was to say, two sides of the same coin.

Thomas Pogge is a liberal philosopher, and liberals tend either to pay scant attention to the insights of Marxists or to dismiss these insights altogether. Though Pogge does agree with the Marxist thesis on the causes of global poverty, he would, I think, write off the remedy that dependency theorists offered to the world: that the erstwhile colonized world can develop only if world capitalism is either smashed or radically transformed because intrinsic to capitalism is the exploitation of labor and raw materials found in the Third World. Pogge's resolution of the problem of global poverty is much more modest, but perhaps more doable. At the same time his resolution may well stop short of what is needed to meet the challenge of global poverty. "There are more things in heaven and earth, Horatio, than are dreamt of in your philosophy," suggests Hamlet in William Shakespeare's immortal play.[10] Does the same gentle advice apply to Pogge? Let us see.

3 Causality and minimalist duties

Of crucial significance to the argument in *World Poverty and Human Rights* is the claim that citizens of the affluent world are morally responsible for the starvation, malnutrition, and deaths that take place in the developing world. Because their representatives have participated in and even determined decisions that have inflicted harm on the global poor,[11] the negative duty of the citizens of the affluent West, the duty not to cause harm, has been violated. (For Pogge, human rights do not impose a fundamental positive duty to help realize the good to which a particular right entitles a rights-holder but rather a fundamental negative duty *not* to cause harm.) It follows that those who are involved in upholding the institutions of the state should discontinue their involvement, challenge the policies of their own government, and compensate for injustice by either working for reform of institutions or working for the protection of the victims. Otherwise, Pogge argues, "we" would be failing "to fulfill our more stringent negative duty not to uphold injustice, not to contribute to or profit from the unjust impoverishment of others."[12]

It is precisely at this point of the argument that we get an idea of Pogge's minimalism. Citizens of the affluent West owe the global poor *only* if a clear and unambiguous causal connection can be established between decision D and consequence E, that is, between policies of global institutions and the production of poverty. Two sorts of implications can be derived from Pogge's notion of causality. One, the extent of duty to the global poor has to be proportionate to the harm caused, and also proportionate to the benefit gleaned from the policy. "The word 'compensate' is meant to indicate that how much one should be willing to contribute towards reforming unjust institutions and towards mitigating the harms they cause depends on how much one is contributing to, and benefiting from, their maintenance."[13] It is, perhaps, an indication of the state of normative political theory today that the transfer of a small amount of resources from the rich to the poor requires such elaborate philosophical justifications. The extent of compensation might also involve complex calculations about what the proportion of compensation to harm caused, and benefits gleaned, is. That is all. But is it enough?

For, and this is the second implication of Pogge's argument, citizens who live and work in the rich countries do not *owe anything* morally to the global poor if they or their governments are not directly responsible causally for harm done.

> When some 800,000 Tutsis and moderate Hutus were slaughtered in Rwanda in early 1994, the world took notice . . . We all felt a bit responsible, but bearably so. The deaths, after all, were brought about by clearly identifiable villains, and we were clearly not among them and also did not benefit from the killings in any way. Deaths caused by global economic arrangements designed and imposed by our governments are a different matter: these governments are elected by us, responsive to our interests and preferences, acting in our name and in ways that benefit us. The buck stops with us.[14]

It follows that the agrarian crisis in India should, and will, invoke negative duties on the part of the citizens of the affluent West. In general, it is difficult to disentangle the complex of factors that contribute to the infliction of grievous harm on people, and allot causal relationship to just one set of factors. In this specific case, however, it is clear that discriminatory policies of the WTO, which is dominated by rich countries, have resulted in a serious agrarian crisis in the developing world. This should serve as a call to arms in the affluent West and summon negative duties (even though, as Pogge regretfully acknowledges, the connection does not always hold).

But whereas Pogge's institutional conception of negative duties holds rather well when a link can be established between (a) global institutions, (b) Western domination of these institutions, (c) decisions that advantage the West, (d) decisions that disadvantage the developing world, and (e) negative duties of Western citizens, it does not work at all when no such causal relation can be established, *not even* when severe poverty entails a severe violation of generic human rights. For Pogge does believe that global poverty *is* a violation of human rights. In a later work on precisely this theme, Pogge writes, "[t]o reach widely sharable conclusions about when severe poverty decidedly *is* a human rights violation, let me focus exclusively then on *negative duties* correlative to human rights: duties not to harm others in certain specific ways."[15]

The problem is that in many cases of severe poverty, which for Pogge represent a violation of human rights, it cannot be conclusively established that poverty is the result of decisions of Western-dominated global institutions. Therefore, these cases do not invoke even negative duties. Take the case of poverty-stricken Mali. The *World Development Report* of 2006 states that a baby born in one of the poorest countries, Mali, in 2001, had approximately a 13% chance of dying before reaching age one. The odds would have declined slightly to 9% *if* the baby had been born to a family in the top quintile of asset distribution. By contrast, a baby born in the US in the same year had less than a 1% chance of dying in the first year. In Mali, 20% of children will not reach age 5, compared to 1% of children in the US.[16] If we begin to investigate the reasons why babies born in Mali have a much lower chance of surviving than babies born in the US, we might be able to identify a host of factors that are responsible for high rates of infant mortality, such as lack of nutrition, or the failure of the government to establish maternity clinics to help both mother and child. But it cannot be definitively established that the unjust global order is directly responsible for infant mortality in Mali. Global institutional mandates that discriminate against Mali might well form one, but not necessarily the determining, factor in explaining infant mortality.

Perhaps finding the specific combination of factors, institutions, and agents that cause poverty is not all that morally relevant. For whatever be the reason for the production and the reproduction of poverty in this part of the world, whichever be the agent that is responsible for this mind-numbing poverty that denies the most basic of rights to little babies, i.e., the right to life, the existence of the absolutely poor is wracked by ill-being. And no one, least of all the state and the societies the poor belong to, seems to take responsibility for remedying the violation of human rights. What is, then, to be done? Pogge has no answer for such cases because he has already covered the metaphorical flanks of his theory of negative duties. He has already suggested that citizens of the Western world were only "bearably" responsible for the thousands of dead in Rwanda for two reasons. The people who caused these deaths were not remotely connected to the West, and the West did not profit. Now a historian of colonialism can find a number of faults with this sort of an escape from responsibility because the enmity between the Hutus and the Tutsis in Rwanda *has* been historically constituted through colonial stereotyping, much as the historical conflict between Hindus and Muslims in India was shaped by colonial formulations on and interpretations of the two-nation theory. Western countries may not be today responsible for, or profit from, the conflict that repeatedly engulfs poor countries, which also happen to be ex-colonies, but they certainly can be held liable for these images and these imaginaries in the past, as much as they profited from the colonial venture. And the past is not another country; it shapes the present, and seems fated to shape the future as well. However, Pogge pays but lip service to the long shadow cast by the history of an appropriative colonialism,[17] so I shall set aside the colonial past and concentrate on a presentist conception of justice and human rights in the following section.

4 Human rights and duties of relevant agents

Let me make four related propositions. One is that large numbers of people who mainly live in the continents of sub-Saharan Africa and South Asia belong to the category of the absolutely poor. The *Human Development Report 2007–8* estimates that one billion people live on less than one US dollar per day, and that 2.6 billion people, or 40% of the world's population, live on the margins of survival; that is, on less than two US dollars per day. This segment of the global population commands less than 5% of the world's income, whereas 20% of the population, which mainly inhabits the affluent Western world, controls two thirds of the global income. The report reiterates that 28% of children in the developing world are underweight and stunted, and 10 million children in this part of the world die before age five from avoidable causes such as poverty and malnutrition.[18] More significantly, over 3.6 billion people in the world not only lack access to a steady income, they also lack access to shelter, to nutritious food, to health care, to education, and to other basic preconditions of living a life that we recognize as distinctively human. It does not require a giant stretch of the imagination to suggest that it is precisely this section of the world's population that suffers from multiple deprivations. The poor are not only denied access to basic material requirements that enable them to live a decent life, they are likely to be socially marginalized, politically insignificant in terms of the politics of voice, humiliated, dismissed, and subjected to intense disrespect in and through the practices of everyday life.

The second and the equally obvious proposition is that human beings have the right not to be poor. Article 25, Clause One of the Universal Declaration of Human Rights states that "Everyone has the right to a standard of living adequate for the health and well-being of himself and of his family, including food, clothing, housing, and medical care, and necessary social services, and the right to security in the event of unemployment, sickness, disability, widowhood, old age or other lack of livelihood in circumstances beyond his control." For Pogge, this clause grants a right to basic necessities.

> A human right to basic necessities, as postulated, for instance, in Article 25 of the UDHR, becomes more plausible when construed along these lines. On my institutional understanding, it involves no duty on everyone to help supply such necessities to those who would otherwise be without them. It rather involves a duty on citizens to ensure that any coercive social order they collectively impose upon each of themselves is one under which, insofar as reasonably possible, each has secure access to these necessities.[19]

Whether we do or do not agree with the concept of negative duties elaborated by Pogge, it is clear that the human rights of 3.6 billion people that have been granted by Article 25 of the UDHR have been left unfulfilled, and thus violated. For the failure to enable the realization of the good that the right is a right to can be justifiably seen as a violation of the right.[20]

The third proposition is the following. Whether or not 3.6 billion people claim their human right not to be poor, the *possession* of this right places obligations/duties on other agents to enable access of the rights-holder to the good to which the right entitles them. Correspondingly, when human rights are violated, agents have the duty of ensuring that this violation is rectified in some way or another. The fourth proposition is that there are very good reasons why agents should consider themselves responsible for the nonfulfillment of basic human rights, or for the violations of these rights.

Most concur with the first proposition that large numbers of people in the world live below the poverty line, even if economists and statisticians quibble about the exactness of this number or about the methodology employed to measure poverty. Most people would also agree that poverty of such magnitude violates a basic human right to a standard of living adequate for the health and well-being of households and communities. The third proposition is that rights place an obligation upon agents. Let me expand on this. P has a right to G and this right places a duty on agents to enable P to realize G. In other words, it would be wrong not to enable P to access G. This obligation can be positive and require agents to aid in the realization of the right on offer. Or it can be negative insofar as agents have the duty of ensuring that people do not come to harm through nonfulfillment, or violations of, human rights. Whatever be the nature of the obligation, the proposition that rights place obligations on agents is a matter of general agreement as well.

Let me now rephrase the issue at hand. Theories of rights establish a relationship between the bearers of rights and agents who are obliged to ensure that the rights-holder is in a position to access the good the right is a right to. Therefore, if every human being is, as Pogge argues, a unit of moral concern, then violations of his or her human rights not to be poor should be of universal moral concern, *irrespective* of what caused this poverty. As the fourth proposition holds, agents should consider themselves responsible for the nonfulfillment of basic human rights, or for the violations of these rights. What is at stake is the question of who these agents are.

Pogge has a clear answer to this question: if people participate in coercive institutions that lead to a violation of human rights, then these people have duties to those who have been harmed. The problem with the concept of negative duties has been well articulated by Gilabert, who notes that, under Pogge's theory of negative responsibility, human rights-based claims do not arise from a human rights deficit but from the element of harmful conduct. Therefore, Pogge's minimalist theory cannot ensure that the goods to which human rights are a right are fully secured.[21]

On the other hand, we can hardly assume that human rights place obligations on everyone, or on every agent. This position is vague at best and irresponsible at worst because it does not identify the duty bearer. Let us therefore assume that the assertion of a right places an obligation on *relevant* agents, relevant agents being those agents who are in a position to ensure the realization of a right. This way we might also avoid, as Pogge does, both minimalist and maximalist notions of rights. Let me elaborate this point. Whereas rights claims place such obligations on society in general, in particular they place such an obligation on the state. Since the state is an institution and a condensate of power, and is therefore able to command resources, it is best able to secure the good to which a right entitles its holders. And a democratic state is so obliged because the legitimacy of democracy hinges on the presumption of participation/representation and accountability.

It follows that if our P has claimed a right, say, to subsistence, the state should be enabling P to access the good or G to which her R is a right. Yet if our abstract state could speak, it might argue that the scale of the realization of the right to G, in this case subsistence, places an unwarranted burden upon propertied citizens because they will have to be taxed heavily. Or our democratic state can argue that whereas P certainly has a claim upon the resources of the state, there is also an urgent need to expend these resources on, for example, sophisticated security systems to counter global terrorism. That is, either the state holds that the realization of the right of subsistence will deplete scant resources, or that these resources are just not there for the asking. However pressing and morally compelling rights claims may be in principle, in practice they are constantly subjected to trade-offs against some factor or other, provided this factor can be justified by the state.

The fact is that political democracies can be perfectly compatible with social and economic inequality, as the case of India shows. India is definitively democratic, and since the early 1990s the growth of the economy has been spectacular. Yet the country is marked by high levels of poverty and rampant inequality, and is highly stratified along the axes of class, gender, caste, religion, and region. High growth rates in the economy have simply not translated into equal opportunities for all. The poor in the process have been denied basic rights. Who do the poor then approach? Which is the relevant agent that can help secure access to the goods that people have a right to, in this case subsistence? Obviously, the global poor cannot approach those who live in the affluent West, and claim that their right to subsistence be realized because this is what the citizens of the West owe them. Cash transfers to the developing world are not available on demand. These are contingent on the realization that citizens who live in the affluent world owe the victims of unjust policies for some specific reason. Will then the poor have to wait for such enlightenment to dawn? Perhaps not, because this option, howsoever significant it may be, is not the only alternative available to the global poor.

Consider the following case. Whereas 94 percent of India's workforce is in the unorganized sector, the Indian Government for at least four decades after independence failed to take the rights of this section of the workforce into account. Policies were enacted for this sector only in the 1980s, that is, at the time when India liberalized and subsequently globalized. Ratna Sudershan has argued that the decade of the 1980s witnessed two paradoxical developments. One, despite the large differences in the situation of the old and the new informal workers, and between workers in the developed and the developing countries, the forging of associative networks between them resulted in the formulation of a definite approach to social protection. Two, although globalization has expanded the informal sector, the process has also provided the space for serious discussion on how to ensure the rights of informal workers to social protection. A number of such discussions in global forums led to the creation of international networks such as Women in Informal Employment: Globalizing and Organizing (WIEGO). Over time, the network began to advocate the adoption of these rights across the world.

Notably, members of WIEGO, who include representatives of several membership-based organizations from different countries, have been engaged in advocating the rights of informal workers not as an act of charity for the informal workers of the developing world, but as a technique for securing the rights of all workers who eke out a living in precarious work situations. International advocacy has played an important role in increasing the visibility of informal workers, and in generating commitment to providing universal social protection, at the very time globalization has created more workers in the informal sector.[22] This strategy seems to have been successful for in December 2008 the government of India finally passed the Unorganized Sector Workers Social Security Bill. The Bill aims to provide social security and job protection to at least 375 million workers in the unorganized sector.

At least three important implications can be drawn from this case. One, across the world people can be bound together in a number of ways, with the binding force ranging from formal regulatory institutions such as the WTO, to mobilization through virtual global civil society networks. If the first sort of (institutional) bringing together of people living in distant spaces generates negative duties in very special circumstances, the second sort of bringing together generates solidarity among different kinds of people, who live and work in different situations, in different countries. Two, these webs of solidarity and networks of advocacy may not lead to a (minimal) transfer of resources from the rich to the poor, but they do something equally significant; they can lead to the grafting of social policy onto political agendas. Three, different strategies of helping the poor need not be mutually exclusive; they can equally complement each other. If citizens of the affluent world contribute to, say, Oxfam, so that the organization can invest in development activities in poor countries, this has to be welcomed. But if concerned citizens across the world come together in and through networks that consolidate solidarity for and with the poor, it is equally good. And if in tandem these different agents can bring about the reform of global institutions, as well as the reform of national governments, it is even better.

For instance, at the end of November 1999, massive protests involving some 700 organizations and about 40,000 students, workers, NGOs, religious groups, and representatives of business and finance brought the third ministerial meeting of the WTO at Seattle to a halt. The WTO was to set in motion a new multilateral round of trade negotiations. Collective anger at the relocation of industries to the developing world, at the unsafe and abusive work conditions in the factories and sweatshops found there, at environmental degradation, at the elitist structure of the organizations, at the underrepresentation of poor countries in global institutions, at the absence of transparency, and at the widespread exploitation of working people exploded in a series of angry demonstrations. Though large-scale protests against the WTO, the International Monetary Fund (IMF), and the World Bank were not new, the scale of mobilization, as well as the intensity of protest, was new. Livid demonstrations by student unions, environmentalists or "tree huggers," economic and xenophobic nationalists, church groups, anarchists, protectionists, consumer groups, NGOs and even business and financial groups validated the new concept that had been catapulted onto transnational vocabularies at the Earth Summit in Rio in 1992, when about 2,400 representatives of nongovernmental organizations came to play a central role in the deliberations, that of global civil society.[23]

This unprecedented agitation compelled the WTO to create a "development round" of talks that were initiated in Doha. The objective of this initiative is to address structural lacunae within the organization, and to ensure that the less developed countries are equal partners in the organization. In this case a move toward institutional reform has been made because activists have made the human rights of the poor their concern, irrespective of whether their elected governments are or are not complicit in the generation of poverty.

Western citizens cannot be held responsible for all the sorts of deprivation that afflict the poor in the developing world but in the ultimate analysis this does not matter, or ought not to matter. What should matter is that a large number of the global poor are condemned to leading lives that are insecure at best and fraught at worst. Should not groups in the Western countries that are concerned about these issues join hands against the denial of human rights, ensure that the poor are not condemned to poverty, or that their rights are not left unfulfilled, particularly if national governments do not do anything about this? Do we always have to be institutionally connected to the causes of someone's ill-being to do something about it? Arguably, the insecurity which stalks the rights of the poor in the developing world should be evoking positive duties on relevant agents irrespective of anything else. As Larry Temkin writes:

> So-called "positive" duties to aid others are often regarded as weak, broad, imperfect, and meritorious while "negative" duties are regarded as strict, narrow, perfect, and unexceptionable. But these divisions are deeply misleading. Positive duties are still *duties,* and one acts wrongly if one *fails* to fulfil them . . . failing to fulfil a positive duty can be significantly more open to moral criticism than failing to fulfil a negative duty, even if the latter involves a rights violation, and hence an injustice, while the former does not.[24]

We can safely assume that many of the activists and NGOs are motivated to act and to confront powerful global institutions and powerful states because they feel that universal human rights impose universal obligations on relevant agents. These agents can secure the realization of a right through a transfer of resources to the poor but they can also secure this transfer through advocacy, and what international human rights NGOs call strategies of "naming and shaming." In other words, a link between rights-bearers and relevant agents can be wrought by the language of human rights, and by the sentiment that, if a right is recognized as human, this is cause enough to evoke duties on the part of relevant agents.

Such an approach accomplishes two things, both of which are compatible with the basic proposition of human rights. One, the global poor are not seen as victims who have to be given cash transfers because the West is guilty but instead are treated as rights-bearers and thus as people who possess irreducible moral status. Secondly, the one factor in politics that engenders awareness of injustice, of rights, and of duties to those whose rights have been violated is political mobilization. This makes people conscious of what is due to them, and what they have been denied. And this is what these networks of solidarity accomplish. There *is* perhaps much more to global justice than the negative duties that Pogge's philosophy admits of. I do not by any means wish to dismiss the concept of negative rights; all I want to do is to argue that violations of human rights place obligations even upon those persons who have not participated, albeit indirectly, in these violations. This might still not be enough but if we can compel recognition that universal rights command universal duties, it might suffice.

Finally, the minor point mentioned in the introduction. Given that the philosophical debate on global justice focuses on the duties of the wealthy West to the poverty-stricken developing world, it is perhaps not surprising that Pogge does not recognize that people who live in this part of the world might also owe the poor in other parts of the world. Despite all the skill that he harnesses to the cause of eradicating the scourge of contemporary humanity – massive poverty – Pogge's philosophy stops short on one count: it just does not conceive of a universal humanity in which all of us make claims via the language of rights on each other, and in which we have duties to each other. Are we, who live and work in the developing world, fated to remain consumers of acts, whether these are acts of harm or of duty, performed by the West? Do those of us who live in India have any kind of duty towards the poor in other countries? And if we do not, do we lack status as moral beings who count? I do not wish to engage in any kind of geographical determinism, or suggest that this philosophical debate is exclusionary just because it originated in the West. I merely register the point in order to engage, in a spirit of friendly criticism, with Pogge's finely crafted philosophical arguments. Whereas the scope of his principles of justice is global, the span of his notion of humanity is, perhaps, not all that global. And this is a matter for some regret, for the reproduction of the distinction between "us" and "them" might well subvert the very project of radical cosmopolitanism.

5 Conclusion

Let me come back to the suggestion made in the introduction. Although Pogge sees his institutional theory of human rights as a distinctive contribution to political philosophy, arguably the more distinctive contribution to the debate on global justice is his theory of shared responsibility. Yet, though the scope of Pogge's principles of justice is global, the span of his negative rights is not. Citizens of the Western world are only concerned about those violations of human rights that can be directly traced to their own governments' actions or inactions. But this concern constricts the scope of negative duties only to cases where clear causality can be proved. In cases where causality cannot be established, millions of people will continue to live lives of extreme deprivation. If the problem I have identified with Pogge's theory of negative duties is correct, then theories of global justice seem to be concerned more about the negative duties of the citizens of wealthy countries than about the human rights of the global poor. The existing world of cosmopolitan democracy is however different, for here agents *do* take up issues which they see of concern, for advocacy, for agitation, and for reform, across the world. If philosophical reflection on global justice should be informing global civil society, the practices of global civil society should, perhaps, also be informing philosophical arguments.

Notes

*I am deeply grateful to Alison Jaggar for her insightful and extremely helpful comments on earlier versions of this chapter.
 1 The research was directed by a senior economist Professor K. Nagraj of the Madras Institute of Development Studies. The findings were widely reported. Here I draw upon the report of the findings in the newspaper *The Hindu:* P. Sainath, 2007, "Farm Suicides Rising, Most Intense in Four States," *The Hindu,* 12 November, Opinion page.
 2 A globalization index was created in the course of a research project that I had conducted. The index was created on the basis of three indicators: statewise per capita exports (value) 2002–3, statewise per capita FDI approved value between 2000 and 2005, and statewise per capita migration

(emigration clearances granted between 1993 and 2001). Maharashtra ranks number one on the index, Karnataka fifth, Andhra Pradesh seventh, and Madhya Pradesh twelfth. The findings of the research have been brought together in an unpublished document titled "Globalisation and the State in India."

3 Cited in P. Sainath, 2007, "Farm Suicides Rising, Most Intense in Four States."

4 Indian Coordination Committee of Farmers Movements, 2005, "Over 50,000 Farmers Protest Against WTO in India" www.indiaresources.org/news/2005/2017.html, accessed on 30 March 2008.

5 UNDP, *Human Development Report, Millennium Development Goals: A Compact Among Nations to End Human Poverty* (New Delhi: Oxford University Press, 2003), p. 23.

6 Cecilia Funtes, 2007, "A Voice of the Developing Nations: Kamal Nath of India Insists WTO Must Establish Fair Trade, Not Free Trade," 12 October, The WIP, www.thewip.net/contributors/2007/10/a_voice_of_the_developing_nations.html, accessed on 29 June 2008.

7 Thomas Pogge, *World Poverty and Human Rights*, 1st edn (Cambridge: Polity, 2002), p. 19. Since Pogge gestures towards the affluent West when he employs the concept of "we," as someone who lives and works in the developing world, I am obviously not a part of the "we." Therefore, the "we" has been put in quotation marks.

8 *World Poverty and Human Rights*, pp. 201–3.

9 The most prominent dependency theorists are: Andre Gunder Frank, *Capitalism and Underdevelopment in Latin America*, rev. edn (London: Modern Reader Paperbacks, 1969); Samir Amin, *Accumulation on a World Scale* (New York: Monthly Review Press, 1974); Paul Baran, *The Political Economy of Growth* (Harmondsworth: Penguin, 1973); and Immanuel Wallerstein, *The Modern World System* (New York: Academic Press, 1974).

10 William Shakespeare, *The Tragedy of Hamlet: Prince of Denmark*, in *The Oxford Shakespeare: The Complete Works*, ed. Stanley Wells, Gary Taylor, John Jowett, and William Montgomery (Oxford: Clarendon Press, 1994), pp. 653–90, Act I, Scene 5, ll. 166–7.

11 The new global economic order, argues Pogge, is harsh on the global poor, because "our representatives ruthlessly exploit their vastly superior bargaining power and expertise, as well as any weakness, ignorance, or corruptibility they may find in their counterpart negotiators, to shape each agreement for our greatest benefit" (*World Poverty and Human Rights*, p. 20).

12 *World Poverty and Human Rights*, p. 197.

13 *World Poverty and Human Rights*, p. 50.

14 *World Poverty and Human Rights*, p. 21.

15 Thomas Pogge, "Severe Poverty as a Human Rights Violation," in his edited *Freedom from Poverty as a Human Right: Who Owes What to the Very Poor?* (Oxford: Oxford University Press, 2007), pp. 11–54, at p. 20.

16 World Bank, *World Development Report: Equity and Development* (World Bank, and Oxford University Press, 2005), p. 56.

17 Countries of the south, writes Pogge, have already been weakened by the "massive grievous wrongs" committed by a common history of colonialism and conquest. Therefore they are simply not in a position of strength to negotiate with the rich countries for policies that would benefit them. *World Poverty and Human Rights*, p. 203.

18 UNDP, *Human Development Report 2007/2008, Fighting Climate Change: Human Solidarity in a Divided World* (Houndmills: Palgrave Macmillan, 2007), p. 25.

19 *World Poverty and Human Rights*, p. 67.

20 I have elaborated this argument in Neera Chandhoke, "Thinking through Social and Economic Rights," in Daniel A. Bell and Jean-Marc Coicaud (eds), *Ethics in Action: The Ethical Challenges of International Human Rights Nongovernmental Organizations*, (Cambridge: Cambridge University Press and United Nations University, 2007) pp. 181–97.

21 P. Gilabert, "The Duty to Eradicate Global Poverty: Positive or Negative?," *Ethical Theory and Moral Practice* 7 (2004): 537–50, at 542.

22 Ratna Sudershan, 2007, "Social Protection, the informal economy, and globalization," paper prepared for the project "Globalisation and the State in India," n. 2.

23 Neera Chandhoke, "The Limits of Global Civil Society," in Marlies Glasius, Mary Kaldor, and Helmut Anheier (eds), *Global Civil Society 2002* (Oxford: Oxford University Press, 2002), pp. 35–54.

24 Larry S. Temkin, "Thinking about the Needy, Justice, and International Organizations," *The Journal of Ethics* 8(4) (2004): 349–95, at 356.

4

What Negative Duties? Which Moral Universalism?

Jiwei Ci*

1 A modest proposal with radical implications

Thomas Pogge presents his philosophical treatment of global poverty as starting from modest moral premises, and his practical solutions as constituting a modest proposal. His account is indeed modest in several ways. First, insofar as the transfer of resources from rich to poor countries is necessary, such transfer, as envisaged in Pogge's proposal of a Global Resources Dividend (204–8),[1] can be highly effective without being very costly to the rich countries. Second, insofar as reforms of global institutions are necessary, even relatively minor reforms can achieve dramatic effects (144).[2] Third, the moral values that can motivate the transfer of resources and the reform of global institutions and form the basis for criticism of the status quo are already available within the tradition of Western normative political thought (211). Fourth, and finally, in keeping with an important strand of this tradition, Pogge accepts the moral significance of the distinction between negative and positive duties, arguing that the measures for dealing with global poverty, as well as the values that should inform such measures, are best conceived in terms of the more moderate requirement of negative duties.[3]

This modesty is significant beyond considerations of mere feasibility. For what is taken by Pogge to be feasible is also taken by him to be morally imperative, and what make it morally imperative are reasons that are both internal to Western normative political thought and of a minimalist kind. That Pogge finds the West seriously wanting by a moral standard that is part of its own self-understanding makes his criticism, if plausible, intellectually unavoidable. That he selects from this self-understanding the minimalist requirement of certain negative duties makes his criticism, if plausible, morally unavoidable.

What is more deeply distinctive of Pogge's position is how he reasons from his deliberately modest starting point. In truth, Pogge's treatment of global poverty is at once modest and radical. Setting off from modest premises, he arrives at radical conclusions, and he does so by pursuing certain familiar concepts with uncommon intellectual rigor and moral integrity. Chief among these concepts are those of negative duties and of moral universalism, which he refines, in combination, into a thought-provoking position on global poverty. I find this position – the way in which radical conclusions unfold from the analysis of negative duties and moral universalism – enormously compelling. But, precisely for this reason, I believe the position taken as a whole requires for its acceptance and implementation a greater transformation in commonsense moral thinking and motivation than Pogge seems fully to anticipate. If this is correct, nothing need be taken away from the cogency of Pogge's position itself but more thought must be given to what has to change in ordinary moral thinking and motivation before a philosophically persuasive position such as this one can be translated into political reality.

2 Negative duties

Pogge takes the distinction between negative and positive duties to be of first importance and holds (or implies) that the fulfillment of negative duties by relevant parties is more or less sufficient for removing severe global poverty. How is a moderate requirement conceived entirely in terms of negative duties meant to go such a long way? The answer lies in Pogge's introduction of a further distinction – the distinction, with regard to negative duties, between an institutional and an interactional understanding.

We should conceive human rights primarily as claims on coercive social institutions and secondarily as claims against those who uphold such institutions. Such an *institutional* understanding contrasts with an *interactional* one, which presents human rights as placing the treatment of human beings under certain constraints that do not presuppose the existence of social institutions (45).

Put another way, "Human rights are . . . moral claims on the organization of one's society," and it follows that "citizens are collectively responsible for their society's organization and its resulting human-rights record" (64). In this way the modest idea of negative duties receives a radical interpretation:

> The most remarkable feature of this institutional understanding is that it can go well beyond minimalist libertarianism without denying its central tenet: that human rights entail only negative duties. The normative force of others' human rights for me is that I must not help uphold and impose upon them coercive social institutions under which they do not have secure access to the objects of their human rights. I would be violating this duty if, through my participation, I helped sustain a social order in which such access is not secure, in which blacks are enslaved, women disenfranchised, or servants mistreated, for example. Even if I owned no slaves or employed no servants myself, I would still share responsibility: by contributing my labor to the society's economy, my taxes to its government, and so forth. (66)

Thus, starting from a strand of Western liberal moral common sense, Pogge arrives at moral requirements that are continuous with such moral common sense and yet involve marked departures from it. The new requirements remain minimal ones in that they still consist entirely of negative duties. Yet, given the institutional understanding of negative duties, the minimal requirements become strangely demanding. On the one hand, more is demanded of moral agents, substantively, in that negative duties now include the duty to uphold just institutions, in addition to the familiar, interactional duty not to cause direct harm to concrete individuals. On the other hand, those who are to carry out negative duties as thus reconceived must not think of themselves as *morally* doing more, in that these duties, whatever they involve, are negative ones and hence represent the least that one should do. Thus, unlike libertarians, Pogge argues for doing more to combat severe global poverty, yet under the description of doing the same. And unlike those on the left who espouse the positive duty to help the global poor, Pogge argues for doing as much (the exact degree of similarity is an open question), yet under a different, at once less elevated and more stringent, description.

What is modest about Pogge's position is the treatment of negative duties as central and perhaps sufficient for taking us as far as we must go and can realistically expect to go in overcoming severe global poverty. If anything appears to be sacrificed as a result of this modesty, it is made up for through the radical reconceptualization of negative duties. To be sure, one is no longer bound by positive duties: "On my institutional understanding, it involves no duty on everyone to help supply such necessities to those who would otherwise be without them" (67). However, this institutional understanding "involves a duty on citizens to ensure that any coercive social order they collectively impose upon each of themselves is one under which, insofar as reasonably possible, each has secure access to these necessities" (67). Provided that this duty is taken care of, it will no longer be necessary to think about global poverty in terms of helping the poor (23), and thus positive duties naturally drop out of the picture. Everything that would otherwise need to be done under a falsely elevated description (helping the poor) is to be done under a more modest description (not harming the poor) once the latter description is revised in the light of the institutional view. As far as the global poor are concerned, the adoption of this revised description is a net gain.

Is this description also one which the rich and powerful have no good reason to reject? This depends on the relative importance of two kinds of moral constraints.

> An *institutional* conception postulates certain fundamental principles of social *justice*. They apply to institutional schemes and are thus second-order principles: standards for assessing the ground rules and practices that regulate human interactions. An *interactional* conception, by contrast, postulates certain fundamental principles of *ethics*. These principles, like institutional ground rules, are first-order in that they apply directly to the conduct of persons and groups . . .
>
> On the interactional view human rights impose constraints on conduct, while on the institutional view they impose constraints, in the first instance, upon shared practices. (170)

Since shared practices make up the context in which individual conduct takes place, their importance is immeasurably greater than that of individual conduct within them. One way of conceiving this priority of shared practices is Rawls's argument for treating the basic structure of society as the primary subject of justice on account of its profound effects on the life prospects of every member of society. From a line of thinking akin in spirit to Rawls's, Pogge derives a conclusion that Rawls for one reason or another is unprepared to draw, namely, that the morally problematic relation in which citizens of the rich countries stand to the global poor is, first and foremost, institutional rather than merely interactional. As Pogge puts it, "The

debate ignores that we are also and more significantly related to them
[the global poor] as supporters of, and beneficiaries from, a global
institutional order that substantially contributes to their destitution"
(117).

Another way of conceiving the priority of shared practices is suggested by Adorno's idea that "there can be no good life within the bad
one."[4] Although Adorno is here discussing the good life rather than
justice, there is a sense in which his remark is true of justice as well. If
the rules of a game are unjust, how can individual players of the game
behave justly within those rules? How much point and consequence
are there in striving to be personally unimpeachable when the shared
practices within which one makes this effort are informed by unjust
principles in the first place? While individuals need not see their personal moral conduct within unjust institutions as entirely pointless,
shouldn't it nevertheless be their first order of business to reform these
institutions and, until such reform is fully successful, compensate the
victims of these institutions? Those who are indifferent to such questions invite the charge of being overly self-regarding, and indeed petty,
in their concern with interactional norms, however scrupulously they
act on this concern.

The unfortunate truth is that such indifference is part of today's
moral common sense, with its unexamined idea that we are not responsible for harms we do not directly inflict and therefore have no negative
duties regarding such harms and need incur no moral blame and suffer
no bad conscience for doing little or nothing about them. It is not
surprising that such moral common sense can provide convenient
refuge for those who have little concern with the effects of injustice
and are mainly interested in preserving the appearance that they themselves are not implicated in those effects. This kind of scenario gives
point to Pogge's question: "How can there be a moral difference
between paying the Saudi clan or General Sani Abacha – the Nigerian
strongman who kept the winner of the annulled 1993 election in jail
and has executed numerous political opponents – and stealing the oil
outright?" (142).[5] Those who are right to see little difference here
should find a powerful explanation of their moral intuition in Pogge's
institutional view of justice.

The institutional view of moral responsibility is all the more ines-
capable in the case of a democratic society. It is a fact of considerable
moral importance that the rich and powerful countries that Pogge
holds accountable for much of the avoidable poverty in the world
happen also to be democracies. While Pogge is aware of this fact and
its implications (21), he nevertheless formulates the institutional view

in general terms. According to it, as we have seen, citizens are implicated in the unjust institutions imposed by their governments if they benefit from these institutions, however unintentionally, and fail to make "reasonable efforts" (172) to resist and reform such institutions or compensate the victims. As Pogge himself puts it, "When undue harms are mandated or authorized by a society's social institutions (e.g., its laws) and when state officials inflict these harms or protect and aid those who do, then citizens who uphold these institutions through their political consent and economic support contribute to the harms" (135). When the institutional view is formulated in general terms, it is quite properly illustrated with the example of Nazi Germany:

> The horrendous crimes inflicted by the Nazis, for instance, were not possible without the economic contributions of many citizens through the tax system, nor without the legitimacy that Nazi laws and officials derived from the consent many citizens expressed by participating in legal and political institutions, by attending rallies, by enlisting in the armed forces, etc. By lending such support, these citizens, too, violated their *negative* duty not to harm others unduly. (135)

If this is true of the citizens of Nazi Germany, as it clearly is to a significant degree, how much more true it must be of members of a democratic society. The latter have greater influence over the conduct of their governments, even over the shape of the basic social institutions of their society, run less or no risk in exercising this influence, and take pride in all this – in the fact that they are free and able to bring about what citizens of nondemocratic societies are not. To the extent that this is the case, it is not only reasonable but also indeed a tribute to the superiority of their political system to ascribe to citizens of democratic societies a greater responsibility, and a greater unavoidability of blame, for any harm caused by their governments and by any institutional arrangements they help impose. Thus, "reasonable efforts" at reforming unjust institutions and compensating their victims must be construed with special stringency in the case of a democratic society.

This does not mean that citizens of nondemocratic societies cannot be held accountable for violating negative duties conceived on the institutional view. On the one hand, they clearly can be, as they are covered by the institutional view as stated in general terms, which has considerable force even in the extreme example of Nazi Germany. On the other hand, to whatever degree that their accountability is attenuated by the lack of democracy in their society, such attenuation by itself constitutes a case for democracy and entails a responsibility to make reasonable efforts to promote democracy. Thus, the link between democracy and citizenly responsibility cuts both ways in the case of a nondemocratic society, much as it does in the case of a democratic one.

Whether understood in general terms or with special reference to democratic societies, the institutional view represents a big leap from the way in which the notion of negative duties is typically comprehended. How else could Pogge have set out from a modest starting point and arrived at conclusions that go considerably against the grain of Western moral common sense? One important reason why I find Pogge's philosophical treatment of global poverty compelling is that his institutional view is plausible and that therefore *the leap is justified*. But the leap, however justified, remains a leap and, as such, will encounter resistance from the entrenched moral thinking and moral psychology that rest on the interactional view. It is thus one thing to show the priority of negative duties as conceived on the institutional view, and something else to appraise the difficulties that will have to be overcome before moral agents as they are presently constituted can be motivated to take up and act on negative duties so conceived. The normative vindication of the institutional view immediately raises the question of the transformation of conventional moral thinking and moral psychology.

It is worth reminding ourselves just how demanding negative duties are when conceived in institutional terms. Once negative duties are given an institutional understanding, they undergo a profound change in what they require of moral agents and the spirit in which they require it. Moral agents will have to acquire a different moral psychology, one in which they do more than is required by the familiar, interactional conception of negative duties, and probably no less than is required by the familiar conception of positive duties and yet in the humbler spirit of discharging negative duties. Under the institutional conception of negative duties, then, citizens of developed countries must do more about global poverty – and yet, strictly speaking, take themselves to deserve no gratitude for doing so, for what they must do, if they do it, falls within the (expanded) category of negative duties.[6] On this (expanded) view of negative duties, citizens of rich and powerful Western countries "do not merely let people starve but also participate in starving them" (214). To correct this, they must do more than they now believe they ought strictly to do (in terms of negative duties according to the interactional view) and take themselves to be doing less than they now believe they are doing (fulfilling positive duties) when providing "aid."

As a revision of the conventional understanding of negative duties, Pogge's institutional view is radical indeed. It is nevertheless understandable why Pogge wants to keep his practical proposal for solving severe global poverty modest: "Modesty is important if the proposed institutional alternative is to gain the support necessary to implement it and is to be able to sustain itself in the world as we know it" (205). There is a sense, as noted at the outset, in which his Global Resources Dividend (GRD) proposal is indeed modest, requiring as it does the transfer of a very small portion of the West's wealth and only relatively minor international reforms. But if the necessary expenditure and reforms are minor, the determination to undertake them requires a major change in moral thinking – a shift in the focus of the sense of justice from the interactional to the institutional.

In the world as we know it, everyday thinking about justice is more interactional than institutional. Under favorable circumstances, to be sure, citizens expect the basic structure of their society not to be "extremely and evidently unjust."[7] As long as this undemanding condition is met, however, most people are consumed with pursuing the so-called freedoms of the moderns within the existing definition and rules of the game. There is little evidence of sustained interest in informed and effectual public discussion concerning the good of the game itself and the justice of its rules, and it would be highly implausible to explain this lack of interest by saying that this is because citizens are happy with the game and its rules upon informed reflection. Most of us are simply too preoccupied, too nearsighted, or too disillusioned to be bothered with reflection upon the institutional context of our everyday concerns and activities. We retain our ability to be upset by institutional injustice that is out of the ordinary, but most of the time we are less demanding of the ground rules of our society than of one another's personal conduct under such rules as happen to prevail, as long as these rules do not conflict with our seldom examined moral common sense. And thus the normal contexts that engage our moral emotion are predominantly interactional: our resentment of injustice is more often directed at, and more easily mobilized against, what is perceived to be the unjust conduct of individuals, especially of course that of public officials, than the injustice of the system as reflected in its ground rules.

We owe largely to Rawls the fact that political philosophers now generally treat the basic structure of a social arrangement as the primary subject of justice. According to Rawls, "From the standpoint of justice as fairness, a fundamental natural duty is the duty of justice. This duty requires us to support and to comply with just institutions that exist and apply to us. It also constrains us to further just arrangements not yet established, at least when this can be done without too much cost to ourselves."[8] It is regrettable that Rawls's emphasis on the basic structure as the primary subject of justice has not made its way into moral common sense. "Rawls is well aware," says the blurb on the back cover of Rawls's *Justice as Fairness*, "that since the publication of *A Theory of Justice* in 1971, American society has moved farther away from the idea of justice as fairness." Even more noteworthy, I would suggest, is the fact that Rawls's treatment of the basic structure as the primary subject of justice has not had much of an impact on everyday moral thinking in America or in the world at large. To this day modern moral common sense remains wedded to the interactional view of justice. Were this not the case, Pogge's argument for the greater importance of institutional than interactional morality would happily lose its point.

Given this moral common sense, it is easier to live with oneself for ignoring the injustice of the global economic arrangements imposed by one's government than for, say, not donating to a charity aimed at helping needy locals, for the former failure involves institutional (if negative) duties while the latter failure involves interactional (if positive) duties, and on the radar of moral common sense the first registers as a much smaller failure, if a failure at all.

This article of moral common sense goes well together with the moral psychology of liberalism, in which cruelty, as Judith Shklar tells us, is the first ordinary vice.[9] Cruelty is, above all, an interactional vice, one that manifests itself in acts perpetrated by one being directly against another. That is why we do not normally ascribe cruelty to those who unknowingly benefit from an unjust institutional arrangement without trying either to reform it or to compensate its victims, nor even to those who knowingly support the arrangement as long as they are not directly engaged in harming its victims. Whatever the fault is, it seldom lends itself to charges of cruelty.

Shklar's privileging of cruelty is of a piece with Richard Rorty's account of moral progress as being caused by hearing sad and sentimental stories.[10] If such stories *directly* motivate people to be more just, they do so by promoting the interactional virtue of justice. Beyond that, sad and sentimental stories can motivate people to reflect on the injustice of institutions but cannot be a substitute for such reflection. And yet it is only through reflection that the injustice suffered by concrete individuals can be raised to a level where the whole system is judged to be unjust and in need of reform. A defining feature of the institutional view of justice is that it comprises second-order principles that are applied to the design of institutions rather than directly to the conduct of moral agents. In this sense, the institutional view is more abstract and less immediately accessible to individual moral consciousness. This is not to say that individual moral consciousness cannot be trained to pay greater heed to the justice or injustice of institutional practices. But such training is more dependent on moral reflection than training in the interactional virtue of justice need be, and moral reflection in turn is of a different order from typical reaction to hearing sad and sentimental stories. The obstacle blocking proper attention to institutional injustice is not cruelty but unreflective comportment to the moral status quo.[11] A liberal moral psychology that fully registers the importance of the basic structure and of the institutional understanding of human rights and negative duties must give equal pride of place to such unreflectiveness as an ordinary vice.

But overcoming such unreflectiveness need not, perhaps should not, be treated, in the first instance, as a matter of individual effort and achievement. Even if individual moral agents overcome the inertia of moral common sense and manage to see themselves as part of the causal nexus of injustice by virtue of being beneficiaries of an unjust order, they then face a further moral challenge, one that does not apply to the familiar, interactional understanding of negative duties. They must, that is, learn to act from a sense of responsibility commensurate with their causal awareness but in the total absence of the prospect of being punished or even of being reasonably singled out for censure. The required sense of responsibility must come from their conscience alone, from an ability to develop a bad conscience for acts which one does not commit or omit individually and for which one is not liable either to punishment or even to individualized criticism. This is an intrinsic feature of the institutional approach, in that an individual agent who does not hold public office will always be at one causal remove from the harm that results directly from the implementation of unjust institutions.

Thus, to develop the kind of sense of responsibility that is necessary to make the institutional approach work is a very tall order indeed, and we cannot pin much hope or blame on moral agents as individuals, to begin with. What is more fitting is the expectation that those institutions of society with an important role to play in moral socialization inculcate the sense of justice as including institutional concerns on a par with interactional ones. As things stand, such institutions fail massively in this task, especially with regard to global justice. There are few societies, if any, in which the acquisition of the institutional view is an integral part of moral socialization and in which the concern with the justice of the basic structure has become a regular component of the everyday sense of justice. It is this failure that makes Pogge's argument for the institutional view as unlikely to receive easy acceptance and implementation as it is timely and worthy of the widest public attention.

3 Moral universalism

The institutional view by itself is not sufficient. Even if this view is accepted for a domestic society, there may yet be resistance to its application across national boundaries. A combination of the institutional view for domestic justice and the interactional view for global justice is a distinct possibility, even though, in reality, I do not think the institutional view has prevailed even domestically in most societies, including Western ones. It is only natural, then, that Pogge's argument for approaching global poverty in terms of negative duties is coupled with his argument for a certain moral universalism. If his insistence on the moral priority of negative duties gains much of its moral power, as we have seen, from his adoption of the institutional perspective, his moral universalism in turn acquires special meaning and force from being combined with the institutional view of negative duties.[12] What characterizes Pogge's position, in other words, is that his moral universalism is defended with respect to negative duties, which in turn are conceived in institutional terms.

The bite of Pogge's universalism comes from the fact, to the extent that this is a fact, that members of Western societies place two minimal requirements of justice – that an economic order be open to change by democratic means and not be coercively imposed by a powerful minority, and that an economic order be so designed that its participants are able to meet their basic needs – on their national economic order and yet they do not place the same requirements on the international economic order and still manage to consider it just (96). It is an empirical matter whether and to what extent this is indeed a fact. Whatever the case may be, those who do not hold the institutional view even in a domestic setting are subject to Pogge's criticism of the failure to give priority to institutional justice. On the other hand, those who do hold the institutional view domestically but refuse to extend it beyond national boundaries are open to the charge of double standards. It is at this inconsistency that Pogge's moral universalism is directed. The precise target is, of course, not the mere adoption of double standards but the adoption of double standards with regard to minimal moral constraints (101, 109, 117, 124–5).

Two different things could be at issue here. One is whether universalism with regard to minimal moral constraints is to be preferred. The other, for those who subscribe to universalism, is what should be the content of minimal moral constraints. On the first issue, Pogge's opponents are nationalists, those who uphold the idea of different standards for different nation-states. On the second issue, Pogge faces opposition from fellow universalists regarding what is to be included in the scope of moral universalism.

In theory, those members of Western societies who place the aforementioned two minimal requirements of justice on their national economic order but do not place the same requirements on the international economic order could be motivated by nationalistic considerations. In reality, however, most of them seem not to be, favoring as they do an alternative universalism that is centered on democracy. If this is the case, then as far as mainstream Western opinion on global justice is concerned, the principal division is not between universalists and nationalists but between those who espouse different versions of universalism.

As Pogge sees it, the problem is that many who favor moral universalism in general fail to apply it to the case of global poverty. "We are quite tolerant of the persistence of extensive and severe poverty abroad even though it would not cost us much to reduce it dramatically. How well does this tolerance really fit with our commitment to moral universalism?" (92). Very poorly, Pogge suggests, treating this as a case of universalists being inconsistent. This assessment works if those whom Pogge takes to task agree that the two minimal moral requirements should indeed fall within the substantive scope of moral universalism. But they may not agree, and this is precisely the issue: the issue of the substantive scope (or core) of moral universalism. It is on this issue, I believe, that Pogge's version of moral universalism is both distinctive and superior.

The predominant moral universalism on the global scene, not least as often advocated by Western governments, pays little heed to global economic justice, leaving economic rights either outside its scope or at least outside its core. What is conspicuous by comparison is that the same universalism displays an irrepressible obsession with democracy and human rights, both in turn very narrowly conceived and often selectively applied. This kind of moral universalism invites the charge that those Western governments and citizens advocating it are opportunistic and self-serving: either they gain ideological advantage vis-à-vis the countries whose record of democracy and human rights they criticize; or they stand to benefit geopolitically or economically if the countries criticized are to adopt the changes they push for in the name of democracy and human rights.

Pogge departs refreshingly from this narrow universalism. Morally minimalist as it is, his universalism is nevertheless appropriately wide-ranging, covering not only democracy but also economic rights. If Pogge puts so much emphasis on economic rights, it is for the very good reason that the dominant universalism of the West does not attach nearly enough importance to them, showing an "easy accep-tance of extensive, severe poverty abroad" (117). Once this corrective emphasis has served its function, there is no reason why Pogge should not be able also to find countries wanting with respect to civil and political rights. The important thing is that, in both cases, criticisms of existing practices and arguments for reform spring from a moral universalism that is free from any convenient and self-serving narrowness.

Pogge thus offers something quite rare: a moral universalism not preached by the West to the Third World but directed first and fore-most at the West itself, given the corrective focus on severe global poverty. This is a valuable reminder that moral universalism is not one uniform substantive position with one uniform political agenda but must be judged on the merit of each instance. There are those in the West who use the discourse of moral universalism almost always to take other societies to task. Then there are those who are as prepared to unmask the self-serving partiality of one's own society in the light of moral universalism as they are to criticize other societies for falling short of what should be minimal standards held in common among all societies. Pogge is an all too rare exemplar of the latter. As someone who is generally suspicious of Western discourses of moral universal-ism and yet also alert to the often expedient particularism of my own culture, I find Pogge's version of moral universalism worthy of unqual-ified respect and the most open-minded and unbiased consideration.

I am less sanguine than Pogge, however, that the West is already morally equipped to embrace this kind of universalism. One reason for hope, according to Pogge, is that citizens of Western countries already have the requisite motivation within a domestic setting. "We accept a weighty negative duty not to impose a *national* economic system that avoidably engenders extreme poverty. Yet, we *fail* to accept a like negative duty with respect to the *global* economic system that we impose, shape, and dominate" (139). If this is the case, then it would seem that reform is largely a matter of extending what people already do domestically to the international arena. Such an extension carries a price for Western countries, however, and the question is whether they are willing to pay this price in the interest of greater moral consistency and improved global justice. One test case in this regard can be constructed out of Pogge's following proposal:

> We might . . . work out an international treaty declaring that rulers who hold power contrary to their country's constitution and without democratic legitimation cannot sell their country's resources abroad nor borrow in its name. Such a treaty would not merely end our complicity. It would also dramatically reduce the rewards and hence the frequency of *coups d'état* and dictatorship in the poor countries. (142)

Whether a concrete proposal such as this one will be adopted is a test of whether citizens of developed countries are willing to pay a significant price for the extension of their professed moral beliefs to the international arena, and in an important sense, for their moral beliefs as such. To the extent that they are not, this will tell a special story about the nature of their moral beliefs.

Central to this story, as I see it, is the idea that real moral progress is to be defined as the removal or reduction of injustice without the same or similar injustice being shifted elsewhere so that the benefits of the abandoned injustice are continued by other questionable means. To the extent, for example, that the ending of colonialism is followed by the Western powers' economic exploitation of the former colonies by other means, such as collusion with authoritarian rulers through the international resource privilege, we have reason to cast doubt on the adequacy of explaining the ending of colonialism, however welcome in itself, in terms of moral progress. How much real moral progress is there if advantages for the rich and powerful are preserved by new means that are seriously unjust even if less directly and blatantly so than the means abandoned? How much real moral progress is there, to take another example, if a minimum wage is introduced in the domestic labor market but those who used to benefit from its absence can happily reap the same old benefits by moving to a foreign labor market without minimum wage legislation? The details of each such case need to be carefully examined, of course, in order to yield anything like a precise assessment, and I cannot provide such assessment here. But if my general point stands, readers can find their own, perhaps more fitting examples. My general point, to say it once again, is this: To the extent that an injustice is shifted elsewhere, there is no moral progress, all sites or means of injustice considered. Only in the absence of such a shift can we speak of the "net" reduction or removal of injustice and hence of real moral progress.

This is especially true if we think of moral progress in terms of improved moral motivation. For a shift of injustice allows the beneficiaries of the old injustice to maintain their advantage without paying any significant price; the price is borne by victims of the new injustice – ordinary Nigerians under General Sani Abacha, say, or cheap laborers without minimum wage protection in another, poor country. The appearance of improved behavior by the rich and powerful that comes about in this way requires little improvement of motivation, in that those who used to enjoy their advantage in one unjust arrangement now enjoy the same or a similar advantage in another. Now that the new unjust arrangement delivers the same advantage to them, the rich and powerful can afford to let go of the old unjust arrangement.

This need not prevent the rich and powerful from interpreting the localized reduction or removal of injustice in terms that suggest moral progress, as if the change in local moral norms had come about independently of the shift of injustice elsewhere. This kind of interpretation is facilitated by the interactional understanding of justice. Blind to institutional injustices, such a limited conception of justice allows the rich and powerful to maintain a sense, or an appearance, of moral cleanliness by not directly engaging in unjust conduct themselves while benefiting from an unjust arrangement which they have no desire to reform. This does not mean that the interpretation is insincere, or the values it comprises superficial. Quite the contrary, and precisely because of this, the new values can come into conflict with the very phenomenon – the shift of injustice to a new place and new direct perpetrator – that seems to have made possible the improvement in local justice in the first place. That the shift of injustice has indeed played this role is suggested by the extreme reluctance on the part of the beneficiaries of the old injustice to put an effective stop to the new injustice – say, to stop extending the resource privilege to predatory, authoritarian governments, or to refuse to shift production to cheaper labor markets without adequate labor protection laws. Something like this is, in my estimation, an important part of the explanation for the kind of inconsistency to which Pogge refers, where "the common moral acceptance of the existing global order is incoherent with firmly entrenched moral convictions about interpersonal morality and domestic justice" (1). Much of the inconsistency is only apparent. This is also, in part, my answer to the question "How can severe poverty of half of humankind continue . . . despite the enlightened moral norms and values of our heavily dominant Western civilization?" (3). The moral norms and values may not be so enlightened after all, having failed the test of the "net" reduction of injustice.

In our age of fast-accelerating globalization, it is not surprising that the shift of injustice typically takes place from centers of power and affluence to places – say, China, and then Vietnam, with potential movement further down the chain – where the poor and powerless are less able to resist unjust institutional practices.[13] What can happen in any society, as Pogge notes, is that the strong "consciously or unconsciously, try to get around the [moral] norms by arranging their social world so as to minimize their burdens of compliance" (5). In a relatively well-ordered democracy, however, the strong face pressure from the domestic weak, sometimes vigilant and persistent pressure that makes burdens of compliance difficult to avoid. One systemic way out of this difficulty is to maintain existing advantage through a shift of injustice elsewhere so that the strong have little to lose from compliance in their own country. The domestic weak too can benefit from this arrangement and hence join the strong in shifting injustice abroad.[14] It is time now for the global weak to exert pressure on the global strong, on all those who benefit systemically from their poverty and helplessness. Only if they too succeed – and succeed in such a way that the injustice removed from their quarter is not shifted elsewhere – will there be a "net" reduction in injustice. But the further down the chain, the more vulnerable and powerless will be the weak, and the less able they will be to put effective pressure on the strong. This is where we are today.[15]

The shift of injustice from the domestic to the foreign can find a philosophical justification in both a narrow universalism and a misguided nationalism. For either position can dictate that, in the case of economic justice, domestic institutions be assessed by standards considerably higher than those applied to global ones. This kind of differentiation is suspect in that it does more to disguise the shift of injustice and to relieve rich and powerful countries of responsibilities toward the global poor than to express genuine respect or tolerance for local values in the poor countries. It is here, above all, that I see the true caliber and integrity of Pogge's moral universalism: it is a powerful philosophical antidote to that all too common yet all too rarely noticed phenomenon of injustice – the shift of injustice from one immediate locus or direct perpetrator to another, especially across the boundaries of strong and weak nations.

That Pogge's moral universalism can play this role is not only because it is appropriately wide-ranging in its coverage of negative duties but also because it raises negative duties to the level of an institutional understanding. If accepted and acted on, this combination of moral universalism and the institutional view will leave no hiding place for the shift of injustice and the moral peace of mind of its beneficiaries. Here lies, I think, the enormous significance of Pogge's philosophical project on global justice. But precisely for this reason, the road leading to the acceptance and implementation of his ideas and proposals will be long and hard.

Notes

*I am indebted to Alison Jaggar, editor of the volume, for comments and suggestions that have greatly helped me improve an earlier version of this paper.

1 All parenthetical references are to Thomas W. Pogge, *World Poverty and Human Rights*, 1st edn (Cambridge: Polity, 2002).

2 To be sure, anything approaching a full and fully just solution to the problem of severe global poverty may well require levels of transfer and institutional reforms that must be considered fundamental. As I understand him, Pogge would not rest content until such fundamental changes are effected, but, equally, he is prepared to settle for considerably less here and now in order to bring immediate relief to those who desperately need it. The modesty of his practical proposals, in the shape of the GRD, seems essentially a function of this realism.

3 "One great challenge to any morally sensitive person today," writes Pogge,

> is the extent and severity of global poverty. There are two ways of conceiving such poverty as a moral challenge to us: we may be failing to fulfill our *positive* duty to help persons in acute distress; and we may be failing to fulfill our more stringent *negative* duty not to uphold injustice, not to contribute to or profit from the unjust impoverishment of others. (197)

Pogge defines negative and positive duties thus:

> I try to draw it [i.e., the distinction between negative and positive duties], within the domain of interpersonal responsibilities, so as to vindicate its moral significance, that is, the popular idea that, given equal stakes for all involved, negative duties have greater weight. I propose, then, to call *negative* any duty to ensure that others are not unduly harmed (or wronged) through one's own conduct and to call *positive* the remainder: any duty to benefit persons or to shield them from other harms. (130)

Pogge comes down decisively on the side of the latter conception: "I agree that the distinction between causing poverty and merely failing to reduce it is morally significant. . . . My argument conceives, then, both human rights and justice as involving solely negative duties: specific minimal constraints – more minimal in the case of human rights – on what harms persons may inflict upon others" (13). In a well-considered ecumenical spirit, Pogge says that in this regard he is in agreement with libertarians (13) and that his is not a leftist critique (24) but one that is Lockean in spirit (23).

4 Theodor Adorno, *Minima Moralia*, trans. E. F. N. Jephcott (London: Verso, 1978), p. 39. In his lectures on *Problems of Moral Philosophy*, ed. Thomas Schröder, trans. Rodney Livingston (Stanford: Stanford University Press, 2001), Adorno refers to this epigrammatic saying of his (p. 1) and discusses it at length in Lecture 17. I have used Livingston's translation here.

5 As Pogge goes on to say, "In fact, paying Abacha inflicted a second harm . . . And having done this, we lavish condescending pity on impoverished populations for their notorious 'failure to govern themselves democratically'!" (142).

6 It is, of course, imprecise to speak of "citizens of developed countries" or "the West," etc., as if there was a single, undifferentiated entity when it comes to ascribing responsibility for the violation of negative duties toward the global poor. It is not my aim here (nor the aim of Pogge's project), however, to make the fine discriminations that any empirical attribution of responsibility would call for. For this reason, I shall continue to use general terms of reference but qualify them from time to time with expressions like "to the extent that. . . ."

7 This expression is borrowed from Stuart Hampshire, *Justice is Conflict* (Princeton: Princeton University Press, 2000), p. 85.

8 John Rawls, *A Theory of Justice*, rev. edn (Cambridge, MA: Harvard University Press, 1999), p. 99; see also p. 497.

9 Judith N. Shklar, *Ordinary Vices* (Cambridge, MA: Harvard University Press, 1984), ch 1.

10 Richard Rorty, "Human Rights, Rationality, and Sentimentality," in *On Human Rights: The Oxford Amnesty Lectures*, ed. Stephen Shute and Susan Hurley (New York: Basic Books, 1993).

11 What I have in mind here bears partial resemblance to the thoughtlessness that Arendt regards as constitutive of "the banality of evil." See Hannah Arendt, *The Life of the Mind*, one-volume edn (San Diego: Harcourt Brace Jovanovich, 1978). In the Introduction, esp. pp. 3–5, Arendt offers philosophical reflections on the phenomenon that she had earlier identified in *Eichmann in Jerusalem*, rev. and enl. edn (New York: Viking Press, 1965).

12 Bringing the two issues together, Pogge argues that "The permissibility of giving priority to the near and dear is quite dubious in the case of negative duties" (130).

13 Of course, the rich and powerful in the developing countries concerned are among the foremost beneficiaries of such practices and have a vested

interest in maintaining them. But this is not the subject of my discussion here.

14 Not always or without qualification, of course, as the shift of injustice can also mean the shift of jobs.

15 As Pogge puts it, "The global poor, who labor all day for a few dollars a month, are unable to cause us the slightest inconvenience and unable even to alert us to their plight. Thanks to our military superiority, they fall outside what Rawls has called the circumstances of justice" (126). Until the global poor come under the circumstances of justice, or are recognized as belonging under them, every apparent improvement in moral norms elsewhere in the world is severely compromised.

5

Non-Egalitarian Global Fairness

Erin I. Kelly and Lionel K. McPherson

1 Asymmetries of justice?

Few political philosophers have been as focused as Thomas Pogge on addressing global poverty. He now emphasizes the negative duty that members of affluent countries have not to harm members of other countries. Such a duty is widely accepted and uncontroversial compared to any positive duty which persons or countries might have to assist the global poor. We will not be concerned with the empirical grounds for Pogge's claims about causes of and solutions to global poverty, claims that have become a source of controversy. Our concern will be his philosophical views, which are an earlier source of controversy.

Presumably, anyone who recognizes such a thing as global justice would agree that there is a duty not to harm members of other countries, at least given a familiar conception of harming behavior. Pogge's influence as a political philosopher is due to stronger, more egalitarian commitments he continues to seem partial to – often in the course of aggressively criticizing liberal, non-egalitarian views of global justice. The impression that he is committed to principles of global justice that are demanding and controversial arises from the body of his work.

For example, Pogge used to characterize his proposed global tax on natural resources as "an egalitarian law of peoples."[1] He also claimed that an "egalitarian" concern that the current world order "generates international social and economic inequalities that are not to the maximum benefit of the world's worst-off persons" is valid given "the significant political and economic interdependencies that exist today and will in all likelihood persist into the indefinite future."[2] More recently, in introducing the representative collection of his work to date, he continues to claim that all human beings should enjoy "a proportional share of the world's natural resources."[3]

Pogge has not repudiated such sensibilities, and there is reason to believe that his shift in focus is more tactical than substantively philosophical. He argues that "you *harm* others insofar as you make an uncompensated contribution to imposing on them an institutional order that foreseeably produces avoidable human rights deficits."[4] This could be construed as a minimalist position, if what counts as an imposition of human rights deficits is construed narrowly – which yields no philosophically distinctive or interesting position, since no thinker imagines that violating basic human rights might generally be permissible. However, the notion of human rights that Pogge relies on to identify harms is more expansive than commonly recognized prohibitions and bears a strong relation to his earlier, more explicit egalitarian commitments.[5] He is drawn to a Lockean account of economic justice, which begins from the idea that persons have equal moral claims on natural resources.[6] Pogge's view appears far from minimal in that an institutional order's willful failure to satisfy these claims would constitute human rights-violating harms.[7]

Egalitarian sensibilities are also evident in Pogge's criticisms of John Rawls. Pogge has persistently criticized Rawls's account of global justice set forth in *The Law of Peoples*. Rawls argues that a principle of distributive justice, which domestically would limit and regulate economic inequality, does not apply at the global level. The main point of contention is whether this type of asymmetry in the requirements of justice is objectionably inconsistent or, instead, plausibly represents differences in the requirements of economic justice globally as compared to domestically. Pogge maintains that proponents of an egalitarian conception of justice in the domestic case cannot in good faith recognize merely a humanitarian duty of assistance in the global case, especially since an emphasis on humanitarianism tends to obscure the causal story of how the global economic order harms members of poor countries.[8] Unless he harbors an egalitarian conception of global justice, along with an uncommon view of what counts as harm, it is not obvious why he should find asymmetries in the requirements of domestic and global justice so objectionable.

Cosmopolitan egalitarians such as Peter Singer and Kok-Chor Tan obviously will take issue with Rawls's account of global justice: Rawls rejects the egalitarianism they take to be fundamental to a reasonable conception of justice, domestically and globally. By contrast, Pogge's work lacks a developed commitment to principles of global economic justice that go beyond a duty to eradicate global poverty. He tries to distance himself from controversial moral considerations of a kind to which cosmopolitan egalitarians might appeal, for example, the notion that accidents of birth should not be permitted to have a substantial effect on the life prospects of persons individually or collectively.[9] Pogge claims that a "universal criterion [of justice] ought to be modest,"[10] shaping the global economic order "to produce an economic distribution such that its participants can meet their most basic standard needs."[11] Achieving this goal, he believes, would require only moderate alterations in the current rules comprising the global order.

Emphasizing a duty to eradicate global poverty is not enough, however, to substantiate the inconsistency line of argument that Pogge runs against Rawls (and most members of affluent countries[12]). The political and economic interdependencies Pogge cites might be viewed as grounds to support a humanitarian duty of assistance rather than a global egalitarian principle. In fact, there are reasons to favor asymmetries in the requirements of domestic and global justice that could be countered, it seems, only by a strong form of egalitarianism. We resist the suggestion that an egalitarian conception of domestic justice implies cosmopolitan egalitarianism and will argue that egalitarianism writ globally risks conflicting with autonomy, toleration, and respect across societies.

We are sympathetic to Pogge's sense of moral priorities. Eliminating global poverty is morally urgent. Moreover, we agree that principles of global justice are not plausibly rooted in egalitarian foundations but, rather, are better elaborated with appropriate notions of cooperation and reciprocity. Thus we will argue forthrightly that commitments to eradicating global poverty and to global fair trade, which are targets of modest principles of global justice, do not imply a commitment to egalitarianism. We also argue that concerns about global poverty can be addressed by what we will call *cosmopolitan cooperationism*. This account of global justice goes beyond Rawls's, yet stops well short of cosmopolitan egalitarianism. Perhaps the Pogge of today would accept our conclusions. Still, the impression persists that he is drawn to cosmopolitan egalitarian commitments.

2 Reckoning with economic inequality

Cosmopolitan egalitarians have criticized Rawls's account of global justice for permitting substantial economic inequality among societies. Rawls almost invites this criticism when reflecting on the fact of inequality within and among societies:

> In itself, it doesn't matter how great the gap between rich and poor may be. What matters are the consequences. In a liberal domestic society that gap cannot be wider than the criterion of reciprocity allows, so that the least advantaged . . . have sufficient all-purpose means . . . to lead reasonable and worthwhile lives. When that situation exists, there is no further need to narrow the gap. Similarly, in the basic structure of the Society of Peoples, once the duty of assistance is satisfied and all peoples have a working liberal or decent government, there is again no reason to narrow the gap between the average wealth of different peoples.[13]

Here the requirements of justice look significantly different than Rawls's presentation in *A Theory of Justice* would lead one to expect. He appears to have backed away from promoting the most striking, egalitarian feature of justice as fairness, namely, the difference principle's requirement that domestic economic and social inequalities be of greatest advantage to persons who are least well off.

Maybe the difference principle is after all not part of a conception of justice that free, equal, and rational persons deliberating behind a veil of ignorance could all be expected to choose.[14] This would resolve the appearance of a stark inconsistency about the requirements of justice domestically as compared to globally. Indeed, given the views Rawls expresses in his later work, characterizing him as a proper egalitarian might be mistaken. Economic inequality, according to the passage above, would be objectionable when it has a substantial negative impact on the lives of truly disadvantaged persons. Such a position is not committed to a requirement of economic equality among persons or societies. In short, an emphasis on the practical consequences of inequality leaves considerable room for economic inequality that would not necessarily be judged unjust or unfair.

Rawls is explicit that members of liberal and decent nonliberal societies, which are presumed to be relatively affluent, have a duty to assist "societies burdened by unfavorable conditions."[15] So the real complaint of cosmopolitan egalitarians like Singer cannot be Rawls's "lack of focus on obligations toward individuals who are currently destitute in other countries."[16] Rawls does deny that a duty of assistance derives from a principle of distributive justice regulating economic inequality among societies, and this is what really bothers cosmopolitan egalitarians. The cosmopolitan egalitarian objection is that departures from economic equality are unfair in that they express a lack of equal regard for persons, wherever they happen to live.

Underlying the cosmopolitan egalitarian commitment to global economic equality is the view that substantial economic inequality among societies is presumptively unjust or unfair to their individual members. To help clarify this view, Tan draws a distinction between justice and humanitarianism. "Justice is concerned with structural equality of some form," he asserts, while "humanitarianism is concerned primarily with the meeting of basic needs."[17] There is no doubt that his focus is economic equality. "What is lacking in Rawls's account of global justice," Tan observes, "is the commitment to *distributive* justice. That is, there are no ongoing distributive principles regulating the inequalities between the rich and the poor of the world beyond the duty of the better-off to ensure that the badly-off are able to meet a certain threshold level of basic needs."[18] The issue is whether humanitarianism, expressed through a duty of assistance to persons as such, falls short of the requirements of a reasonable conception of global justice.

Pogge seems sympathetic to two strategies for advancing the cosmopolitan egalitarian mode of criticism, despite his disavowal of controversial moral foundations. The first strategy is to argue that societies should have a fair opportunity for economic growth, where the criteria for fair opportunity should be decided by an agreement that representatives of all persons would reach when situated behind a global veil of ignorance.[19] This would be to extend to questions of global justice the move that Rawls makes in *A Theory of Justice* to arrive at his domestic difference principle. Although Pogge is reluctant to endorse a global difference principle, he utilizes this strategy to charge Rawls with inconsistency.

The second strategy is to argue that humanitarianism deflects attention away from the sources of economic inequality among societies – sources that often are not morally innocent. Burdened societies might be victimized externally, for instance, by colonialism or neocolonialism and its legacy, or by coercive international trade arrangements that greatly favor economically powerful countries. In addition, disadvantaged persons in burdened societies might be victimized internally, for instance, by kleptocratic or tyrannical regimes. Rawls hardly mentions these various circumstances that can figure into an explanation of global inequality. When he does, his discussion of the sources of global inequality places much of the responsibility for economic inequality among societies on burdened societies themselves:

> I believe that the causes of the wealth of a people and the forms it takes lie in their political culture and in the religious, philosophical, and moral traditions that support the basic structure of their political and social institutions, as well as in the industriousness and cooperative talent of its members, all supported by their political virtues. I would further conjecture that there is no society anywhere in the world – except for marginal cases – with resources so scarce that it could not, were it reasonably and rationally organized and governed, become well-ordered.[20]

This strong conjecture about the causes of domestic wealth seems, as Pogge has argued, empirically implausible.[21]

Nevertheless, and we stress, the wealth conjecture is tangential with respect to Rawls's account of global justice. Critics have failed to see through his defensive and misleading presentation. Rawls introduces the conjecture as a rationale for rejecting a principle of distributive justice that would regulate economic inequality among societies. But his rejection of a principle of global distributive justice does not depend on the conjecture: his fundamental view is that *whatever* the (morally unobjectionable) causes of domestic wealth, justice does not inherently exert pressure to promote global economic equality. The aim of the duty of assistance, Rawls believes, is "to realize and preserve just (or decent) institutions, and not simply to increase, much less to maximize indefinitely, the average level of wealth, or the wealth of any society or any particular class of society."[22] The evidence could lead him to accept, without material compromise, Pogge's point that "even if country-specific factors fully explain the observed variations in the economic performance of the poor countries, global factors may still play a major role in explaining why they did not on the whole do much better or worse than they did in fact."[23] Furthermore, as we will argue later, Rawls could acknowledge a duty of just engagement and a duty of reparations – duties that would address corresponding, morally objectionable sources of global economic inequality. There is no deep dispute between Rawls and his cosmopolitan egalitarian critics on this front. The wealth conjecture is a distraction in the presentation of his account of global justice.

The deep dispute between Pogge and Rawls must lie not in their causal accounts of global inequality but, rather, in their philosophical conceptions of global justice. For Pogge, the judgment that affluent societies harm the global poor is made relative to a baseline of entitlements.[24] Insofar as these entitlements might extend beyond the threshold that a duty of assistance would ensure, the question is what justifies them. Pogge believes that they derive from an account of global justice that includes fair rules for economic engagement.[25] Specifically, the entitlements presuppose that each society is to have a fair opportunity for economic growth.[26] If fair opportunity can be illuminated from the perspective of representatives of all societies behind a global veil of ignorance, the consistency argument and the harm argument converge.[27]

Much of the rhetorical force of Pogge's work can be tied to a certain conception of fairness. When leveraging the charge of inconsistency against Rawls, Pogge relies on a premise of "moral universalism," which maintains that the same, basic moral principles apply to all persons.[28] He thus presents moral universalism as a formal requirement. In fact, however, his moral universalism appears to express a substantive conception of fairness. Moral universalism, as Pogge presents it, requires equality in the distribution of benefits and burdens: "equality remains the default – the burden of proof weighs on those favoring specific departures."[29] So fairness would require an equal distribution of social and economic benefits, except when there is a morally compelling rationale for departures from equality. This represents what we refer to as "the default view of fairness." In its spirit, Pogge implies that permitting substantial global inequality is unfair to persons who are relatively worse off.

Instead of presuming the default view of fairness, we begin from a minimalist concept of fairness that goes back to Plato: fairness consists in persons getting what they are due. This minimalist concept draws attention to the fact that determining what it is that persons are due in a particular domain almost always calls for substantial argument. The default view of fairness, which may seem self-evidently true, requires the support of background views about morality or justice. We will argue that in the domain of global justice, appeals to fairness fall short of supporting an egalitarian principle of distributive justice. At the same time, we argue that a humanitarian duty of assistance should be supplemented with a duty of just engagement and a duty of reparations. We sketch this account of global justice in the final section.

3 Fairness via asymmetries of justice

In games, fairness generally requires that players play within the rules, though expectations can vary depending on the game. Some games, such as American football, largely leave it to officials to decide when play violates the rules. Technical violations of the rules are not considered unfair when officials do not call them. Other games, such as golf, largely place a duty to abide by the rules on the players themselves. Outside the self-contained realm of games, the requirements of fairness become more difficult to determine. No freestanding appeal to fairness serves as common ground since fairness is more or less a placeholder concept: it does not have much content of its own but instead must point to specific values that ground some conception of fairness.[30]

We do not deny, of course, that philosophers recognize there can be different conceptions of fairness. Yet some philosophers, particularly those who are egalitarian-minded, would appear to reject our view that fairness is virtually a placeholder concept: they may believe that quite a lot of content, while the subject of dispute, is built into the concept.[31] Specifically, egalitarian-minded political philosophers often appeal directly to fairness to make the point that departures from equality naturally require special justification. With apologies to readers who need no convincing, we feel compelled to elaborate why recognizing that fairness is better construed as a placeholder concept is important in thinking about domestic vis-à-vis global justice.

The extent to which fairness is a placeholder concept is obscured by the default view of fairness. According to the default view, fairness generally requires an equal distribution of benefits. Children are said to have a natural sense of fairness that expresses this view. They know, for instance, that all the kids in a classroom should get an equal piece of cake; or, if they do not get equal pieces, a bigger piece might go to a birthday child to signify her special day. But surely, the story goes, the size of pieces should not be determined by factors that are morally arbitrary or irrelevant. Similarly, a recent study purports to show that "a sense of fairness is deeply ingrained in human evolutionary history rather than the idea that it's a more cultural response."[32] The basis for this finding: capuchin monkeys throw a fit when their peers get more desirable treats (in the study, grapes rather than cucumber). The scientists conducting the study take for granted that fairness consists in an equal distribution of benefits.

Actually, the default view of fairness often functions as a placeholder concept. This describes the sense in which the default view can be shared across the political spectrum in a democratic society. Where progressives and conservatives typically disagree is over the factors that permit departures from equality – for instance, talent, hard work, inherited wealth, and social group disadvantage. Apart from establishing some form of equality or other as the default position, appeals to fairness hardly advance such debates. In the absence of shared background views about morality or justice, appealing to fairness does not do much to establish what persons are due.

Whether the default view represents a substantive egalitarian conception of justice or a mere placeholder concept depends on: (1) the basis of a default presumption of equal division; and (2) the nature and strength of considerations required to override it. This brings us back to Pogge. He employs a burden-shifting argument that charges Rawls with offering woefully inadequate justification for treating questions of global economic justice with different principles than Rawls advocates in his liberal account of domestic justice. Without an adequate justification for treating the two cases differently, Pogge argues, Rawls's conception of global justice is unfair to the global poor.[33] After all, they would have no objection to policies that would benefit them economically. Yet Pogge has a serious criticism of Rawls only if the default view represents more than a placeholder concept of fairness – and Pogge has not shown this. He has not shown why a substantive egalitarian conception of fairness must be accepted as a principle of global justice.

Rawls did not always make clear that his account of justice and its two principles are subject to qualifications about scope and content.[34] At the outset of *A Theory of Justice* he declares, "Justice is the first virtue of social institutions, as truth is of systems of thought."[35] Such statements have contributed to the misimpression that he understands his theory of justice to hold universally; consequently, his theory of justice could seem to provide a universal benchmark of what is substantively fair. But in later works Rawls corrects this misimpression. He acknowledges that there might be reasonable disagreement about the scope and content of his two principles of justice – and that this disagreement is bound to widen once it is not bounded by the elements of a liberal political culture. In *Political Liberalism*, he claims that the content of

> a political conception of justice . . . is expressed in terms of certain fundamental ideas seen as implicit in the public political culture of a democratic society. This public culture comprises the political institutions of a constitutional regime and the public traditions of their interpretation . . . as well as historic texts and documents that are common knowledge.[36]

Simply put, what justice as fairness substantively requires will reflect a standing commitment to the core political ideals and practices of a democratic society.

The Law of Peoples, in contrast, elaborates the possibility of a just global society not restricted to liberal societies. A nonliberal society does not conceive of its members as free and equal citizens. Nevertheless, such societies may count as decent.[37] Rawls argues that insofar as decent peoples honor "the law of peoples" that holds among liberal societies, denying their inclusion in a just global society would be unwarranted. Their exclusion would run contrary to the purposes of this global society, which seeks to promote peace and political equality among societies, and human rights and a "well-ordered" basic structure within societies. Thus Rawls finds that toleration and mutual respect would be due decent societies by recognizing their full, participatory membership in a just global society. Further, he believes that their inclusion would encourage them to adopt politically liberal reforms.

Pogge remains dissatisfied with these aims of Rawls's conception of global justice. In addition, as we have indicated, Pogge argues that all societies must have a fair opportunity for economic growth. Fair rules for a global economy, Pogge suggests, are those that would be chosen behind a veil of ignorance in a global original position. To reiterate, his argument for this criterion of substantive fairness relies on his moral universalism, which affirms that any discrepancy in the requirements of domestic and global justice must be justified. But this moral universalism, we have argued, is insufficient to support the notion of fair economic arrangements that Pogge favors. A more substantial argument is required – and it should not be at odds with social autonomy, reasonable toleration, and respectful cooperation. We have been unable to find such an argument, though he does offer promissory notes such as this:

> I lack the space . . . to develop and defend a complete criterion of global justice and to show what specific institutional arrangements would be favored by this criterion. I will therefore employ a little shortcut. I will make an institutional proposal [his "global resources tax"] that virtually any plausible egalitarian conception of global justice would judge to be at least a step in the right direction.[38]

Perhaps Pogge believes that Rawls starts from a fundamental commitment to egalitarianism and is bound, on pain of inconsistency, to extend that commitment from the liberal domestic case to the global case. This reading of Rawls would be mistaken: his egalitarianism derives from a conjecture about what members of a liberal domestic society, conceived of as free and equal citizens, would accept under ideal conditions. The global "society of peoples," by contrast, is one whose member peoples have fundamental interests that overlap but are not equivalent to those of persons in a liberal domestic society.[39] This difference grounds, as we characterize it, asymmetries in the requirements of domestic as compared to global justice. We will now outline and defend a substantive conception of global justice that, while reflecting this type of asymmetry, is more robust than Rawls's and would seem to address some of Pogge's major concerns.

4 Cosmopolitan cooperation

We propose a *cosmopolitan cooperationist* account of global economic justice that includes a duty of assistance while introducing a duty of just engagement and a duty of reparations. This account holds that global trade practices (1) should benefit partner societies so as to leave them stably better off than burdened, and (2) should be consistent with (reasonable) policies they have agreed upon or affirmed. Furthermore, societies that have helped to cause or have proximately benefited from the poverty of other societies may have a corrective duty, along with a globally applicable duty of assistance, to help lift those burdened societies out of poverty.

It is helpful to compare the duty of just engagement with Rawls's duty to assist burdened societies and Pogge's requirement of a fair opportunity for economic growth. The duty of assistance that Rawls endorses is in one respect stronger than Pogge's fair opportunity requirement. Unlike Pogge's requirement, Rawls's duty applies even in the absence of economic relations between particular societies: any society with adequate means would be required to assist burdened societies, whether or not the burdened societies participate or aspire to participate in the global economy. In another respect, Rawls's duty to assist burdened societies might be weaker. Unlike a principle of distributive justice, Rawls claims, a duty of assistance has a "defined goal, or cut-off point, beyond which all aid may cease."[40] The threshold set by this duty of assistance might seem to represent a bare minimum that would fall short of what would ensure over time a fair opportunity for economic growth. Our cooperationist account supplements a duty of assistance with a duty of just engagement. Economic relations introduce reciprocal duties to ensure that the global economy protects fair opportunity for economic growth. Still, fair opportunity does not presume cosmopolitan egalitarian distributive justice as the default.

Although Rawls does not describe a duty of assistance as being humanitarian, conceptualizing it this way highlights its independence from established cooperative relationships among societies. A humanitarian duty of assistance recognizes the moral arbitrariness, on some level, of national boundaries with regard to the basic needs of persons. Active concern for basic needs would seem to represent a moral minimum in the domestic and global spheres of justice. Discounting the moral significance of national boundaries – that is, regarding basic needs – emphasizes that a humanitarian duty of assistance is directly responsive to persons, not to states and not to the instrumental aim of promoting a just global society of liberal and decent nonliberal states.[41] This discounting also expresses a standard of moral urgency that does not depend on a luck egalitarian conception of justice.[42] For luck egalitarians, justice requires that persons be compensated, when feasible, for any disadvantages beyond their control – including disadvantages (e.g., lack of talent) that may register well above any humanitarian threshold of basic needs.

Less contentious than luck egalitarianism, our cosmopolitan cooperationist account of global economic justice supplements a straightforward, humanitarian duty of assistance with a duty of just engagement. This duty of just engagement rests on a requirement of reciprocity in trade relationships. We take this reciprocity requirement to be both realistic and fair, as we will now explain. The reciprocity requirement on which the duty of just engagement rests is realistic in that the aim of trade is construed primarily as societies commonly profess it: in terms of mutual, collective self-interest. Each partner society is in the first place motivated to pursue global trade, in a competitive environment, in order to advance the economic interests of its own members. That substantial benefits accrue at the macro level, society-to-society, is not necessarily a mark of just engagement. Indeed, when the benefits are greatly concentrated among power elites, the justice-based, collective self-interest rationale for global trade is undermined. Hence the benefits are to be widely distributed among the members of a partner society. This rules out, for example, morally indifferent trade with dictatorial regimes that would abuse, for their own enrichment, their international resource and borrowing privileges.[43]

The reciprocity requirement is fair in the following respects. It expresses a commitment to "fair play": global trade practices should be consistent with (reasonable) policies that partner societies have agreed to follow. Powerful societies cannot give themselves a mulligan – for example, by imposing import tariffs in an effort to protect domestic industries that are especially vulnerable to foreign competition – while insisting, through threat of retaliation, that weaker societies expose their vulnerable industries to the forces of free trade. No global difference principle or the like is needed to recognize the illegitimacy of a society leveraging its power, in an effort to secure even more disproportionate gains for itself, by refusing to adhere to reasonable agreements it has made. Surely, Rawls would agree. Nothing more than a minimalist concept of fairness is needed to ground this claim.

How to characterize a commitment to reciprocal economic benefit is less straightforward. The problem is familiar enough: poor societies will be inclined to settle for global trade practices that would leave them relatively better off than they otherwise would be given their current circumstances, even when this would still leave poor societies poor or only marginally better off than poor. Such a situation seems plainly at odds with reciprocity – where reciprocity is understood as mutually respectful cooperation. That desperate societies (or persons) will accept economic arrangements that leave them relatively better off is no reliable indicator of mutually respectful cooperation: being better off than some desperate alternative is not good enough for justice. The situation is akin to sharecropping, which leaves the working poor in a perpetual state of poverty or near-poverty and overwhelming dependence.

So the challenge is to construe a plausible criterion of reciprocal economic benefit. A deep justification of this criterion would have to appeal to moral foundations that might not prove much less controversial than egalitarian foundations – neutralizing what we take to be a significant advantage of our cosmopolitan cooperationist account. The criterion we propose, then, reflects nothing deeper than good faith judgments about the significant interests and needs of members of trading partner societies. Undoubtedly, these judgments are susceptible to the usual, self-serving biases. The following procedure is designed to control for such biases under realistic circumstances of mutual knowledge of each society's relative trading power.

Partner societies participate in a transparent lottery to select a criterion of reciprocal economic benefit with respect to their industries of trade, including labor. Each partner society openly specifies the least it deems necessary for sustaining good lives for its members in those industries. The "winning" entry determines the economic benefit through trade that partner societies can expect to receive at a minimum. Inequalities might accumulate above this point. In order to help partner societies resist submitting entries geared solely to their own relative trading power – since more affluent societies will be disposed to specify terms that would allow greater inequality, while less affluent societies would specify more egalitarian terms – they agree in advance to accept a penalty for exiting trade arrangements after the winning entry has been selected. This penalty in effect dissuades societies from negotiating, after the fact, more favorable terms with new partners. But each society retains, without threat of penalty, a general right to strike for more favorable terms within its current partnership group. Partner societies therefore have an incentive to act in good faith in proposing mutually satisfactory terms. Add to this the assumption that the representatives of each society are rational, nonideological fiduciaries: they simply want to make sure, under the lottery conditions, that the members of their society are able to lead good lives. In short, the lottery aims to compel reciprocity in the arena of international trade.

We recognize that in the actual world, economically powerful countries are unlikely to enter voluntarily into a process that could significantly counteract their relative bargaining advantages. The lottery process we have described is better understood as a hypothetical measure of good faith about judgments of reciprocity in trade. It sets an ethical standard that may be deployed to challenge varieties of wishful, self-serving thinking about flimsier notions of reciprocity.

Our conjecture is that the procedure would yield a threshold, beyond that of humanitarian relief, at which partner societies are stably better off than burdened. What is a solid measure of such stability? One measure, at least, is whether the economic benefit to a society is sufficient generally to enable its members to save after their basic needs have been met. The capacity for savings represents a buffer between being burdened and being neither burdened nor highly vulnerable to being burdened.

This criterion of reciprocal economic benefit expresses a substantive conception of fairness. It will not satisfy cosmopolitan egalitarians, who adopt a maximalist approach in supporting a global difference principle. As we have presented it, a reciprocity requirement expressing mutually respectful cooperation need not be egalitarian. Nor will it approximate principles that would be chosen behind a veil of ignorance by all decent societies. The duty of just engagement that we have introduced does not guarantee that the global economy would be to the greatest benefit of societies (or persons) who are least well off, and some societies might have greater bargaining power, which they could use to advance their own interests. Instead, it requires something like the golden rule for international trade: a partner society, operating within a market scheme, seeks trade arrangements that are no less favorable to its partners than the least that society judges would be acceptable for its own members.

A more demanding duty of just engagement, one that cosmopolitan egalitarians would prefer, is likely to be in tension with the value of collective self-determination.[44] Insofar as certain reasonable domestic practices are most conducive to economic prosperity, it would seem acceptable to set potentially strong conditions – e.g., for democracy, or gender and ethnic equality – on participation in an egalitarian global economy. Otherwise, continual transfers of wealth could reasonably be unacceptable to better-off societies. But imposing strong conditions on participation in the global economy could be hard to square with the value that persons typically attach to the political and social self-determination of their societies. A society committed to a widely shared conception of the common good of its members would seem to warrant a fair opportunity to participate in the global economy.[45]

The corollary of this argument on behalf of the self-determination of liberal and decent nonliberal societies is that better-off societies should not be required to cooperate with less affluent societies on a more strongly reciprocal, egalitarian basis. More strongly reciprocal terms express a sense of common membership or joint enterprise that extends beyond due respect for the well-being of persons as such and recognition of the value of self-determination for societies. It is not unjust for members of one society to lack a sense of common mission and fate with members of other societies. To suppose otherwise could be contrary to a society's not unreasonable adherence to distinctive political and cultural values. Of course, societies legitimately may establish stronger common bonds with one another (e.g., the European Union), but it seems doubtful that such bonds should be required as a matter of global justice. Here the charge that cosmopolitan cooperationism amounts to a neo-Westphalian enterprise would seem hyperbolic and misplaced. Cosmopolitan cooperationism does not entail or imply a descriptively outmoded and normatively inadequate attachment to the notion of an essentially sovereign state. Only a certain kind of utopian could deny that many societies (e.g., England, France, Norway, Saudi Arabia, China, Quebec, Puerto Rico, and the continental US, among many others) are anxious to maintain their relative political and cultural autonomy in a globally interdependent world.

We certainly are not suggesting that international relations should be conceived of as some kind of state of nature. When societies lack common bonds or a sense of mutual commitment, this provides no warrant or excuse, currently or historically, for doing unconscionable harm to another society. So a plausible account of global justice will not be entirely forward-looking: societies that have suffered colonial or neocolonial exploitation or egregious breaches of fair play in trade, for example, may well have claims to reparations. These claims become especially pressing for burdened societies: presumably, past injustice often plays a role in helping to explain why poor countries are poor or, at least, not better off than they otherwise could have been.

Even if and when past injustice among societies does not largely explain their relative wealth or poverty today, there may remain legitimate claims to reparations on grounds of corrective justice. The idea is not that countries as such may have claims to reparations, though countries are likely to be the entities charged with satisfying these claims. Rather, members of societies that have suffered unconscionable harm would have such claims. Since reparations claims are most urgent in the case of burdened societies, relatively affluent societies – when confronted with multiple claimant societies – have reason to prioritize the claims of societies that are least well off. This reflects the priority that our account of global economic justice places on eradicating poverty. That is, the primary aim of the corrective duty of reparations, as we construe it, is to lift burdened societies out of poverty. The primary aim is not to promote corrective justice in a more comprehensive sense. Thus the duty of reparations is not tied to, for instance, an estimation of actual damages based on accumulated disadvantage within a society.

It might be asked why – if the duty of reparations has the same, basic aim as the duty of assistance – there is much point in recognizing the corrective duty. The forward-looking humanitarian duty would seem less fraught with complications than the backward-looking corrective duty. Nevertheless, there is a significant, practical reason to include the corrective duty. Affluent countries are often derelict or belated in their response to humanitarian crises; not infrequently, precious time and energy are spent debating how international responsibility for the amount and the means of response is to be divided. The corrective duty of reparations recognizes a special, further, less mediated responsibility that relatively affluent countries have to assist those burdened societies to which they have done unconscionable harm.

Few philosophers who work on global justice would deny the need to address global poverty through urgent, effective measures. Humanitarian concern about the plight of the global poor should be taken for granted. But we have tried to show that a commitment to dealing with global injustice on the ground does not depend on a commitment to cosmopolitan egalitarianism and a principle of global distributive justice. Nor, philosophically, are claims in support of an egalitarian principle of justice, whether domestically or globally, beyond considerable challenge.

Questions of global economic justice are intertwined with less obvious questions about the nature and value of political and social autonomy, reasonable toleration, and respectful cooperation. There also are difficult questions about the extent to which societies are required to make common cause morally, politically, and materially. Grappling with these questions has led us to a non-egalitarian view that allows for asymmetries in the requirements of reciprocity, domestically and globally. Cosmopolitan egalitarians will still be dissatisfied with our view. The underlying issues require discussion in greater detail, and we do not claim to have resolved them. But our cosmopolitan cooperationist account does put pressure on Pogge to explain his evident dissatisfaction with a duty of humanitarian assistance, particularly when such a duty is supplemented with cooperationist duties of just engagement and reparations. Neither his appeal to a negative duty not to harm, nor his appeal to the default view of fairness, nor his appeal to moral universalism establish that the global poor are due more than this.

Notes

*We would like to thank Andreas Follesdal and Alison Jaggar for comments on earlier drafts.
1 Thomas W. Pogge, "An Egalitarian Law of Peoples," *Philosophy and Public Affairs* 23 (1994): 195–224.
2 Pogge, "An Egalitarian Law of Peoples," p. 196.
3 Thomas W. Pogge, "Introduction," in *World Poverty and Human Rights: Cosmopolitan Responsibilities and Reforms*, 1st edn (Cambridge, UK: Polity, 2002), p. 16; see also pp. 23–4.
4 See Thomas Pogge, "Severe Poverty as a Violation of Negative Duties," *Ethics and International Affairs* 19 (2005): 55–83, at 61. See also Pogge, "Cosmopolitanism and Sovereignty," p. 170, "How Should Human Rights be Conceived?" p. 70, and "The Bounds of Nationalism," p. 144, in *World Poverty and Human Rights*.
5 See Pogge, "Eradicating Systemic Poverty: Brief for a Global Resources Dividend," in *World Poverty and Human Rights*, p. 201, "The Bounds of Nationalism," pp. 136–9, and "Cosmopolitanism and Sovereignty," p. 176. See also Pogge, "Severe Poverty as a Violation of Negative Duties," pp. 74–8. See criticism by Alan Patten, "Should We Stop Thinking about

Poverty in Terms of Helping the Poor?," *Ethics and International Affairs* 19 (2005): 19–27, and by Deborah Satz, "What Do We Owe the Global Poor?," *Ethics and International Affairs* 19 (2005): 47–54, at 53–4.

6 Pogge, "The Bounds of Nationalism," pp. 137–9.

7 Pogge, "Severe Poverty as a Violation of Negative Duties," pp. 55–6.

8 Thomas Pogge, "Moral Universalism and Global Economic Justice," in *World Poverty and Human Rights*, pp. 105–8.

9 Pogge does not express sympathy for the view that persons be compensated for any disadvantages beyond their control, but he does seem drawn to egalitarianism in the space of resources. On the contrast between these views, see Thomas W. Pogge, "Can the Capability Approach be Justified?," *Philosophical Topics* 30 (2002): 167–228.

10 Pogge, "Human Flourishing and Universal Justice," in *World Poverty and Human Rights*, p. 36.

11 Pogge, "Moral Universalism and Global Economic Justice," p. 96.

12 See, e.g., Pogge, "Moral Universalism and Global Economic Justice," pp. 96–7.

13 John Rawls, *The Law of Peoples* (Cambridge, MA: Harvard University Press, 1999), p. 114.

14 See John Rawls, *Justice as Fairness: A Restatement*, ed. Erin Kelly (Cambridge, MA: Harvard University Press, 2001), pp. 95, 132–3.

15 Rawls, *The Law of Peoples*, p. 106.

16 Peter Singer, *One World: The Ethics of Globalization* (New Haven: Yale University Press, 2002), p. 176.

17 Kok-Chor Tan, *Justice without Borders: Cosmopolitanism, Nationalism, and Patriotism* (Cambridge: Cambridge University Press, 2004), p. 68.

18 Tan, *Justice without Borders*, p. 65.

19 See Thomas W. Pogge, "Rawls on International Justice," *The Philosophical Quarterly* 51 (2001): 246–53; Thomas W. Pogge, *Realizing Rawls* (Ithaca, NY: Cornell University Press, 1989), ch. 6, esp. pp. 246–54; and Pogge, "An Egalitarian Law of Peoples," pp. 208–14. On this point there is continuity across these works.

20 Rawls, *The Law of Peoples*, p. 108. He cites the Inuit as a marginal case.

21 See Tan, *Justice without Borders*, p. 70. His criticism follows Pogge's. See, e.g., Thomas W. Pogge, "'Assisting' the Global Poor," in *The Ethics of Assistance: Morality and the Distant Needy*, ed. Deen K. Chatterjee (Cambridge: Cambridge University Press, 2004).

22 Rawls, *The Law of Peoples*, p. 107.

23 Pogge, "'Assisting' the Global Poor," p. 263.

24 For Pogge's critical discussion of an array of possible baselines, see "'Assisting' the Global Poor."

25 Pogge writes, for example, "Partiality is legitimate only in the context of a *fair* competition . . . national partiality is morally acceptable only on condition that the fairness of international competition is continually preserved"; "An Egalitarian Law of Peoples," pp. 221–2.

26 See Pogge, "Rawls on International Justice," p. 252.

27 Pogge prefers to construe a global original position as representing individual persons rather than peoples or societies; see *Realizing Rawls*, ch. 6.

28 Pogge, "Moral Universalism and Global Economic Justice," pp. 93–4.

29 Pogge, "Moral Universalism and Global Economic Justice," p. 93.

30 Roughly, the concept of fairness illustrates what W. B. Gallie called an essentially contested concept. See W. B. Gallie, "Essentially Contested Concepts," *Proceedings of the Aristotelian Society* 56 (1956): 167–98. As we would put the idea, though, the concept of fairness is not so much contested as are conceptions of fairness.

31 For instance, after proposing the merit of a minimalist definition of "fairness," Brad Hooker concludes that fairness is narrower than all-things-considered moral rightness but that it brings in certain substantive requirements, including priority for the needs of the worst-off; Brad Hooker, "Fairness," *Ethical Theory and Moral Practice* 8 (2005): 329–52, at 350. Hooker is largely responding to John Broome, who seems to propose a theory of the *concept* of fairness. See John Broome, "Fairness," *Proceedings of the Aristotelian Society* 91 (1990): 87–102.

32 Jeanna Bryner, "Monkey Fuss over Inequality," LiveScience.Com, 13 November 2007.

33 On Pogge's reading, "it seems clear, then, that Rawls endorses double standards" because Rawls allows "a global economic order that generates strong centrifugal tendencies and ever increasing economic inequality, provided we 'assist' the societies impoverished by this order just enough to keep them above some basic threshold" (Pogge, "Moral Universalism and Global Economic Justice," p. 107).

34 The first principle of justice requires "equal basic liberties" for all; the second principle of justice requires "fair equality of opportunity" and also includes the difference principle; Rawls, *Justice as Fairness*, pp. 42–3. Also see Rawls, *A Theory of Justice*, p. 266.

35 Rawls, *A Theory of Justice*, p. 3.

36 Rawls, *Political Liberalism* (New York: Columbia University Press, 1996), pp. 13–14.

37 Rawls, *The Law of Peoples*, p. 61.

38 Pogge, "An Egalitarian Law of Peoples," p. 199.

39 In particular, Rawls emphasizes "amour-propre," which he describes as "a people's proper self-respect of themselves as a people, resting on their common awareness of their trials during their history and of their culture with its accomplishments"; Rawls, *The Law of Peoples*, p. 34.

40 Rawls, *The Law of Peoples*, p. 106.

41 For criticism of Rawls on this point, see Charles R. Beitz, "Rawls's Law of Peoples," *Ethics* 110 (2000): 669–96, at 677–85.

42 See, e.g., G. A. Cohen, "On the Currency of Egalitarian Justice," *Ethics* 99 (1989): 906–44, at 922.

43 See, e.g., Pogge, "Moral Universalism and Global Economic Justice," pp. 112–16.

44 See Andreas Follesdal, "Justice, Stability, and Toleration in a Federation of Well-Ordered Peoples," in *Rawls's Law of Peoples: A Realistic Utopia?*, ed. Rex Martin and David A. Reidy (Malden, MA: Blackwell, 2006), especially pp. 310–12.

45 For discussion of the value of collective self-determination, see Joshua Cohen, "Is There a Human Right to Democracy?," *The Egalitarian Conscience: Essays in Honor of G. A. Cohen*, ed. Christine Sypnowich (Oxford: Oxford University Press, 2006), pp. 233–5.

6

Realistic Reform of International Trade in Resources

Leif Wenar

Many readers of Thomas Pogge's work have found it opens what is for them a new world:

> We live in extreme isolation from severe poverty. We do not know anyone earning less than $30 for a 72-hour week of hard, monotonous labor. The one-third of human beings who die from poverty-related causes includes no one we have ever spent time with. Nor do we know anyone who knows and cares about these deceased – someone scarred by the experience of losing a child to hunger, diarrhea, or measles, for example. (4)[1]

This is the world of 18 million premature deaths every year from poverty. "If developed Western countries had their proportional shares of these deaths, severe poverty would kill some 3,200 Britons and 16,000 Americans per week. Each year, 14 times as many US citizens would die of poverty-related causes as were lost in the entire Vietnam War" (104).

It is in fact our world, which we never knew was there.

How could it be that this world is there without our realizing that it is the same world on which we stand every day? "The global poor," Pogge says, "who labor all day for a few dollars a month, are unable to cause us the slightest inconvenience and unable even to alert us to their plight" (133). These parts of the planet have been kept, for us, out of sight: "Our world is arranged to keep us far away from massive and severe poverty and surrounds us with affluent, civilized people for whom the poor abroad are a remote good cause alongside the spotted owl."[2]

Pogge's greatest public impact over the past 20 years has been to force the world's rich to see the world's poor. His statistical inventories and depictions of the manifestations of poverty in powerlessness, disease, and death have been startlingly eye opening.

Having made vivid these distressing realities, Pogge adds a second, disturbing thought. We are, to some extent, responsible for our world being as awful as it is:

> There is a simple two-part explanation for why our new global economic order is so harsh on the poor. The design of this order is fashioned and adjusted in international negotiations in which our governments enjoy a crushing advantage in bargaining power and expertise. And our representatives in the international negotiations do not consider the interests of the global poor as part of their mandate . . . Our representatives ruthlessly exploit their vastly superior bargaining power and expertise, as well as any weakness, ignorance, or corruptibility they may find in their counterpart negotiators, to tune each agreement for our greatest benefit . . . The cumulative result of many such negotiations and agreements is a grossly unfair global economic order under which the lion's share of the benefits of global economic growth flows to the most affluent states. (26–7)

Our world is not just bad, Pogge says, it has been made bad. And it has been made bad by people working for us who use our great collective power to wring from the world more wealth for us while squeezing the poor to death. This thought is resisted even by many who admit the intolerable nature of global poverty. For Pogge, this resistance is again the result of a kind of blindness. The mechanisms by which the global order is formed and then reformed in our favor are largely unseen by most citizens. Part of the genius of Pogge's writing is to connect dark events like the renegotiation of a convention on the law of the sea, or the implementation of an international treaty on intellectual property rights, with the painful fading from existence of thousands of human lives (131–2, 224–9). We squint at the world while allowing our politicians to continue to fill our pockets. We in this way help to create, Pogge suggests, a counter-Panglossian dystopia: "the worst of all possible worlds to which the strong can morally reconcile themselves" (6). We help to create, that is, "the vast evil of global poverty" (142).

1 Pogge's work

Anyone surveying Pogge's writings on justice for the past 20 years will be struck first by the range of its subjects. More than any other contemporary theorist, Pogge has vetted power, poverty and disadvantage, and advanced progressive proposals for reforms. Pogge caused a storm with an article on the moral priorities of international aid organizations, where he argued that these NGOs should focus their resources on projects that favor the poor who can be cheaply aided instead of the poor whom it is expensive to help. He examined the ethics of Western pharmaceutical companies testing new drugs on poor foreigners. He scrutinized the propriety of armed humanitarian intervention, paying particular attention to the actions of the UN and the US during the Rwandan massacres. He lectured on the real implications of the West's "war on terrorism." He excoriated the World Bank's methodology for assessing the extent of global poverty, and outlined an alternative framework. He asked what claims people with disabilities have on the social institutions of their countries. He studied what language instruction should be given in public schools to children whose home language is not the dominant one in the society. He explored whether democracy could be made more robust by making constituencies self-forming instead of leaving them geographically defined.[3] And more as well – and no doubt there is more still to come.

Beyond the range of Pogge's work, what strikes the reader is its tone. The moral tone of everyday life for many born in rich countries is complacency. In Pogge's writing one feels moral urgency. This urgency can be felt in the stylistic feature of Pogge's writing most present to his readers which is its relentlessness. The style is dense and demanding. The style says: "This is hard, but important; and we can do something about it." Should we not be impatient with a global plan – progressively and disingenuously watered down by the governments of rich countries – to reduce severe poverty by only half over a span of almost two decades (11–13)? Let's get on this, Pogge's writing suggests, and stay on it. On issues like these we must be uncompromising.

There are two further features of Pogge's work that stand out, this time viewing this work from a theorist's perspective. The first is how well stocked this work is conceptually. Pogge gives us (at times almost in passing) ready analyses of some of the hardest ideas in the international theory: of human rights, for example, and of cosmopolitanism, and of sovereignty (52, 70, 175, 183). Moreover, in order to describe the realities of the global order, Pogge has also fashioned new concepts: explanatory nationalism, loopholes in moralities, the "sucker exemption," the distinction between institutional and interactional understandings of moral constraints, the might-is-right principle, radical inequality and more. Every theorist can appreciate, both while working and on reflection, this new collection of conceptual tools.

The second feature of Pogge's writing that commends it to theorists can only be called its honesty. Pogge always calls them as he sees them. One gets a sense of how deeply this is true by surveying Pogge's many discussions of Rawls.[4] Pogge is at once one of Rawls's most fertile interpreters, and also one of Rawls's severest critics. Aristotle, at the start of his critique of Plato's doctrine of the forms, exhibits the honesty that characterizes Pogge's writing in this passage:

> Perhaps we had better examine the universal and consider critically what is meant by it; although such a course is awkward, because the forms were introduced by friends of ours. Yet surely it would be thought better, or rather necessary (above all for philosophers), to refute, in defense of the truth, even views to which one is attached; since although both are dear, it is right to give preference to the truth.[5]

2 The harm argument and feasibility

What has attracted so many to Pogge's writings are his studies of particular global institutions, why these institutions have such great impact on the lives of the poor, and how they might be reimagined. Concerning Pogge's argument that the affluent are harming the world's poor, the reaction has been more mixed. This is the argument that affluent individuals are harming the poor insofar as they actively cooperate in designing or imposing institutions that foreseeably cause human rights deficits that they (the affluent) know could be avoided. There have been several scholarly appraisals of this argument, to which Pogge has replied forcefully.[6] My sense, however, is that many who hear Pogge's arguments remain uncertain about the claim of harm itself. Many find the descriptions of the human rights deficits compelling, and the proposal for reform intriguing. Yet they tend to understand the appeal to "harm" as only the idea that things are bad and we might be able to do something to make them better.

In part this hesitancy about the harm argument seems rooted in the fact that the natural home for the concept of harm is what Pogge would call an interactional setting, not an institutional one. Hitting is harming; paying taxes may not seem available for that kind of evaluation. This hesitancy may also result from most affluent individuals feeling that they have no rational strategy to relate differently to national or global institutions. Even fairly wealthy people feel that (short of risking prison) they have little choice but to support national and global institutions by paying taxes and obeying other laws. So even if these wealthy people were to agree that they harm by upholding the global order, they may feel that they are being forced to harm. And being forced to harm normally cancels any moral responsibility to compensate for harms caused.

The main source of hesitancy in accepting Pogge's harm argument, however, appears to come from uncertainty that his proposals for the reform of global institutions are realistic, and that they will bring the advantages that he asserts they will. In order to carry through on his harm argument, Pogge must show not only that current global rules generate very bad consequences, but that we can be fairly certain that different rules would do better. As he says, in order to prove harm, "We must be able to be confident that the alternative institutional design would do much better in giving participants secure access to the objects of their human rights" (26). Without this confidence in the possibility of a superior alternative we are left with the conclusion only that things are bad, instead of the conclusion that we are making them worse than we know they should be.

It is the feasibility of Pogge's recommendations for institutional reform that will be studied here, with a focus on one area of possible reform in particular. One can see the issue of feasibility absorbing increasing amounts of Pogge's attention as his work on global justice has unfolded over the past 20 years. In the articles of the 1990s, a concern for feasibility is present but certainly not central. For example, in "Cosmopolitanism and Sovereignty," there is only a single paragraph asserting that the article's major reform agenda to disperse sovereignty away from the state will produce greater global peace and security than the statist status quo (187–8). And in Pogge's proposal for the Global Resources Dividend, there are but two paragraphs that sketch how countries that fail to meet their obligations to contribute to the scheme should be sanctioned by other countries (213–14).

By the time we reach the work of the 2000s, however, Pogge has made feasibility the hub of his investigations. In some articles, one can see Pogge working through possibilities for reform on the page. For example, in the article on incentivizing the creation of essential medicines to combat the diseases that afflict the poor, Pogge first asks whether differential pricing of drugs in rich and poor countries could work. He shows why this is a dead end, and starts afresh. He then presents an entire reconceptualization of the global patent system for essential medicines, paying equal attention to how this new system *would* work and why it *could* work given the capacities and interests of the major players involved.

Pogge's proposal for a parallel drug patenting system has grown into a major research initiative, which is one of the most progressive and potentially beneficial contemporary proposals for reform of global institutions.[7] Feasibility is here center stage. Pogge has worked with epidemiologists, economists, lawyers, corporate leaders, and representatives of international health organizations to ensure that the initiative is more than a theorist's dream. This initiative now sets a standard for serious, innovative responses to global poverty. Pogge has created by example the sense that morally alive researchers should either be critiquing his proposals in order to improve them, or should be advancing proposals for institutional reform as bold and sophisticated as his own.

Whether Pogge's proposals for reform are feasible is crucial for his harm argument. As above, unless Pogge can give us confidence that better institutions are available, he cannot prove that we are harming the poor by imposing the current institutions upon them. Yet the importance of Pogge's proposals also transcends the harm argument. Those who feel the awful toll of poverty, and understand the malleability of institutions, will look for ways to make global institutions better for the poor. If Pogge has put forward feasible proposals for reducing severe poverty, those proposals will attract people of good will even if they do not follow Pogge in pursuing the harm argument.

3 The international privileges and the claim of imposition

Pogge singles out two features of the current global order as particularly ripe for reform: the international resource and borrowing privileges. In the world as it is:

> Any group controlling a preponderance of the means of coercion within a country is internationally recognized as the legitimate government of this country's territory and people – regardless of how this group came to power, of how it exercises power, and of the extent to which it may be supported or opposed by the population it rules. . . . [This means] that we accept this group's right to act for the people it rules and, in particular, confer upon it privileges freely to borrow in the country's

name (international borrowing privilege) and freely to dispose of the country's natural resources (international resource privilege). (118–19)

Pogge says that these "two aspects of the global economic order, imposed by the wealthy societies and cherished also by authoritarian rulers and corrupt elites in the poorer countries, contribute substantially to the persistence of severe poverty" (121).

The remainder of this chapter will examine one of these privileges – the international resource privilege – and proposals for how it can be restructured. This is a vital topic because Pogge is clearly right that the current international resource privilege generates a great deal of misery, and that if it can be reformed it must be. Before turning to the specifics of the resource privilege, however, we might pause to consider Pogge's assertion that these privileges "are imposed by the wealthy societies." Is it in fact correct that "the citizens and governments of the wealthy societies" (121) dictate that these two international privileges must be in force?

In order to show that wealthy societies are imposing the international privileges on the world, it is of course not sufficient to show that wealthy societies are benefiting from these rules. (Disaster victims put first in line for medical attention benefit from the rules of triage, but this does not establish that disaster victims impose those rules.) Nor is it sufficient to show that rich countries could, if they tried, change those rules. To take an analogy, the American president could, if he made it a high enough priority, likely change any number of features of global institutions: getting India a permanent seat on the UN Security Council, for example, or expanding the drug-testing regime of the Olympic Games. Yet these facts do not in themselves show that the American president imposes the global institutions that we now see. And the mere fact that the ideas of the national borrowing and resource privileges originated in the rich northern countries (if indeed they did) does not show that these rich countries are imposing these features of institutions, any more than origination of ideas would show that the North is imposing on the world the international rules for postage stamps.

The question of how Pogge would redeem his assertion that rich countries are imposing the international privileges on poor countries is interesting because from a *historical* perspective the truth seems to be closer to the reverse. This is apparent from the history of the twentieth century. The twentieth century saw two monumental movements for progressive reform of international institutions, and of these Pogge focuses preponderantly on only one: human rights. The second movement, which was at least as important for advancing human well-being and dignity, was anticolonialism. The rule for resources before the anticolonial movement was that the colonial powers had rights to dispose of the resources of their colonies.

The epochal and bloody struggle of anticolonialism was, to a great extent, nothing less than the struggle to replace the old colonial rules for resources with the national resource and borrowing privileges that we have today. These two privileges were seen by the anticolonial movements as crucial incidents of self-determination. The significance of this transition from colony to self-determining nation can be seen in the urgency, even the pride, with which these crucial anticolonial rights are asserted within the international legal instruments that proclaim the former colonies' victory. For example, the important African (Banjul) Charter of 1981 declares that:

> All peoples shall freely dispose of their wealth and natural resources. This right shall be exercised in the exclusive interest of the people. In no case shall a people be deprived of it . . . States parties to the present Charter shall individually and collectively exercise the right to free disposal of their wealth and natural resources with a view to strengthening African unity and solidarity. . . . States parties to the present Charter shall undertake to eliminate all forms of foreign economic exploitation particularly that practiced by international monopolies so as to enable their peoples to fully benefit from the advantages derived from their national resources.[8]

As a matter of historical fact, the international borrowing and resource privileges were wrested by the poorer countries away from the wealthier ones, often through violence and at the cost of many thousand lives. It would not be inaccurate to summarize this history by saying that the great triumph of many poor societies in the twentieth century was to impose the current order of international privileges on the wealthy societies that had formerly denied these privileges to them.

Now Pogge might not believe that this historical narrative affects his assertion that the rich are imposing the two-privilege system on the poor. His readers will know that he has argued against using historical baselines to analyze whether the rich are currently *harming* the poor.[9] Pogge might similarly argue that we should not take a historical perspective when evaluating whether the rich are currently *imposing* these major structural features of the current global order. He might favor instead a more complex subjunctive analysis of what imposition comes to. He might, for example, identify the agency that imposes a system of rules as that set of agents who could and would together effectively resist attempts by others who are bound by the rules to change those rules (or, perhaps, as that set of agents that appears in all or almost all such sets).

Subjunctive analyses of "imposition" would be intriguing, if extremely complex, analyses to carry through. Analyzing who in this sense imposes the TRIPS Agreement that regulates the intellectual property regimes of WTO members would be one level of complexity. Analyzing who imposes major structural features of the global economy like the two international privileges would be an order of magnitude more complex. These analyses might well point to "the citizens and governments of the wealthy societies." They could possibly point to other agents (say, members of the G20 developing nations) as well.[10] Without some serious empirical discussion it is difficult to say.

What we can say is that Pogge's assertions of "imposition" will be very controversial among social scientists, however the subjunctives are cashed out. For, in passages like the ones quoted at the beginning of this section, Pogge cuts against the foundational premise of mainstream international relations theory. This is the premise the global order is anarchic.[11] According to Pogge, the citizens and governments of the rich countries (perhaps in concert with the leaders of poor countries) impose the major structural rules of the global economic order like the two international privileges, meaning that in some sense these actors have coercive control over setting and enforcing these rules. According to mainstream international relations theory, there is no agent that has such coercive control – any more than there is such an agent in classic state of nature theories.[12] Pogge could perhaps draw on minority views within international relations (e.g., dependency theory) to support his denial of anarchy at the global level. Yet victory against the dominant theories in international relations – realism and liberalism in their many elaborations – will require a real fight.

My view is that the redemption of the claim of "imposition" would be worthwhile, but that this is again not the prime interest in Pogge's work. Like the harm argument, Pogge's assertion of imposition is not the main event. Pogge's most urgent investigations concern whether the rules of the global order, like the international privileges, are in fact leading to significant oppression and poverty – and, if so, whether there are feasible paths to improving these rules. If Pogge has put forward realistic proposals for institutional reform, then, again, those proposals will attract people of good will even if they do not follow Pogge in pursuing the claim of "imposition."

4 The resource privilege and the resource curse

The resource privilege is the international legal convention that any group sufficiently powerful to maintain coercive control over a territory's population holds the legal right to sell off that territory's natural resources. According to this customary rule, *might makes right*: specifically, might vests the legal right to sell a territory's resources to foreigners. Pogge contends that the resource privilege is very unlikely to be a rule that is part of a morally acceptable global economy:

> How, for instance, can our ever so free and fair agreements with tyrants give us property rights in crude oil, thereby dispossessing the local population and the rest of humankind? . . . Not only is the oil taken away for our consumption (and much environmental damage done) without [the consent of the people of the country], but their tyrant is also propped up with funds he can spend on arms and soldiers to cement his rule. What is more, we are offering a prize to every would-be autocrat or junta anywhere: whoever can gain effective power by whatever means will have the legal power to . . . confer internationally valid ownership rights in the country's resources. . . .
>
> We authorize our firms to acquire natural resources from tyrants and we protect their property rights in resources so acquired. We purchase what our firms produce out of such resources and thereby encourage them to act as authorized. In these ways we recognize the authority of tyrants to sell the natural resources of the countries they rule. We also authorize and encourage other firms of ours to sell to the tyrants what they need to stay in power – from aircraft and arms to surveillance and torture equipment. (148)

The resource privilege, as Pogge says, is both suspect in principle and pernicious in its consequences. Indeed the resource privilege is a major contributing factor in one of the most significant poverty traps in the contemporary world: "the resource curse."

The resource curse can afflict countries that derive a large portion of their national income from exporting high-value extractive resources such as oil, natural gas, and minerals. Less developed countries that gain a large portion of their national incomes from these extractive resources are subject to three overlapping resource "curses." They are more prone to authoritarian governments; they are at a higher risk of civil wars and coup attempts; and they exhibit lower rates of growth.

Elsewhere I have reviewed some of the empirical research that establishes the correlations between resources and authoritarianism, civil conflict, and lower growth. I also described Equatorial Guinea as a particularly dramatic example of these curses. The ruler of Equatorial Guinea, Teodoro Obiang, sustains his remarkably repressive rule over the country's impoverished population by selling hundreds of millions of dollars of the country's oil to American corporations like Exxon and Hess, and the prospect of seizing that revenue stream has attracted coup attempts (which have so far failed).[13]

I will not repeat here the review of the empirical research or of Obiang's reign, but will instead just draw a historical parallel. In the twentieth century, colonies fought to end colonial oppression and exploitation by wresting the resource privilege away from the colonial powers. Today, within countries like Equatorial Guinea, the resource privilege is in turn being used by bad regimes to oppress and exploit the country's population. These countries suffer from a kind of "internal colonialism," whereby bad regimes (funded by rich outsiders) treat the territory as a colony in the old style. These bad regimes exercise their coercive power, as the old metropolitan centers did, to maintain control over resource revenues for their own purposes. And like the old colonial powers, these bad regimes do whatever they must both to and for the people in order to keep the resources flowing. In countries like Equatorial Guinea, Sudan, and Burma, what these regimes have been willing to do to the country's people is nearly unlimited, and what they have done for the people is often very little indeed. Whether Spain's past colonial rule of Equatorial Guinea was more inhumane than is Obiang's current "internal" colonial rule is a live question.

5 Pogge's Democracy Panel

Pogge's work has been pivotal in bringing the contribution of the resource privilege to the resource curse to the attention of political theorists. Pogge has also been a leader in insisting on reform to the resource privilege so that it no longer does such great damage. To be feasible, as Pogge says, a reform to this aspect of the global order would have to generate its own support by being morally and prudentially appealing to the major players who would be affected by it (224). The question of feasibility is particularly intense with respect to the resource privilege because of the tremendous economic and political stakes involved in the international trade in extractive commodities.

Oil, for example, is by far the most valuable resource that is traded across borders. Oil accounts for over half the value of all global primary commodity transactions.[14] Ninety percent of the world's transportation runs on oil. Any proposal to deny the resource privilege to regimes in resource-rich countries will disrupt some of the current flow of oil. Such action will therefore need to be able to withstand the tremendous commercial and so political pressures to bring ever more oil to market. Oil companies are very powerful transnational actors. Four of the top five, and seven of the top ten, largest privately traded corporations in the world are oil companies. Their priorities are to locate as much oil as they can, extract as much as they can, and send as much as they can on to consumers. When one adds that any reform to the resource privilege will also have to be enforced for international sales of extractable resources beyond oil (such as natural gas, diamonds, copper, and tin), the demand that such a reform be resilient only intensifies. The resource privilege, so deeply implicated in how rich countries get their most vital resources, will not be easily restructured.[15]

The challenge in framing a proposal to reform the resource privilege is to find a way to transform the current system in which anyone with sufficient power within a territory can sell off that territory's resources into a system that makes distinctions: *these* regimes can sell resources, while *those* cannot. This challenge is in fact four separate problems. The first is the *grounding value problem*: to which values should reformers appeal to distinguish among the regimes currently offering resources on the international market? The second is what Pogge calls *the criterial problem*: what conditions determine whether a territory is or is not above the line that marks legitimate resource sales. The third is the problem of *authoritative notice*: what is the decisive public indication that the criterion used is or is not satisfied? The fourth problem concerns *enforcement*: what institutions could possibly be powerful enough to enforce a judgment that trade in resources with some regimes should stop?

Pogge's proposal for meeting these challenges turns on two mechanisms: an amendment to national constitutions of resource-rich developing democracies, and an international panel to decide when this amendment has been activated. Imagining himself to be a political leader of a fledgling resource-exporting democracy, Pogge recommends: "A constitutional amendment in which our country declares that only its constitutionally democratic governments may effect legally valid transfers of ownership rights in public property and forbids any of its governments to recognize ownership rights in property acquired from a preceding government that lacked such constitutional legitimacy" (169).

Such an amendment, Pogge says, would reduce the resource revenues that predatory authoritarians could expect from overthrowing the fledgling democratic regime. Should a nondemocratic regime seize power after such an amendment is passed, that regime's sales of resources will not be recognized as valid within the country if democracy is restored thereafter. Now as Pogge says, a nondemocratic government that seizes power may revoke this amendment and transfer the country's resources at will. But the amendment will signal to international actors who might buy resources from the nondemocratic government that their title to the goods will be questioned should a democratic government return to power.

Pogge's plan is that this amendment would make potential purchasers of a country's resources more wary of dealing with any authoritarian who gains power. Potential authoritarians, aware of this reduced demand, would then be less likely to attempt to destabilize the democracy in the first place.

The grounding value of this proposal is democratic governance. To solve the criterial problem and the problem of authoritative notice, Pogge describes a "Democracy Panel." This is "an international panel, composed of reputable, independent jurists living abroad who understand [the country's] constitution and political system well enough to judge whether some particular group's acquisition and exercise of political power is or is not constitutionally legitimate" (162). Not all transitions away from democracy are as dramatic as a *coup d'état*, and the Democracy Panel is intended to provide swift, authoritative determination of when a country that has passed Pogge's amendment has gone from above to below the democratic line. Once a Democracy Panel ruled that a country was no longer democratic, all potential purchasers would be on notice that resource sales from that country will not be not viewed as legitimate (until the Panel ruled that democracy had been reinstated). Any fledgling democracy could empower such a Democracy Panel; if enough countries used the same panel, then Pogge suggests it could naturally find a home within the United Nations system.

Pogge's proposal to reform the resource privilege through a constitutional amendment and a Democracy Panel is characteristically imaginative and careful. Pogge attends to the incentives this proposal would create, as well as to the unintended consequences that the proposal might engender.

Indeed Pogge is so scrupulously honest about his own proposal that, in the end, he states it cannot work as intended. The main obstacle that he points to is enforcement. It would be a "miracle," he

says, if the envisioned amendment and panel could stop Shell, for
example, from buying oil from some future authoritarian regime that
overturned the democracy in Nigeria (171). There is just too much gain
to be made from these purchases of petroleum. No ruling from an
international panel that some country was insufficiently democratic
could, in itself, be weighty enough to convince a Western oil major to
stop dealing with the regime in that country. And, we might add, a
panel's ruling would be even less likely to halt the national oil companies of China, which are quickly becoming major players in the extraction of African oil. Without credible enforcement mechanisms, the
panel's judgments would be ignored by those engaged in international
resource trade.

There are also further limitations to Pogge's proposal. First, any
solution that turns on a democratically passed amendment can only
help in those countries that have already achieved democratic governance – so not Equatorial Guinea, for example, which has never been
democratic.[16] Second, the proposal is not entirely *incentive compatible*:
it creates incentives which work against its own grounding value.
Consider the incentives of rich-country leaders whose corporations are
buying oil from a poor-country despot who seized power after Pogge's
amendment was democratically passed. These rich-country leaders
know that, if democratic governance returns to the poor country, their
corporations will face accusations of misappropriation of foreign
goods. These leaders will then have significant political incentives to
assure that democratic governance does not return to the poor country.
And potential authoritarians, aware of these future incentives to
entrench them, will be more likely to attempt to destabilize the democracy in the first place. So the proposal would generate significant
incentives that point in a counterproductive (antidemocratic)
direction.[17]

Pogge suggests that his Democracy Panel proposal should be implemented despite its limitations, so that the current moral situation can
at least be clarified. Such clarification may, he offers, eventually bring
about change in public opinion in the rich world, which in turn may
bring unspecified improvements. But this hope for gradual reform of
the current global economic order through changes in public opinion
is not sufficient as proof of the feasibility of Pogge's proposal. Indeed,
this rather vague hope does not meet Pogge's own standards for
success. To return for a moment to the harm argument, recall that by
Pogge's own standards in order to prove harm, "We must be able to
be confident that the alternative institutional design would do much
better in giving participants secure access to the objects of their human

rights" (26). Pogge's proposal for an amendment and a Democracy Panel cannot, as it stands, give us this confidence.

Elsewhere I have set out an agenda for reforming the international resource privilege that draws on Pogge's work but points in a different direction. This agenda frames the resource curse not as a democratic deficit but rather as a violation of property rights and national self-determination.[18] I believe that we can have more confidence in the feasibility of this agenda. Unless Pogge endorses that agenda, or some other proposal that is even more promising, he cannot make good on his claim that the members of wealthy countries are harming the world's poor by imposing the international resource privilege. And, more significantly, without a feasible proposal, we will be missing a crucial asset in the drive to change global institutions so as to reduce repression and severe poverty.

6 Grounding values, authoritative notice, and enforcement

Part of the difficulty with Pogge's proposal for replacing the resource privilege is the proposal's grounding value: democracy. Democracy is too strong a value to ground a feasible proposal for reform of international institutions. By Pogge's criterion even the nondemocratic but relatively decent Kuwaiti government, for instance, could not legitimately sell its country's oil to foreigners. A universal requirement of democracy is too contestable a premise on which to rest a realistic proposal for the reform of the global economic order.

The alternative for reforming the international resource privilege turns, as mentioned, not on democratic rights but on property rights. The criterial question here is whether the political conditions in the country in question are good enough for it to be possible for the citizens of the country to agree to some regime selling off the country's natural resources (which, in international law, the people have the ultimate right to control). Property is better than democracy as a grounding value because the proposal based upon it will disqualify fewer regimes, and so will be more feasible. More significantly, the value of enforcing property rights is a value that no corporation or rich government can credibly deny.[19] The proposal presents itself as a demand that the major players in the global market correct large-scale violations of property rights. Such a demand is considerably less contestable than a demand to boost democracy in resource-rich countries.

We can now take a wider perspective on strategies for meeting the other challenges facing proposals to reform the resource privilege. Whether democracy or property is used as the grounding value, any proposal for reform of the resource privilege will need to give some account of what will put outsiders on notice that the minimal criterial conditions for purchase of natural resources do or do not obtain within some country. Authoritative notice that the minimal conditions do not obtain will signal to all outsiders that they cannot deal in good faith with any regime in that country, and so that they cannot legitimately take possession of any of its natural resources. A very large question for any proposal to reform the resource privilege is what that source of authoritative notice could be.

As Pogge says, we cannot rely on institutions within the poor country itself to provide authoritative notice that the minimal conditions have not been met. For, if the minimal conditions are not met, the domestic institutions that might be used (such as the judiciary) will likely themselves be controlled by the regime. There must be some source for authoritative notice outside of the country, and this source must have some degree of political independence from the powerful actors who want the resource transfers to go through.[20]

Pogge's suggestion is that notice be given by an international panel composed of reputable, independent jurists. Such a panel would investigate whether the minimal conditions had been met within suspect countries, and Pogge's hope is that this panel would have sufficient standing that its rulings would carry weight in the international community. The panel's judgment that a certain country did not fulfill the minimal conditions would put all international actors on notice that natural resource transfers from that country must be illicit. Ideally the panel should be permanently established: Pogge says the United Nations might be a natural home for it.

Shafter also opts for a panel model in the parallel context of the international borrowing privilege and "odious debt."[21] Shafter is not as sanguine as Pogge about the United Nations: he worries that the inclusiveness of the UN would mean that the panel would be put under pressure by governments that do not meet the minimal conditions or that would have no compunction about subordinating the panel's aims to political bargaining.[22] Shafter's alternative suggestion is for the panel to be embedded in a self-standing international organization, with a membership composed of "diplomatic political appointees from member states to the organization."[23]

Both Pogge's and Shafter's proposals run significant risks of institutional capture. Wherever the panel is located, if the member states that supply the panel's members are mostly rich countries, then the panel may be captured by commercial interests (perhaps working through the ministries of the rich countries) that want resource transfers to go through regardless of whether the countries in question actually do meet the minimal conditions.

The political pressure on an international panel is clearly one area of concern – a concern about the "input" to the panel's decisions. Another concern is enforcement: what would happen to an international panel's "output?" A panel ruling that some country does not meet the minimal conditions of legitimacy could feed into the institutions of resource-importing countries through two routes: through their political institutions or through their judiciaries. Shafter looks to the political route.[24] The panel he posits would have enough standing among importing-country governments that these governments would enforce against their own corporations the panel's negative rulings that the regimes in some places were not to be dealt with.

Shafter's proposal faces real difficulties, most obviously with compliance by the United States (although compliance by China and other fast-growth developing countries is also a major concern). The more independent an international panel is (the purer its "input"), the less likely it is that the US government will agree to be bound by its rulings. Both the US executive and legislative branches have proved robustly suspicious of international panels that the US does not control.[25] And this suspicion, it must be admitted, is also widespread within the American citizenry. Yet without American support for its judgments, the effective authority of any international panel's decisions will be limited. The governments of resource-hungry countries are unlikely to enforce the decisions of an international panel that the minimal conditions in some country have not been met if doing so will limit their own resource imports but not (because of continuing US trade with that country) lift the resource curse in that country.

It might be thought that the output of the international panel could better feed into the judicial systems of resource-importing countries. On this judicial route, the negative judgments of the panel would be decisive in importing-country courts in actions charging that some party had illegitimately received extractive resources from a resource-cursed country. The advantage of this direct judicial solution is that it resolves the question of enforcement. Unlike an international panel, the rulings of domestic courts immediately bind all actors that operate within that court's jurisdiction.

The difficulties of going this judicial route are also evident from the American case. The US judicial branch has been at least as reluctant as the executive and legislative branches to accept the standing of international panels as conclusive for their own judgments. Although one could imagine a day when it might be otherwise, it would presently require an American judge of considerable professional courage to rule that the decision of some international panel was decisive in allowing an action to proceed, for example, against ExxonMobil for its oil contracts in central Africa.

Until a credible proposal for an international panel has been put forward, we should be alive to other solutions. The alternative suggestion for solving the problems of notice and enforcement is that we find independent sources of evidence that can be used to ground judgments by domestic courts. Here it will be domestic courts themselves that rule that there is public and conclusive evidence that the minimal conditions within some country are not met, and so that no regime within that country can legally sell off its resources. For example, an American judge will rule that the political conditions in Equatorial Guinea are so bad that Obiang cannot legitimately sell the country's oil, and that no American corporation could possibly gain good title to the oil by dealing with him.

The concern for this suggestion is that domestic courts may not seem to be up to the task that that is assigned to them. Domestic judges and juries cannot be presumed to be experts in political science or foreign affairs. For courts to rule that the minimal conditions are not met in some country, their decisions must be supported by independent and weighty evidence that bears directly on the minimal conditions. Yet where could such evidence be found?

The evidence required would have, to as high a degree as possible, two features. First, domestic courts will be helped by *bright-line* standards: by standards that clearly state that the minimal conditions for legitimate sales have or have not been met. Second, courts will look for bright-line standards that are of sufficient *status* to secure what will after all be very dramatic judicial decisions. To be of sufficient status, the standards should be recognized by domestic and international agencies at the highest levels. In the ideal case, an American court ruling against an American oil company would be able to rely on standards that the American government had officially and publicly endorsed.

This ideal might seem a distant hope, again especially in the American case. However the ideal can be realized – even in the American case – when property is used as the grounding value for the reform. There currently exist public, bright-line ratings that indicate for every country in the world whether the minimal conditions for resource sales have been met. Moreover, these ratings have sufficient status to ground secure judgments by American courts. In fact, American courts could tomorrow be presented with evidence that is clear enough and decisive enough to support a ruling that all parties bound by American law may not legitimately purchase natural resources from regimes like Obiang's in Equatorial Guinea. I will describe this source of evidence for courts, and then close by noting how it could also be used within trade policy to complete the agenda of reforming the resource privilege.

7 The Freedom House ratings

The central principle of the property-based framework is that the natural resources of each country ultimately belong to the people of that country. This principle is deep within international law, and is here taken as read.[26] Accepting this principle that the citizens of a country should have final control over the country's resources, the legitimacy of resource sales then turns on whether these owners could authorize anyone to sell their resources abroad. The argument of the property-based framework is that, unless certain minimal political conditions obtain within a country, the people could not possibly authorize such sales.

The argument begins along familiar propertarian lines. For an owner to be able to authorize sales, the owner must at least:

1 be able to find out about the sales;
2 be able to stop the sales without incurring severe costs; and
3 not be subject to extreme manipulation by the seller.

If these minimal conditions do not obtain, neither the assent nor the silence of the owner can possibly authorize any sale of that owner's property. In the context of peoples and their resources these three conditions require that citizens must have at least minimal civil liberties and political rights. There must be, that is, at least some absolutely minimal press freedom if citizens are to have access to information about what resource deals the regime is making. The regime must not be so deeply opaque that it is impossible for the people to find out what happens to the revenues from resource sales. Citizens must be able to pass information about the regime to each other without fear of surveillance and arrest. The regime must put some effective political mechanisms in place through which the people can express their unhappiness about resource sales: at least a non-elected consultative legislature that advises the regime, or at the very least occasions on which individuals or civic groups can present petitions. There must also be a minimally adequate rule of law, ensuring that citizens who wish to protest resource sales publicly and peacefully may do so without fear of cruel judicial punishment, disappearance, serious injury, or death.

If these minimal conditions do not obtain in a country, then the silence of the people when a regime sells its resources cannot signal the people's authorization. Absent these conditions, the people's silence is just silence. In countries where these minimal political conditions do not obtain, the people cannot authorize resource sales, and so no regime can pass good title of the territory's resources to an international corporation. Therefore absent these conditions, any corporation that accepts resources from a regime in that country is receiving stolen goods. Possession of stolen goods will then be the subject of litigation in rich-country jurisdictions against international resource corporations such as the oil majors.

The strategy of litigation returns us to the questions of what standards can be used as evidence in, for example, American courts that the minimal political conditions above are lacking within some country. To rule that an international resource corporation has received stolen resources from a foreign regime, American courts will, as we have seen, be aided by public, bright-line standards that establish that these minimal political conditions in some country are unfulfilled.

The US government has authorized just such standards. It has authorized for official use an independent report that gives bright-line ratings of the political conditions in every country in the world. And these ratings measure exactly the factors that determine whether the citizens of a country could possibly consent to their resources being sold off.

In 2002, the Bush administration established the Millennium Challenge Account (MCA) as a mechanism for distributing development aid to poor countries. President Bush required that the MCA choose countries to receive aid based on "a set of clear and concrete and objective criteria" on political conditions that would be applied "rigorously and fairly."[27] For the criteria concerning civil liberties and political rights, the US government selected the ratings of Freedom House.

Freedom House is an independent NGO established in 1941 by Eleanor Roosevelt and Republican presidential candidate Wendell Willkie. Today the organization is prominent in Washington; it has a regional headquarters in Europe and field offices in several developing countries. Its Board of Trustees is filled with well-known figures of the American establishment.

Since 1972, the organization has published *Freedom in the World*, an annual evaluation of political conditions in countries around the world. The survey uses indicators drawn from the Universal Declaration of Human Rights to rate each country in two broad categories: civil liberties, and political rights. The Freedom House ratings are widely cited by journalists, academics, and nongovernmental agencies: "most scholars of comparative politics consider the Freedom House index to be the best measure available."[28] The US government has used the Freedom House ratings not only for the MCA but also, for example, for setting official targets for the performance of the State Department.

The Freedom House report assigns each country a rating from 1 (best) to 7 (worst) on civil liberties and on political rights. The index on civil liberties measures to what degree citizens are free from arbitrary political coercion, violence, or manipulation. The report describes countries with the worst two scores on civil liberties in this way:

> *Rating of 6*: People in countries and territories with a rating of 6 experience severely restricted rights of expression and association, and there are almost always political prisoners and other manifestations of political terror. These countries may be characterized by a few partial rights, such as some religious and social freedoms, some highly restricted private business activity, and relatively free private discussion.

> *Rating of 7*: States and territories with a rating of 7 have virtually no freedom. An overwhelming and justified fear of repression characterizes these societies.[29]

Among the countries rated 6 on civil liberties in the 2009 Freedom House report are Iran, Syria, and Zimbabwe. Among the countries with a rating of 7 are Burma, North Korea, Somalia, and Sudan.

The Freedom House index of political rights measures how much the people's informed and unforced choices control what those with power in the country do. The descriptions of countries that receive the worst scores on political rights are as follows:

> *Rating of 6*: Countries and territories with political rights rated 6 have systems ruled by military juntas, one-party dictatorships, religious hierarchies, or autocrats. These regimes may allow only a minimal manifestation of political rights, such as some degree of representation or autonomy for minorities. A few states are traditional monarchies that

mitigate their relative lack of political rights through the use of consultation with their subjects, tolerance of political discussion, and acceptance of public petitions.

Rating of 7: For countries and territories with a rating of 7, political rights are absent or virtually nonexistent as a result of the extremely oppressive nature of the regime or severe oppression in combination with civil war. States and territories in this group may also be marked by extreme violence or warlord rule that dominates political power in the absence of an authoritative, functioning central government.

Among the countries rated 6 on political rights in the 2009 report are Angola, Iran, and Rwanda. Among the countries rated 7 are Burma, Equatorial Guinea, North Korea, Sudan, and Zimbabwe.

In order to build the strongest legal cases, we make the least controversial assumptions, focusing on the countries where it is certain that the minimal conditions are not met. We can say with confidence that a Freedom House rating of 7 on either civil liberties or political rights should be conclusive for establishing that the people of that country are not in conditions under which they could possibly authorize resource sales. Therefore no regime within a 7 country can legitimately sell resources from that country, and any corporation that receives resources from such a regime is legally liable for possessing stolen goods.

The Freedom House ratings are secure criteria, based on a scale that the US government has declared to be useful as an official, objective, and reliable standard. The Freedom House ratings provide evidence that is clear enough and decisive enough to support rulings that parties bound by American law may not legitimately purchase natural resources from regimes in certain countries, or from anyone in a chain of transactions stretching back to those regimes. These ratings can underpin rulings that would significantly curtail America's contribution to the resource curse.

8 Resistance and support in the property-based framework

One central concern about the property-based approach to reforming the resource privilege is that Freedom House would come under pressure to change its ratings if successful legal actions were brought against large multinational corporations. Should the current proposal be effected, a great deal of money would turn on how different countries fared on the Freedom House scales. The difference between a country being rated 6 rather than 7 could mean the difference to deals worth hundreds of millions of dollars. Freedom House does have friends in high places and, should their ratings start to block big resource contracts, one would suspect that these friends would start requesting that certain countries have their ratings raised. This concern is, again, one of institutional capture.

One way that the property-based approach protects Freedom House from capture is to generate counterpressures for it to raise its scores. Power is normally required to balance power, and the full implementation of the property rights approach to the resource curse (which involves trade duties and "Clean Hands Trusts") will generate just such counterpressures.[30] This balance of forces can create open space for the staff of Freedom House to continue to act in accordance with the organization's self-image as an independent evaluator of political conditions.

Moreover, there is another reason to be optimistic here. One thing we know for certain is that the *current* (2009) Freedom House survey is not warped by commercial and political pressures of the type just mentioned. Neither the present administration nor large American corporations have realized that the Freedom House scores call the legitimacy of extractive resource sales into question. This can be confirmed by the fact that several countries (e.g., Equatorial Guinea, Libya) with whom American companies have signed large contracts are currently rated 7. Given that the present ratings are not distorted by the relevant pressures, and that everyone would know that pressure will be applied on Freedom House to revise its ratings, much of the organization's reputational credibility will turn on its proving publicly that revisions of the ratings are justified. The Freedom House ratings now have a long track record, so it is known how much the scores can be expected to change year on year and how much the index overall can be expected to track similar indices. Academics and nongovernmental organizations will scrutinize and criticize each new annual survey, increasing the organization's motivation to resist surreptitious suasion.

What is more, pressure on Freedom House to raise its ratings may for two reasons not in fact be as strong as initially feared. First, what every corporation resists most is state action that puts it *in particular* at a competitive disadvantage. Yet the court rulings described above would restrict the activities of all American corporations equally, and so will meet with less resistance. New rules that bind all firms, especially if credibly enforced, can be accepted fairly quickly as defining the framework of business practice.

Second, international resource corporations might in fact welcome the property-based reforms since these promise to improve the business environment in which these firms operate. What resource corporations want above all in resource-rich countries is the predictability of the rule of law and the enforcement of property rights. Capricious dictators and the threat of civil conflict greatly increase their business risks. By requiring minimally decent governance as the condition of any resource transfers, the property-based legal actions will incentivize regimes in resource-cursed countries to improve the political economies of their countries in ways that will increase the expected profitability of resource contracts for the international corporations. These firms may see the property-based reforms as means to solve some of their own collective action problems and so reduce risks.[31]

It will also be useful here that ratings of a number of indices that rate political conditions strongly reinforce one another. Courts can be presented not only with the Freedom House ratings but with concurrent ratings from, for example, the Bertelsmann Transformation Index, the Transparency International Corruption Perceptions Index, and the World Bank's Worldwide Governance Indicators.[32] Discursive country reports from ministries like the State Department and the Energy Department describe the same sets of facts. There is in fact no controversy among any of these indices and reports that the political conditions in Equatorial Guinea, for example, are abysmal. The agenda for reforming the international resource privilege can make good use of this consensus by presenting these indices as weighty, independent sources of information about the political conditions in foreign countries in front of domestic courts.[33]

Once the judicial strategy has been successful within a country like the United States, the resource corporations of that country will then agitate not to lose competitive advantage with respect to corporations based elsewhere. This is where the second stage of the agenda for reform would begin. Here the United States (for example) would use its trade policy to levy duties on imports from countries (such as China) whose corporations receive stolen resources from a disqualified regime, or from any country in a chain of transactions that stretches back to such a regime. These duties would discourage other countries from dealing with disqualified regimes, and so again exert a counter-pressure to the resource curse.

This trade agenda, which revolves around the Clean Hands Trusts, faces important questions about feasibility that are too far-reaching to be answered here.[34] Two key supports for the agenda are that it, like the litigation strategy, can be presented as a regime for enforcing property rights in global trade; and that it aligns with the interests of powerful domestic industries such as manufacturing, agriculture, and banking. It should also be appealing to the public across the political spectrum in a country like America, from left to right. This trade agenda is designed to work with the grain of dominant domestic interests and partisanships, and so to offer a promising approach to the reform of international trade in natural resources. It merits further scrutiny.

9 Conclusion

Thomas Pogge has made visible to many a world of vast poverty and inexcusable domination. The rules by which the contemporary world operates generate much of the misery which we now see. These rules are not immutable and, as with the resource privilege, they often run counter to the ideals on which those in the affluent world pride themselves. Pogge has vivified the costs in human well-being and dignity that result from failing to live up to our own principles. The imperative is to join Pogge in working to make the world that we now see more tolerable for both the poor and the rich who share it.

Notes

1 All parenthetical references are to pages in Thomas Pogge, *World Poverty and Human Rights*, 2nd edn (Cambridge: Polity, 2008).
2 Pogge, *World Poverty and Human Rights*, 1st edn (Cambridge: Polity, 2002), p. 26.
3 See the list of Pogge's publications at pantheon.yale.edu/~tp4/index.html.
4 To date Pogge has over twenty publications on Rawls, ranging in critical posture from *Realizing Rawls* (Ithaca, NY: Cornell University Press, 1991) to "The Incoherence between Rawls's Theories of Justice," *Fordham Law Review* 72(5) (2004): 1739–59.
5 Aristotle, *Nicomachean Ethics*, trans. J. Barnes (New York: Penguin, 2003), p. 10.
6 See for example the critical essays and Pogge's reply in the symposium on *World Poverty and Human Rights* in *Ethics & International Affairs* 19(1) (2005).

7 See www.healthimpactfund.org.
8 African (Banjul) Charter on Human and Peoples Rights, Article 21, clauses 1, 4, 5.
9 Pogge, "Recognized and Violated by International Law: The Human Rights of the Global Poor," *Leiden Journal of International Law* 18(4) (2005): 717–45, 728–9.
10 The G20 developing countries are Argentina, Bolivia, Brazil, Chile, China, Cuba, Egypt, Guatemala, India, Indonesia, Mexico, Nigeria, Pakistan, Paraguay, Philippines, South Africa, Tanzania, Thailand, Uruguay, Venezuela, and Zimbabwe.
11 As Hedley Bull famously put it, "[A]narchy it is possible to regard as the central fact of the international system and the starting place for theorizing about it." (Hedley Bull, "Society and Anarchy in International Relations," in *Diplomatic Investigations*, ed. Herbert Butterfield and Martin Wight, London: George Allen and Unwin, 1966, pp. 35–60, at 35).
12   International politics takes place in an arena that has no central governing
       body. No agency exists above individual states with authority and power to
       make laws and settle disputes. States can make commitments and treaties,
       but no sovereign power ensures compliance and punishes deviations. This
       – the absence of supreme power – is what is meant by the anarchic environ-
       ment in international politics.

   (Robert Art and Robert Jervis, *International Politics*, 3rd edn, Boston, Harper Collins, 1992, p. 1)
13 Wenar, "Property Rights," *Philosophy and Public Affairs* 36(1) (2008): 3–7.
14 The percentage of trade figure is from WTO, *International Trade Statistics 2007*.
15 Pogge suggests in passing that a poverty-reducing alteration in the resource privilege would be a "minor reform" (263); but surely in terms of either political difficulty or divergence from current legal practice this must be an understatement.
16 Pogge's proposal could also only help in countries with a written constitution, since only a written constitution can be explicitly amended in the way that Pogge suggests.
17 Pogge's proposals for using a Democracy Panel and Democracy Fund to reform the international borrowing privilege has similar difficulties with counterproductive incentives. (Pogge's Democracy Fund is a pool of money which temporarily services the debts of democratic governments that have passed the constitutional amendment, in the event that uncon-stitutional rulers take over and refuse to honor these debts.) Consider the incentives of a large bank (call it "Bank") based in, and influential with the government of, a G8 country. If Bank sees that there is a large pool of money from which it can be reliably paid when the democratic govern-ment is overthrown (the Democracy Fund), then it has an incentive to work to undermine that government. If Bank believes that any debts that

a predatory authoritarian government owes to it will not be honored if the predator government is replaced by a democratic government, then Bank has incentives to keep the predator government in power. And, most importantly, if Bank sees that a Democracy Panel will have the authority to annul large debts on its books, it will work against the establishment of this panel or work to capture it.

18 See cleantrade.org.
19 Wenar, "Property Rights," p. 16.
20 Pogge, *World Poverty*, pp. 155–8.
21 Jonathan Shafter, "The Due Diligence Model: A New Approach to the Problem of Odious Debt," *Ethics and International Affairs* 21(1) (2007): 49–67.
22 Shafter has similar worries about the UN Security Council filling the role of the panel. But see Seema Jayachandran and Michael Kremer "Odious Debt," *American Economic Review* 96(1) (2006): 81–92.
23 Shafter, "The Due Diligence Model," p. 59.
24 Pogge leaves this question open, mentioning both the political and judicial branches of rich countries' governments; Pogge, *World Poverty*, pp. 164–5.
25 The major exceptions to this generalization are the WTO dispute resolution panels (which are part of an organization that the US government regards as operating broadly in the national interest) and the UN Security Council (where the US has veto power).
26 The principle of national ownership is discussed in Wenar, "Property Rights," pp. 9–12. The principle is affirmed in, for example, Article 1 of both of the major human rights covenants.
27 Speech by George W. Bush, March 14, 2002 (http://georgewbush-whitehouse.archives.gov/news/releases/2002/03/20020314-7.html, accessed April 2010).
28 Cynthia McClintock and James Lebovic, "Correlates of Levels of Democracy in Latin America During the 1990s," *Latin American Politics & Society* 48(2) (2006): 29–59, at 31.
29 Freedom House, *Freedom in the World 2008: Selected Data from Freedom House's Annual Global Survey of Political Rights and Civil Liberties* (Freedom House, 2008).
30 See Wenar, "Property Rights," pp. 26–31.
31 "Governance issues, the transparency of operations, and political stability matter in every oil-producing country, not just Saudi Arabia and Kuwait. It's a concern everywhere. [Reforms] don't just produce benefits for the citizens, but they create a more stable investment climate." (Richard Karp of the American Petroleum Institute in Esther Pan, "The Pernicious Effects of Oil," Council on Foreign Relations, 2005, www.cfr.org/publication/8996/pernicious_effects_of_oil.html.)
32 See www.bertelsmann-transformation-index.de/16.0.html?&L=1, www.transparency.org/policy_research/surveys_indices/cpi, info.worldbank.org/governance/wgi/index.asp, all accessed April 2010.

33 The congruence of the various indices also means that compelling evidence can now be presented to courts even in countries where no index is in official use. The legal framework of the proposal here can thus be translated, for example, into European courts as well.

34 See cleantrade.org for more on these issues of feasibility.

7

Realizing (Through Racializing) Pogge

Charles W. Mills

Few if any contemporary political philosophers have done as much as Thomas Pogge to translate the abstract ideals of the just *polis* into practical prescriptions and concrete recommendations for institutional change. If Rawlsianism in particular has seemed to inhabit a realm as otherworldly and remote from the applied as Plato's republic, Pogge has sought, in different ways, to "realize Rawls," both locally, and, especially in his writings of the last decade, globally.[1] Moreover, whereas Rawls seemed to many in his later work to be retreating from the powerful and inspiring social-democratic vision of *A Theory of Justice*,[2] Pogge originally argued for radicalizing it and, in a post-Marxist world marked by the triumph of neoliberalism, applying it on a planetary scale. More recently, however, Pogge has taken up, if only for strategic reasons, a more minimalist ethico-political position that he still sees as having radical implications for the remedying of global poverty.

Since I am in complete sympathy with Pogge's enterprise, my aim in this chapter is not so much critique as it is friendly amendment, supplementation, and expansion. Somewhat presumptuously, I am going to suggest that the project of "realizing Pogge" could be considerably assisted by his making race (and gender, though I will have less to say about that) more central to his theorizing than it currently is. Precisely because of his recent shift to a discourse more acceptable to political centrists and conservatives – the correction of injustices

arising from "negative" rights violations rather than the globalizing of
social democracy – a focus on racial and gender justice would significantly enhance his work and strengthen his case against his critics.
White supremacy and patriarchy as overarching non-ideal social institutions profoundly affecting the actual "basic structure" both locally
and internationally need to be recognized as historical realities with
lasting contemporary effects for justice not merely at the material level
but also, reflexively, at the ideological level, in how we *theorize* about
justice.

1 Ideal vs. non-ideal theory

The appropriate starting point, in my opinion, is the distinction
between ideal and non-ideal theory, and its relation to Rawls, race and
gender, and Pogge's revisionist Rawlsianism. As I have argued in
greater detail elsewhere,[3] my own belief is that the ideal-theory orientation of Anglo-American political philosophy in its post-Rawls resur-
rection of the last few decades has overall been a disaster, or, at the
very least, has greatly hindered rather than helped the project of theorizing and bringing about social justice.

Ideal theory, in Rawls's famous formulation, is concerned with the
demands of justice in "a perfectly just society." Non-ideal theory, by
contrast, is concerned with the remedying of injustice (the demands of
justice in an *unjust* society) and "questions of compensatory justice."
Rawls's lifetime corpus is centered almost exclusively on ideal theory,
his rationale being that "it provides, I believe, the only basis for the
systematic grasp of these more pressing problems [of non-ideal
theory]."[4] So it is important to appreciate that – whatever its subsequent career – the development of ideal theory was, even for Rawls,
never originally intended to be an end in itself but rather instrumental
to the more this-worldly goal of adjudicating the correction of
injustices.

But a growing body of work has begun to question its necessity and
even its utility for such a task.[5] Some of the criticisms would include
the following:

1 First, just as a matter of fact, it is evident that for many political
   philosophers today, ideal theory *has* become an end in itself, with
   theorists quite happy to ring the conceptual changes indefinitely on
   variations and permutations that are not only tediously familiar by

now but increasingly stratospherically removed from real-world problems.

2 In terms of prioritizing an allocation of energies, surely problems originally conceded to be "pressing" (and far more pressing today) should be precisely those getting most of our theoretical attention.

3 In many cases of injustice, we do not need to know what an ideal world would look like to correct them.

4 More strongly, an ideal world will be so distant from our actual world that a conceptual array based on its idealized picture of the workings of sociopolitical institutions (one that abstracts away from social oppression) may offer little guidance, or positively harmful guidance, in the task of reforming these actual institutions. Ideal theory may simply be theoretically blinded by its conceptual apparatus.

5 Relatedly, in its failure to advert to the ways in which moral agents' consciousness and material interests will typically have been shaped by their respective locations in these systems of oppression, ideal theory handicaps itself in the task of attaining a realistic assessment of different groups' openness to moral suasion.

6 Finally, insofar as both race and gender have historically involved the denial of equal moral status to certain human beings, their systemic exploitation, and the justification of that exploitation by ideologies opposing a superior (white, male) self to an inferior (nonwhite, female) other, an idealized contract model predicated on egalitarianism, mutually advantageous cooperation, social transparency, and reciprocal respect is going to be so utterly removed from sociopolitical reality that it will basically mis-orient us from the beginning.

If the "basic structures" established and consolidated in modernity are both white-supremacist and patriarchal, if racial and gender injustices are not deviations from a flawed but basically sound institutional architecture but constitutive of that architecture itself, then to start from ideality is to guarantee that we will never attain it. Racial and gender justice should be at the center of our attention rather than the periphery.

Now both in his original expositions and extrapolations of Rawls, and in his more recent work, Pogge makes various remarks that seem to me quite consonant in principle with a recognition of the desirability of moving racial and gender subordination to the center of our concerns. He points out that "race- and gender-induced inequalities" are "neglected in *A Theory of Justice*," and that Rawls's theoretical distinction between natural and social contingencies is somewhat misleading in this context, since these inequalities "are based on natural facts that, absent certain social facts, might never have had the slightest social importance."[6] And in his more recent expository, *John Rawls*, he clarifies a peculiar feature of Rawlsian ideal theory that may not be immediately apparent to the reader:

> [W]hen assessing alternative public criteria of justice, Rawls is asking not how well each would guide and organize people as they are now, shaped by existing social institutions. Rather, engaging in *ideal theory*, he is asking how well each candidate criterion would guide and organize human beings as they would come to be if they grew up in a society governed by this criterion. . . . *This criterion is not meant to be used for guiding the reform of an unjust basic structure design: for judging the relative urgency of various institutional reforms by examining which reform would result in the least unjust design* [my emphasis]. . . . The focus on ideal theory complicates the comparison among criteria, because it requires envisioning and assessing social worlds that are remote from our own. It also involves neglect of questions that seem important: Which of the social worlds envisioned through such candidate public criteria are reachable from where our society is now, and on what path?[7]

So, contrary to what one might have expected of a book (*the* book) on social justice, it is *not* the case that these ideal Rawlsian principles of justice can serve without modification, or perhaps at all, as normative guideposts for making our own unjust world more just. They are principles that, in effect, presuppose *as already accomplished* the creation of the idealized world in which they are to be applied. But Rawls, as Pogge tells us elsewhere, is supposed to be sketching out "a *realistic* utopia, an ideal social world that is reachable from the present on a plausible path of transition and [which], once reached, could sustain itself in its real context."[8] How then is such a transition going to be possible without a mapping of the optimal route, an identification of the major obstacles along the way, and some indication of how they are to be overcome? It seems to me that Pogge points here to the fundamentally flawed nature of the project of ideal theory without drawing the appropriate conclusion, viz., that this whole approach needs to be jettisoned. For given the *non*recognition of the moral equality of most human beings for the past few thousand years or so, given the centrality of exploitation of various kinds to *all* societies past the hunting and gathering stage,[9] then the orientation toward ideal theory is a fundamental mistake because its social ontology presupposes a successful dismantling of the metaphysics of a racialized and gendered world when its very epistemology (that ignores the non-ideal) blocks us from successfully recognizing, identifying, and eliminating the primary obstacles to such a dismantling. Non-ideal theory in the form of rectificatory racial and gender justice should be our priority because it is only through such a normative project that the way to the ideal can even come into view.

2 Society as a noncooperative venture

Rawls's characterization of society in the opening pages of *A Theory of Justice* must therefore be unequivocally repudiated. He famously says there that "a society is a cooperative venture for mutual advantage," so that though "it is typically marked by a conflict as well as by an identity of interests," nonetheless the governing "rules of conduct" "specify a system of cooperation designed to advance the good of those taking part in it."[10] But this claim is simply absurd, and that it has not for the most part been immediately seen as such speaks volumes about the unbalanced race and gender demography of the profession and the implications of its whiteness and maleness for majoritarian philosophical cognition.

Even if one were to focus just on class, it would be obvious that, given the prevalence of slavery in antiquity across the world for thousands of years, the claim is false.[11] Nor, moving to the medieval period, can feudal Europe's serfs or Afro-Asia's peasants or those subordinated in the great pre-Columbian Meso-American empires be plausibly represented as freely cooperating in systems aimed at the common good. So the simple fact of class domination in the premodern epoch on its own suffices to refute the thesis as a valid historical generalization. But once one takes a feminist perspective seriously, according to which women have been deprived of basic rights in most societies, and adds their numbers – half the population – to the numbers of (male) slaves and other premodern classes subordinated even by mainstream liberal (non-Marxist) standards, then its ludicrousness becomes even more flagrant. And though entry into the modern period may render controversial claims from the left about continuing unfair (white male) working-class disadvantage through the rule of capital, the emergence of race as a new system of domination means that tens of millions of nonwhite indigenous peoples and African slaves now (presumably uncontroversially) have to be added to the ranks of the oppressed as well. (In the eighteenth century, for example – well within modernity

– my native Jamaica was a slave society in which the Amerindian population had been completely wiped out by the Spanish conquistadores, later replaced by the British conquistadores, and organized around the production of sugar in an intensive coerced labor regime in which imported African slaves outnumbered the free white population ten to one. Was this society a "cooperative venture for mutual advantage"?)

Now in *Realizing Rawls*, Pogge recognizes the dubiousness of Rawls's claim here: "This explication [of society] seems narrow, for there are surely many historical societies (standardly so-called) whose rules fail either to be designed for mutual advantage or to be recognized as binding by all participants. For example, the rules may be designed for the advantage of a minority, and compliance by the remaining participants may be due to coercion or religious superstition."[12] And he goes on to suggest that we work with the concept of a "social system" instead, and allow that the economic interactions "may be largely coercive rather than genuinely cooperative."[13] But though he makes this recommended correction, he does not draw the more radical conclusion which I think is appropriate, viz., that since domination and exploitation are central to most (not just "many") if not *all* societies post the hunting-and-gathering stage, then our starting point for determining justice should be the analysis of domination and exploitation.[14] In other words, Pogge's recognition that Rawls has gotten something so basic so wrong should not take the form of an offhand remark but should be center stage to his revisionism. Given that the "basic structure" is our normative focus, we should recognize not merely that the "basic structure" is profoundly shaped by gender and race, but, more startlingly (if like Rawls one thinks of both as natural) *that gender and race are themselves artifacts of an unjust basic structure.*

As Pogge emphasizes, in examining social disadvantage, Rawls's focus is almost exclusively on class, and class conceived of not (obviously) in Marxist terms, as one's relationship to the means of production, with a ruling class and ruled classes, but rather as social stratification determined by education and natural ability. For Rawls, both gender and race are natural, and not appropriately dealt with in ideal theory: "Suppose, for example, that certain fixed natural characteristics are used as grounds for assigning unequal basic rights. . . . Those characteristics cannot be changed, and so the positions they specify are points of view from which the basic structure must be judged. Distinctions based on gender and race are of this kind."[15] Pogge's comment, cited above, hints at the problematic nature of this conceptualization. But he does not push his criticism far enough. The standard scholarly judgment is that variations in skin color, hair texture, and morphological features are not crystallized into "racial" differences until the modern period, and genealogically linked to slavery and colonialism. So a naturalistic metaphysics here is back to front, reversing the actual direction of the causal vector. A social ontology in which races are existent is a social ontology in which the basic structure is *already* racialized, since it is the basic structure that creates race in the first place. It is not that we have these naturally pre-existing discrete groups – whites, blacks, browns, reds – who then exist in different possible locations and relations generated by alternative public policy principles. Rather, these groups are ontologically (not merely locationally) dependent on choices already made and *would not have existed as groups* absent these public policy decisions. They are metaphysical manifestations of a basic structure founded on a particular kind of domination. And correspondingly, when Rawls says that he has not dealt with race and gender because he has been "mainly concerned with ideal theory: the account of the well-ordered society of justice as fairness,"[16] what he fails to understand is that in an ideal society, it would not merely be the case that no race or gender would be discriminated against, but that, more radically, races would not even exist (as against people ranged on a continuum of clines), nor people formally assigned different gender roles (as against people possessing different genitalia).

My claim is, then, that Rawls's failure to deal with race and gender is not merely an "omission," as he characterizes it, but structurally related to a social ontology that gets things wrong at the most basic level. Pogge comments that:

> Rawls's explication of fair equality of opportunity pays little attention to race and gender, despite their great historical and ongoing importance. One reason . . . is that Rawls works within ideal theory, where race and gender have no special salience. . . There are millions of possible personal characteristics that might, merely on account of prevalent negative attitudes, diminish professional prospects: all kinds of physical characteristics, sexual preferences, marital status, religious and political convictions and affiliations, and so on.[17]

But as indicated, this judgment seems to me to misread the historical significance of race and gender. They are not merely two of "millions of possible personal characteristics" that might be used to justify discrimination but two of the historically most fundamental variables in

152 Charles W. Mills

shaping (and being shaped by) the basic structure itself. Their very existence (unlike, say, sexual preference, marital status, religious and political convictions) is a testimony to the *noncooperative* nature of most societies. Racial and gender systems will typically be regulated by social rules and conventions predicated not on voluntary consent and reciprocal advantage, but force (conquest, enslavement, colonization, segregation, rape and the threat of rape) and ideological socialization. So to ignore their reality in one's normative theorizing is to ignore the most obvious challenge to one's normative architectural model. This would be true even if the total population in question were a minority, since we would expect a discourse on justice to be particularly concerned about the fate of oppressed minorities. But of course, given that women constitute half the population to begin with, even before the racialized male population is added, the group in question actually makes up the *majority*. Moreover, by contrast with a controversial left-liberal program, relying on appeals to the "moral arbitrariness" of our natural assets, the situation of women and the racially excluded directly contravenes the *uncontroversial* mainstream liberal principle, common to all varieties of liberalism, not to harm. It is because of social oppression, not bad luck in the natural lottery, that they occupy the position they do.

So once one puts all these factors together – that the very existence of race and gender gives the lie to the "cooperative venture" characterization of society, that women of all races and males of color will constitute the majority of the population, that their situation is the result of a social oppression that patently violates liberal principles (once de-gendered and de-racialized), and that they will be disproportionately at the bottom of the social order – then surely they collectively make an overwhelming case for making the remedying of these inequities a priority for us.

3 The moral inequality of the contractors

Once we admit the nonconsensual nature of society even in the modern period, then, it forces us to revise the orthodox narrative of modernity encapsulated in contractarianism and liberal theory more generally. It is white men who become morally equal, not humanity as such, and this necessarily has implications for the actual schedule of rights presupposed to be central to the modern contract.

In the standard Western periodization of the past few thousand years, antiquity and feudalism may be marked by ascriptive hierarchy, but modernity is distinguished by the acceptance as a basic principle of the socially recognized equality of human beings. So *moral* equality is supposedly uncontroversial, with any deviations from this norm being nonrepresentative if deplorable anomalies that require no theorization in their own right, nor demand any fundamental rethinking of the orthodox account. The real issue is allegedly the debate between right and left as to whether only legal and political equality should be juridically codified or whether the practical realization of these liberal equalities calls for (greater or full) economic equality as well. Material egalitarianism is controversial; moral egalitarianism is not.

But the supposed truism of modernity's establishment of recognized universal human moral equality is completely false, as is the narrative within which it is embedded. Only by concentrating exclusively on white men could it be taken seriously for a second. (Once again, we see how far-reaching are the implications of the relegation of gender and race to the sidelines of mainstream justice theory.) Even white women were not seen as equal in any substantive way, considering how recently in historical terms they have gotten the vote, been given the right to own property, run for office, been freed of the legal burden of coverture, and so forth. And in the case of people of color, of course, both male and female, the exclusion has been even more flagrant, since they did not even benefit from the derivative rights (arising from their whiteness, their link with the white male) enjoyed by white women. Basically, the history of the West is being retroactively sanitized by white political philosophers so as to deny the centrality of racism, and in its classic form, racism can be thought of as expressing a moral claim: some humans are so unequal because of their race that it is appropriate that they should *not* have equal rights.

If one historical episode definitively sums up this history of racial exclusion, it is the following: the vetoing by the "Anglo-Saxon" nations (Britain, the United States, Canada, Australia, New Zealand, South Africa) of the Japanese proposal at the 1919 post-World War I Versailles conference that a "racial equality" clause should be inserted in the League of Nations' Covenant.[18] (Thomas Pogge is the only white political philosopher I have ever seen to cite this episode.[19]) Think of it. We are well into the twentieth century, in the aftermath of a war ostensibly prosecuted to make the world safe for democracy. We are hundreds of years deep into modernity, which has supposedly established the moral equality of all human beings as an uncontroversial principle. And yet *racial* equality – not socialism, not even decolonization – is so controversial, so threatening to the planetary order, that it must be vetoed! As Frank Füredi has pointed out, this history has been written out of existence in order to deny the recency of the Western commitment (to the extent that there is a commitment) to transracial moral equality.[20] What has actually prevailed for several hundred years is a commitment to *white* moral equality, not the equality of humans as such.

But a narrative revised to reflect this reality would have drastic implications for the liberal contractarian story. It would force us to acknowledge that the "actual" contract that has shaped modernity has been an exclusionary sexual and racial one, so that what has been taken for granted by white men has been denied to white women and people of color.[21] Pogge's 1989 critique of Rawls for his "(increasing) conservatism" and growing "resistance" to the "progressive power" of his own "two central ideas," the "focus on the basic structure, combined with the priority concern for the least advantaged," centered above all on Rawls's "treating national borders as moral watersheds" and "let[ting] his lexical priority of the basic liberties . . . undermine his priority concern for the least advantaged."[22] But once we switch fully to non-ideal theory, as I have recommended we do, Pogge's enterprise of trying to establish the institutional injustice of global poverty should be considerably advanced and facilitated for the simple reason that in the real (non-Rawlsian) world a large proportion of the worst off will be so *because of historic violations of the lexically prior first principle*. This poverty is to a high degree a consequence of the institutional refusal – not just nationally but (contra Rawls) transnationally – to recognize the full personhood of nonwhites.

So given the supposed uncontroversiality of normative as against material egalitarianism, and the centrality of Kantian respect for all persons to liberalism(s) across the spectrum, it follows that the achievement of a genuinely universalist, nongendered and nonracially coded, schedule of rights would itself demand dramatic global transformation. For non-ideal theory, the thought-experiment would become the working out by free and equal persons of what measures of rectificatory justice would be required to dismantle a basic structure *already* organized around unfair principles that deny freedom and equality to the majority, and bring into existence socially subordinated superpersons identified as "women" and "nonwhites." Even before invoking anything as controversial as the difference principle, simply demanding corrective measures for violations of the first principle would require radical, indeed revolutionary, changes.

Secondly, and relatedly, the material consequences of the systematic social disadvantaging of white women and people of color arising from their moral inequality as subpersons and the corresponding nonrecognition of their basic rights and freedoms would have to be traced. Once we admit the systematicity of gender and racial subordination in the juridico-political sphere, we are forced to recognize its implications for access to the marketplace also. If exploitation is absent from an ideally just society, it is ubiquitous in actual non-ideal societies. So before even tackling such questions as the appropriateness of compensating for the natural lottery, we would need to examine how systemic exploitation reproduces unfair advantage and disadvantage at opposite poles.

As Alan Wertheimer has pointed out, exploitation has not been the subject of much discussion in the liberal tradition in recent years.[23] It is tainted by its association with Marxism, now so seemingly discredited, and in any case marginalized by the Rawls-inspired concentration on ideal theory. But a liberal concept of exploitation can easily be developed, predicated not on the labor theory of value but on standard Kantian norms about violations of norms of equitable treatment and corresponding unjust enrichment, though expanded to take account of *group* relations. (Two recent liberal treatments of exploitation by Wertheimer and Ruth Sample, by contrast, focus almost exclusively on individual exploitation.[24]) The shift to non-ideal theory requires as a correlate the revision of some of the standard conceptual cartographies of the Western sociopolitical tradition. Mapping the multidimensional exploitation of women, for example, requires us to reject the conceptual dichotomization of economy and household that goes back to Aristotle, and to recognize that the differential treatment of women in the household is itself an internal "economic interaction" that deprives women of equal chances to compete in the external economy, or, perhaps better, that the "economy" has to be rethought as having both internal and external aspects. Similarly, I have argued elsewhere that racial exploitation needs to be thought of in terms much broader than traditional Marxist or Leninist concepts of sub-proletarianized labor and super-profits, since slavery and aboriginal expropriation are transactions not involving wage labor that benefit whites as a whole, not just the capitalist class, having the cumulative effect of privileging the white population at the expense of the population of people of color, so that there is a continual net transfer of opportunities and wealth to the former.[25]

The point is, then, that once we recognize the centrality of exploitation to society's actual workings, it becomes theoretically incumbent upon us to track its various mechanisms in their multifaceted interaction and self-reproducing effects. Exploitation cannot be a residual category for us, as it is for Rawls, since exploitation is a continuing violation of the norms of justice that must be eliminated for us to realize the ideal of a just society. Pogge's case for the injustice of the global order could thus be considerably enhanced by making racial and gender exploitation more central to his work, since these varieties of exploitation, unlike the classical Marxist variety, should be uncontroversial within a liberal framework.

Finally, the third major implication of the moral inequality of the contractors for orthodox contractarianism is its impact on the moral psychology of the privileged. In the quotation from Pogge cited near the start, he emphasizes that Rawls's principles are *not* intended to guide people "as they are now, shaped by existing social institutions." The indifference of ideal theory to its own realization marginalizes such considerations: it is a shining beacon whose role is, perversely, to blind us to the appropriate path rather than illuminate it. But once, as in non-ideal theory, we *are* concerned with practical implementation problems, then issues of moral psychology and the receptivity (or lack thereof) of different groups to moral suasion become a legitimate part of the overall argument. In the opening pages of *World Poverty and Human Rights*, Pogge asks a crucial question: "Why do we citizens of the affluent Western states not find it morally troubling, at least, that a world heavily dominated by us and our values gives such very deficient and inferior starting positions and opportunities to so many people?" The answers he reviews do include people's "interests and situation" and the all too human "rationalizing tendency" for people to "tend to interpret their moral values in their own favor and tend to select, represent, and connect the facts so as to facilitate the desired concrete judgment."[26] But he does not specifically mention gender and race. What I would claim is that the architectural centrality of race and gender to the real-life basic structure affects the moral economy as well as the political economy of the social order, so that apart from general human moral weaknesses, one also has to take account of the particular racial and gender psychologies of those privileged by the social order.[27]

The intimate and interdefinitional relationship between masculinity and femininity, between the respective constitutive norms articulating what it is to be a man and a woman, is obvious, and has been the subject of a vast amount of literature since the second-wave revival of feminism. Masculinity as a social construct that deeply affects male psychology, and provides a prism of cognitive interpretation and affective response, is therefore obviously crucial to understanding men's resistance to gender equality. What may be less appreciated today is that there was originally a comparable dialectic of race, not just locally but globally. In the heyday of colonialism, one was, as a white man, self-conscious of one's superior global status and the need never to let oneself be lowered to the level of the native. In his famous preface to Frantz Fanon's *The Wretched of the Earth*, Jean-Paul Sartre writes "there is nothing more consistent than a racist humanism . . . On the other side of the ocean there was a race of less-than-humans."[28] Similarly, in his classic *Culture and Imperialism*, Edward Said points out that "there was virtual unanimity that subject races should be ruled, that they *are* subject races. . . . [T]his secondariness [of the non-European] is, paradoxically, essential to the primariness of the European."[29] Oppositional relationships – we are what *we* are above all by not being what *they* are – become crucial in this non-ideal world of power and hierarchy.

And even if this reciprocal interrelation of white self-respect and disrespect for nonwhites no longer obtains, these racial-normative distinctions arguably continue to influence the scope of affect. In the Kantian ethical ideal, we should be motivated to do our duty by our apprehension of universal law, not through feelings of benevolence and empathy. But such a picture is highly incongruent with our actual formation as moral agents. In practice, such feelings are crucial to our moral education, and boundaries of concern and unconcern are established through practices of social subordination which teach us from our childhood onwards that the fate of certain entities need not concern us because of their subordinate (if not zero) moral status. And originally, these boundaries would have been highly racialized. White settlers in a white settler state displacing and killing native peoples, free whites in a society of black slaves, white Europeans detachedly contemplating the squalor of the teeming millions over whom they rule: all these populations learn to limit their concern to their fellow whites. So even in the present postcolonial, (supposedly) postracist stage, this history of white indifference to nonwhite suffering needs, I suggest, to be considered as at least a potential contributory causal factor to Western indifference.

4 Explanatory internationalism

Moreover, this racial history is arguably also pertinent for Pogge's critique of what he calls "explanatory nationalism," the assumption that societies are largely autarkical entities, so that their subsequent fates can be explained exclusively or largely with respect to endogenous variables. As Rawls says in *The Law of Peoples*: "I believe that the causes of the wealth of a people and the forms it takes lie in their political culture and in the religious, philosophical, and moral traditions that support the basic structure of their political and social institutions, as well as in the industriousness and cooperative talents of its members, all supported by their political virtues."[30] Pogge rightly finds this claim absurd, and his work on international justice is to a significant extent predicated on regarding European colonialism as a "global institutional scheme," an unjust planetary institution "based upon racial superiority."[31] But his references to race are more episodic than systematic. What I would like to propose is that his case could be strengthened by the formal recognition of race – white supremacy – as *itself* an international institution, with effects both material (in determining possibilities for achieving wealth) and ideological (in providing pseudo-explanations for these outcomes).

The idea of race as a social institution of any kind – let alone one of an international character – will sound odd from the perspective of a mainstream liberal discourse on race for which *racism* is the preferred theoretical locution, usually conceived of in the subjective terms of individual attitudes, values, and beliefs. But a growing body of work in what has come to be called critical race theory argues that it is more theoretically illuminating to conceive of race in terms of objective racialized social systems, which both tendentially generate racial attitudes ("racism") and create race itself. Different global histories would have generated different racial systems, but in our own world it is clearly European domination that has been the most important one. Slavery, conquest, colonialism were all in part racial institutions, and for this reason alone, race should be seen as international.

The term "white supremacy" is usually restricted to South African apartheid and the Jim Crow American South. But as I have argued in greater detail elsewhere, once we modify the reference to denote systemic and structural white advantage, which may be de jure or de facto, then a case can easily be made that European domination can illuminatingly be conceived of as a white supremacy that is global in reach.[32] "Race" becomes social-structural and socially explanatory – not, of course, in biological terms but as a social identity with real causal effects in determining people's consciousness, self-conception, motivation, and life chances. In effect, the "basic structure" of individual nations is heavily shaped by its interaction with an international "basic structure" and this global structure privileges whites and white nations. Thus as late as the 1940s most of the planet was formally controlled by the European empires, people categorized as "white" ruling over people categorized as "nonwhite," while whites were dominant in independent nations, overtly in white nations like the United States, Canada, Australia, and New Zealand, and more subtly in the *mestizo* Latin American countries which gained their independence in the nineteenth century.

Historian Thomas Borstelmann speaks of "the era of global white supremacy," "the long era of legalized white rule over people of color," producing an "international consciousness" in "white supremacists," and giving rise by World War I to "a global struggle for racial equality," to "what might be called the international civil rights movement of anticolonialism": "Continuing differences in the racial distribution of power and wealth confirm the ongoing relevance of this theme to contemporary international history."[33] Similarly, two Australian historians, Marilyn Lake and Henry Reynolds, describe "the spread of 'whiteness' as a transnational form of racial identification," "the basis of geo-political alliances and a subjective sense of self."[34] They cite Benedict Anderson's well-known *Imagined Communities*,[35] and comment: "Paradoxically, one outcome of Anderson's argument has been to naturalize the nation as *the* imagined community of modern times, an effect that has obscured the ascendancy of transnational racial identifications and their potency in shaping both personal identity and global politics."[36] So, as earlier emphasized, the very existence of race points beyond national boundaries to transnational institutions and practices, to a global "whiteness." Race cannot be understood "autarkically" because race and the categories of white and nonwhite are created by European expansionism. These are global categories that transcend national borders, dividing the planet into the privileged and the subordinated, the beneficiaries and the victims of transcontinental racial exploitation.

In this context, then, "explanatory nationalism" needs to be recognized as the contemporary sanitized version of what would once have been the cruder and more blatant thesis of "explanatory *continentalism*," the so-called "European miracle,"[37] which attributes the modern history of global white domination to the special virtues of Europeans at home and in the nations they found abroad. If the basic structure is a just one, as in ideal theory, then mystifying ideologies have no functional social role. But if the basic structure is unjust, as in nonideal theory, then such a role obviously becomes crucial, since this injustice needs to be denied. And race provides not just a hierarchy of moral statuses but a set of explanatory schemas as well. The inferiority of nonwhites manifests itself not just in their lesser humanity but in their lesser competence. In the work of figures not at all marginal but at the very center of Western thought we can find representations of

Native Americans as "savages" still in the state of nature and incapable of seeing the need to construct a polity (Hobbes), as "lazy" (Kant), and unwilling to fulfill the divine mandate to appropriate the world and increase its value (Locke), of sub-Saharan Africa as a benighted continent with no history (Hegel), of Indians as not competent to rule themselves (Mill), and so forth. These themes are taken up and developed in what become full-fledged theories of geographical and biological determinism that explain why it is impossible to find developed civilizations, or any civilization at all, in these blighted parts of the world. Thus the most important justification of colonialism becomes the civilizing mission, the need to bring the benefits of a more advanced social order to nonwhite savages and barbarians incapable of making proper use of the resources of their own country (when their existence and their ownership was even conceded – see the doctrine of *terra nullius*[38]). Race as an international basic structure, global white domination, justifies itself in terms of international nonwhite deficiency.

Today, of course, such theories are officially discredited, just as racism is officially discredited. But milder culturalist versions survive (as in Rawls) whose ultimate point is the same: the uniqueness of the West and the denial of the role of exploitation and structural constraint in accounting for the fate of the Rest. In a world marked for centuries by white success and (seeming) nonwhite failure, it will inevitably be the case that such accounts recapitulate, if in disguised form, long-established claims of European specialness and non-European ineptitude. After all, it can hardly escape First World attention that the countries most needing assistance are nonwhite ones, that the starving children with flies circling their heads on our television screens are black and brown, not white. So given the centuries-long history of derogation of these countries and these peoples, how could it not be the case that stereotypes of national (because racial) inability will continue to shape First World cognition? Vijay Prashad summarizes the precepts of 1960s' "modernization theory": "Modernization theory typically put the onus for development on the cultures of the so-called traditional societies, and thereby excised the history of colonialism. This elegantly returned the emergence of capitalism to its pristine European setting, for . . . modernization theory contended that the darker world did not have the culture of frugality and thus willed itself into poverty."[39]

But as anthropologist Jack Goody points out in his comparativist study on what he calls "the theft of history," European claims to be the unique inventors of various institutions that are supposedly responsible for their differential success (democracy, mercantile capitalism, freedom, individualism) are not at all supported by the historical evidence.[40] Rather, once Europe is located in the larger context of Eurasia, the extent of intercultural borrowings makes clear that the standard Orientalist and anti-Africanist conceptions in this literature are simply manifestations of an ethnocentrism which, as a result of the rise of Europe to global domination (primarily through "advances in guns and sails"), then becomes so entrenched that "world-domination in various spheres . . . was often looked upon as almost primordial": "[N]otions of Asiatic despotism, of Asiatic exceptionalism, of distinct forms of rationality, of 'culture' more generally. . . . prevent 'rational' enquiry and comparison by means of the recourse to categorical distinctions; Europe had this (antiquity, feudalism, capitalism), they (everyone else) did not."[41] The structural barriers to other nations following the European route, the role of colonialism and slavery, are then denied in the name of supposedly deficient national cultures.

The point is, then, that there is nothing at all new about such claims, which merely repeat in more abstract and nominally de-raced form assumptions of European specialness that go back for centuries. Pogge's critique of contemporary versions could be sharpened by greater advertence to their long history and originally overtly racist incarnation.

5 Rethinking liberalism

Finally, I want to bring these themes together and urge a rethinking of liberalism that would be conducive to Pogge's social justice project, as well as that of others interested in genuine reform.

In Rawls's own rethinking, the most important shift is that from comprehensive to political liberalism, and the corresponding meta-political reconsideration of how we should revise theoretical terms and normative aspirations given this more restricted scope of the theory.[42] Pogge, rightly concerned that this shift has only further exacerbated the retreat from realizing the radical potential of Rawls's original normative vision, wants to force liberalism to deal with the pressing issues of global poverty and injustice. As emphasized throughout, my belief is that the reorientation he seeks can be greatly facilitated by formally making the transition from ideal to non-ideal theory, beginning with the recognition of how distant actual societies are from the Rawlsian ideal, and how misleading liberalism's official self-advertising has always been. The shift I am proposing, then, can be thought of as the shift from a liberalism both racial and patriarchal (in actuality though not in self-conception), which takes for granted – when not outright rationalizing – racial and gender injustice, to a de-racialized and de-gendered liberalism, which makes the remedying of these injustices its priority.

Note how such a framing inverts the standard approach. It is no longer a matter of starting from a liberalism self-conceivedly abstract and universalist and then – taking it at its word – asking (assuming the question is ever asked) how to bring race and gender in. This framing puts one at a hopeless disadvantage from the outset. Rather, we would be rejecting existing liberalism's misleading self-conception, and contending that actual historic liberalism has been so profoundly shaped by the needs, perspectives, and priorities of a white male minority that it has been conceptually and normatively structured so as to accommodate systemic exploitation and injustice along racial and gender lines. So it is not a matter of *bringing in* race and gender but of *taking them out*, not a question of (tentatively, hesitantly) seeking to "import" color and sex into a colorless and sexless discourse but of recognizing that the supposed colorlessness and sexlessness has been white and male all along. The challenge then becomes how to reconceptualize liberalism so as to correct for this legacy and its structural manifestations in terms of foundational assumptions, concept formation, overarching narrative, and normative orientation. In what follows, I will focus on race, because the greater representation of (white) women in the profession means that there is already a large body of feminist liberal work engaged in this enterprise.[43]

To begin with, I would suggest, the complicity of liberalism with imperial domination needs to be exposed, and incorporated into histories of liberalism: the underlying assumptions and overarching narrative need to be revised. Various scholars in political science have recently begun tackling this task – for example, Uday Singh Mehta's *Liberalism and Empire* and Jennifer Pitts's *A Turn to Empire*[44] – but the implications for political philosophy in general and for liberal contractarianism in particular have not, I would claim, been systematically thought through. Insofar (not very far) as these issues are discussed within political philosophy, they are represented as a deviation from the Western tradition of egalitarian inclusiveness – in the phrase of Rogers Smith, a classically "anomalist" view of racism.[45] But once we recognize that race is symbiotically incorporated into the thought of such key architects of this tradition as Locke, Hume, Kant, Hegel, Mill, Tocqueville et al. – their conceptions of personhood and property rights, their assumptions about fitness for self-government, their spatial mappings, and temporal periodizations – then we will appreciate that a liberalism founded on such values will be a liberalism that is white.[46] Racial exclusion and disrespect for people of color are part of the apparatus.

At various places in his writing, Pogge refers to the great atrocities of imperialism and colonialism, and uncompromisingly characterizes them as the crimes that they are, rather than passing over them in an embarrassed silence (if they are even remembered in the first place) as most contemporary white political philosophers do: "The North Atlantic states have, rather brutally, imposed a single global system of military and economic competition, destroying in the process the social systems indigenous to four continents. . . . [Their assets] were in fact acquired in a history involving genocide, colonialism, slavery, unjust wars, and the like."[47] Such condemnation is welcome, but we also need to ask what their nonrecognition *as* crimes says about the (actual, non-idealized) liberal apparatus. One of the distinguishing features of the contractarian polity is supposed to be the norm of epistemic transparency, in keeping with the Kantian ideal of a sociopolitical order constructed not for the aggregative common good but to guarantee respect for the personhood of all citizens. And this is a transparency both contemporary and retrospective, since there should be nothing to hide in the past. But obviously this only holds true if society *has* genuinely been a "cooperative venture for mutual advantage," free of structural oppression and systemic exploitation. If it has not, if the actual contract has been a racial one, then different epistemic norms are generated. So if social transparency is the ideal appropriate for the Kantian *Rechtsstaat*, social opacity is the norm required for states founded upon a white *Recht*, the *Rassensstaat*. These polities are, in Stanley Cohen's phrase, "states of denial," not merely contingently, but as a matter of principle.[48]

From this perspective, then, what might at first seem to be Rawls's astonishing failure in his book on international relations, *The Law of Peoples*, to say anything about the Atlantic Slave Trade, European imperialism, and the genocide of native populations becomes less a mysterious omission than a straightforward implication of a framework built on mystifying the past and present. If you begin by conceiving of society as a cooperative venture, which rules out structural oppression and systemic exploitation; if you continue by assuming the recognized moral equality of all humans, which rules out the actual normative subordination of the majority of the population; if you postulate autarkical nations, which rules out the history of imperialism; if you take ideal theory to legitimate ignoring both gender and race, whose very existence shows that they are constitutive of the basic structure you are supposed to be prescribing for; then how after all that can you possibly afford to pay any attention to the real world, when every assumption you have made is so flagrantly contradicted by it? It would mean that you would have to tear everything down and begin again, recognizing that historically the most important "outlaw states" have been the very Western nations which are your key normative reference point, and that your apparatus is hopelessly inapplicable once the actual experience of people of color is taken into account. And that, in effect, is precisely what I am saying we need to do with liberalism: to rethink it in a way that admits the centrality to its development of imperialism, racial exploitation, and the denial of personhood to the majority of the world's population, with corresponding consequences for its framing assumptions and normative priorities.

So the reconstitution of social memory – retrospective transparency – will be a crucial part of this rethinking. In Pogge's native Germany, one of the most crucial postwar debates was the *Vergangenheitsbewältigung* about the Jewish Holocaust, and a central theme was the importance of not forgetting the genocide, both to avoid repeating it and as a sign of respect for the dead. Thomas McCarthy has argued that these principles should be extended to the United States, in the memorialization through a rewriting of conventional histories of the black victims of American slavery.[49] Indeed the need for such a rewriting and the potential application of such principles is obviously global, given what was the planetary reach of imperialism. But the problem is that the politics of colonial exploitation are less congenial than the politics of Nazi genocide for such a mnemonic exercise, too centrally linked to the histories of the victors, as against a defeated Third Reich with none but fringe defenders. Better to forget a history that is so uncomfortably continuous with the present, and whose retelling might encourage people to make the conceptual connections now so carefully blocked. Since it is through such engineered amnesia that the racial character of racial liberalism is obfuscated and perpetuated, a self-conscious remembering is required for its exposure. Certainly it is not the case that the educational systems of these nations can be relied upon to inform their students about the ugly facts of the imperial past (and present).

Adam Hochschild's *King Leopold's Ghost* brought back to Western attention the killing of ten million people in what was then the Belgian Congo in the late 1890s/early 1900s.[50] But one of the main points of his book is the remarkable extent to which this great genocide has been written out of Western history. Near the end, Hochschild describes how a Belgian ambassador to West Africa in the 1970s came across a reference to the slaughter in an African newspaper, and was bewildered about the motivation for this "strange slander" on his country, which he had never heard before. As Hochschild explains: "There is no hint of these deaths anywhere in Brussels. . . . And yet the blood spilled in the Congo, the stolen land, the severed hands, the shattered families and orphaned children, underlie much that meets the eye. . . . The Congo offers a striking example of the politics of forgetting."[51]

The point is that rethinking liberalism in the light of this history should force us to recognize that the normative priorities of contemporary political philosophy are inverted, an artifact of white male racial and gender privilege. We should begin with non-ideal theory, not ideal theory, and with rectificatory rather than distributive justice. Once the completely counterfactual character of Rawls's assumptions about society and history are acknowledged, it should move us to reject his meta-normative hierarchy also. Society is not a cooperative venture for mutual advantage; the contract is not consensual; women, half the population, do not really agree to a patriarchal basic structure; and people of color certainly did not agree to white expropriation, colonization, and enslavement. Those already included in the contract (white males) can indulge themselves with speculations about how a society *already* conceived of in idealized terms as a cooperative venture (and somewhat so for them, at least in the modern period) could be made even better. Those excluded from the contract from the start will have as their immediate priority the remedying of their exclusion. Perfect justice is not even on the table – we're too far away from that for it even to be a live issue. The categorical imperative should be the correction of what, by mainstream liberal standards (once de-racialized and de-gendered), is flagrant racial and gender injustice, the denial of equal personhood, which affects the majority of the population and disproportionately determines the composition of the worst-off group. Making race and gender more salient to our accounts of historical injustice would go a long way towards bringing about a world better than our own and thus helping to "realize Pogge."

Notes

1 Thomas W. Pogge, *Realizing Rawls* (Ithaca, NY: Cornell University Press, 1989); Thomas Pogge, *John Rawls: His Life and Theory of Justice*, trans. Michelle Kosch (New York: Oxford University Press, 2007); Thomas W.

Pogge, *World Poverty and Human Rights: Cosmopolitan Responsibilities and Reforms*, 1st edn (Cambridge: Polity/Blackwell Publishers, 2002); Thomas Pogge (ed.), *Freedom from Poverty as a Human Right: Who Owes What to the Very Poor* (Oxford: Oxford University Press, 2007).

2 John Rawls, *A Theory of Justice* (Cambridge, MA: Harvard University Press, 1971).

3 See Charles W. Mills, "'Ideal Theory' as Ideology," *Hypatia: A Journal of Feminist Philosophy* 20(3) (2005): 165–84, and my chapters in Carole Pateman and Charles Mills, *Contract and Domination* (Malden, MA: Polity, 2007).

4 Rawls, *Theory*, p. 9.

5 For some recent work, see: Amartya Sen, "What Do We Want From a Theory of Justice?," *The Journal of Philosophy* 103 (2006): 215–38; Colin Farrelly, "Justice in Ideal Theory: A Refutation," *Political Studies* 55 (2007): 844–64; *Social Theory and Practice*, Special Issue: Social Justice: Ideal Theory, Nonideal Circumstances, ed. Ingrid Robeyns and Adam Swift, 34(3) (July 2008).

6 Pogge, *Realizing Rawls*, pp. 164, 252 n. 15.

7 Pogge, *John Rawls*, pp. 40–1.

8 Pogge, *John Rawls*, p. 27.

9 Though the evidence is ambiguous, some feminist anthropologists have argued that there is an inequitable gender division of labor in most or all hunting and gathering societies also – in which case, of course, the argument goes through even more forcefully.

10 Rawls, *Theory*, p. 4; see also p. 126.

11 See, for example, Orlando Patterson, *Slavery and Social Death: A Comparative Study* (Cambridge, MA: Harvard University Press, 2007 [1982]).

12 Pogge, *Realizing Rawls*, p. 30. In footnote 10 on the same page, Pogge emphasizes that he sees this as Rawls's definition of "what a society *is*," not "what a society ought to be."

13 Pogge, *Realizing Rawls*, p. 21.

14 I think this conclusion follows even if, in Rawls's later work, a case can be made that he *is* intending his conception to be limited to just societies. For the challenge still remains: how does an idealization so distant from the actuality assist us in realizing the actuality?

15 John Rawls, *Justice as Fairness: A Restatement*, ed. Erin Kelly (Cambridge, MA: Harvard University Press, 2001), p. 65.

16 Ibid.

17 Pogge, *John Rawls*, p. 124.

18 For a recent account, see chapter 12 of *Drawing the Global Colour Line: White Men's Countries and the International Challenge of Racial Equality* (New York: Cambridge University Press, 2008) by two Australian historians, Marilyn Lake and Henry Reynolds.

19 See, for example, Pogge, *World Poverty*, p. 92.

20 Frank Füredi, *The Silent War: Imperialism and the Changing Perception of Race* (New Brunswick, NJ: Rutgers University Press, 1998).

21 Carole Pateman, *The Sexual Contract* (Stanford: Stanford University Press, 1988); Charles Mills, *Racial Contract* (Ithaca, NY: Cornell University Press, 1997).

22 Pogge, *Realizing Rawls*, pp. 9–10.

23 Alan Wertheimer, *Exploitation* (Princeton: Princeton University Press, 1996).

24 Wertheimer, *Exploitation*; Ruth J. Sample, *Exploitation: What It Is and Why It's Wrong* (Lanham, MD: Rowman & Littlefield, 2003).

25 Charles W. Mills, "Racial Exploitation and the Wages of Whiteness," in Maria Krysan and Amanda E. Lewis (eds), *The Changing Terrain of Race and Ethnicity* (New York: Russell Sage, 2004).

26 Pogge, *World Poverty*, pp. 3–4.

27 In an endnote to a comment about the "academic justice industry's" "stunning failure" in ignoring the phenomenon of millions of deaths annually from global poverty, Pogge remarks: "But not unprecedented: many highly independent and progressive thinkers of the past saw nothing wrong with what we now regard as paradigm instances of severe injustice (e.g. slavery and the oppression of women)" (Pogge, *World Poverty*, pp. 145, 245 n. 248). I think he should ask himself whether the current failure might not be more than merely analogous.

28 Jean-Paul Sartre, Preface to Frantz Fanon, *The Wretched of the Earth*, trans. Constance Farrington (New York: Grove Weidenfeld, 1968), p. 26.

29 Edward W. Said, *Culture and Imperialism* (New York: Knopf, 1993), pp. 53, 59.

30 John Rawls, *The Law of Peoples with "The Idea of Public Reason Revisited"* (Cambridge, MA: Harvard University Press, 1999).

31 Pogge, *Realizing Rawls*, p. 279.

32 Mills, *Racial Contract*.

33 Thomas Borstelmann, *The Cold War and the Color Line: American Race Relations in the Global Arena* (Cambridge, MA: Harvard University Press, 2001), pp. 15, 6, 13, 21, 46, 6.

34 Lake and Reynolds, *Drawing the Global Colour Line*, p. 3.

35 Benedict Anderson, *Imagined Communities: Reflections on the Origins and Spread of Nationalism* (New York: Verso, 2006 [1983]).

36 Lake and Reynolds, *Drawing the Global Colour Line*, p. 6.

37 Eric Jones, *The European Miracle: Environments, Economies and Geopolitics in the History of Europe and Asia*, 3rd edn (New York: Cambridge University Press, 2003); orig. edn 1981.

38 Carole Pateman, "The Settler Contract," ch. 2 of Pateman and Mills, *Contract and Domination*.

39 Vijay Prashad, *The Darker Nations: A People's History of the Third World* (New York: The New Press, 2007), p. 65.

40 Jack Goody, *The Theft of History* (New York: Cambridge University Press, 2006).

41 Goody, *Theft of History*, pp. 5, 4.

42 Rawls, *Political Liberalism* (New York: Columbia University Press, 1993).
43 See, for example, Amy R. Baehr (ed.), *Varieties of Feminist Liberalism* (Lanham, MD: Rowman & Littlefield, 2004); and Lisa H. Schwartzman, *Challenging Liberalism: Feminism as Political Critique* (University Park, PA: The Pennsylvania State University Press, 2006).
44 Uday Singh Mehta, *Liberalism and Empire: A Study in Nineteenth-Century British Liberal Thought* (Chicago: University of Chicago Press, 1999); Jennifer Pitts, *A Turn to Empire: The Rise of Imperial Liberalism in Britain and France* (Princeton: Princeton University Press, 2005).
45 Rogers M. Smith, *Civic Ideals: Conflicting Visions of Citizenship in US History* (New Haven: Yale University Press, 1997).
46 See Charles W. Mills, "Racial Liberalism," *PMLA (Publications of the Modern Language Association of America)* 123(5) (October 2008): 1380–97.
47 Pogge, *Realizing Rawls*, pp. 262–5.
48 Stanley Cohen, *States of Denial: Knowing about Atrocities and Suffering* (Malden, MA: Polity, 2001).
49 Thomas McCarthy, "*Vergangenheitsbewältigung* in the USA: On the Politics of the Memory of Slavery," Part I, *Political Theory* 30(5) (2002): 623–48; Thomas McCarthy, "Coming to Terms with Our Past: On the Morality and Politics of Reparations for Slavery," Part II, *Political Theory* 32(6) (2004): 750–72.
50 Adam Hochschild, *King Leopold's Ghost: A Story of Greed, Terror, and Heroism in Colonial Africa* (New York: Houghton Mifflin, 1998).
51 Hochschild, *King Leopold's Ghost*, pp. 293–4, 297.

8

Responses to the Critics*

Thomas Pogge

1 Response to Cohen

1.1 The Strong Thesis and the Conventional Thesis

Josh Cohen's forceful critique seeks to defeat what he calls my "Strong Thesis," formulated as follows: "Most of the global poverty problem could be eliminated through minor modifications in the global order that would entail at most slight reductions in the incomes of the affluent" (p. 19).[1] His response does not mince words: "The Strong Thesis is . . . entirely speculative, unwarranted by available evidence and argument. I see no reason to accept the claim that changes in global rules would suffice to lift most of the terrible poverty that so many people suffer from" (p. 20). Cohen advocates abandoning the Strong Thesis via two revisions. He wants to see "most poverty" replaced by "some poverty." If we follow Cohen, then, instead of saying that, with minor modifications to the design of the global order, the number of chronically undernourished people and the number of poverty-related premature deaths could be lower by at least one half, we ought to say merely that such modifications could avert the severe poverty of some persons. This is Cohen's "Conventional Thesis": "*Some* global poverty could be eliminated by changes in global rules that would not themselves result in serious moral injuries" (p. 26; emphasis in text).[2] In addition, Cohen also recommends dropping (as a "theological distraction," p. 29) the claim that Western citizens are *actively* responsible for whatever excess poverty in the less developed countries is due to global institutional arrangements, that we are *harming* the global poor in violation of a *negative* duty of justice.

Josh Cohen is an especially useful critic, for two reasons. First, he expresses a reaction to my work that I have found to be very typical, especially in the United States. This reaction consists of the judgment that my claims about our responsibility for world poverty are obviously grossly overstated and underjustified, mixed with some annoyance at such flimsy claims being put forward and taken seriously in some intellectual circles. Secondly, Cohen does not merely express this reaction, but seeks to justify it – vigorously and elaborately. He thereby gives me an opportunity to address a carefully stated defense of that typical reaction in detail, which in turn enables our readers to judge the issue with the benefit of a detailed debate.

For the sake of perspicuity, I will adopt Cohen's labels for our two theses, though I note that neither label is innocent. The "Strong Thesis" label he attaches to my view suggests that it is a daring one on which a high burden of proof should be imposed. The label thus helps motivate Cohen's suggestion that we should feel obliged to accept and act upon this thesis only in the face of conclusive social-scientific evidence in its favor. The criticism in *WPHR* of the unfortunate dearth of research on the role of global institutional arrangements in generating severe poverty (*WPHR* 17, 27) makes clear that I did not take my argument to rest on abundant such research. Indeed, I offered alternative reasons (to be reviewed below) for accepting it.

By calling his view the "Conventional Thesis" and "relatively uncontroversial" (p. 27), Cohen suggests that it is widely accepted. I would think that the Purely Domestic Poverty Thesis (PDPT), which ascribes the persistence of severe poverty solely to domestic causes, is in fact more widely held among affluent populations. Cohen is right that the PDPT is "pretty obviously wrong" (p. 23) – once one thinks about it. But as repeatedly stated in *WPHR*, many people, at least in my anecdotal experience, do *not* think about it: They unthinkingly and implicitly assume it.[3] This is revealed when the issue of global poverty is discussed even among well-educated citizens of wealthy countries. Why do we not do more to help the poor abroad? The proffered reason is that such efforts are bound to be ineffective until poor countries first fix their own corrupt and ineffective domestic institutions. Such a response is then typically accompanied by a casual citation of the ineffectiveness of foreign aid as "evidence" for the claim. Now this reaction is not an express endorsement of PDPT. But it clearly relies on something like it in the background. So what to Cohen seems "pretty obviously wrong," as an explicit, reflective view of the world, is also pretty widely held as an implicit, unreflective view of the world among many citizens of the wealthy countries.

Accepting Cohen's labels with these caveats, I proceed as follows. In Section 1.2, I recapitulate the more important elements of my Strong Thesis and comment on the high evidentiary burden Cohen proposes to impose on it. With these preliminaries as a background, I then respond to the substance of Cohen's critique in Section 1.3.

1.2 The Strong Thesis and how to assess it

First, the global poverty problem. Somewhere around a quarter of the world's population are living in life-threatening poverty. They appear in statistics such as the following: 1,020 million people are chronically undernourished;[4] 884 million lack access to safe drinking water;[5] 2,500 million lack access to improved sanitation;[6] 2,000 million lack access to essential medicines.[7] 924 million lack adequate shelter;[8] 1,600 million lack electricity;[9] 774 million adults are illiterate;[10] 218 million children are child laborers;[11] 1,377 million people consume less per month than could be bought in the US for $38 in 2005;[12] and about 18 million deaths annually, or nearly one third of all human deaths, are due to poverty-related causes.[13]

Second, the global order. A central element of this order is the international state system in which any person or group exercising effective power in a national territory – regardless of how violently they came to power and how badly they exercise it – is recognized as entitled to act on behalf of its people: to sell their resources, to borrow and to sign treaties in their name, and to import the means of internal repression. Another central element of the present global order is the international trading regime as codified in the rules of the WTO Treaty and the TRIPS Agreement, which was made a condition of WTO membership. Other central elements of the present global order are the rules and treaties governing global resource extraction as well as the international banking and finance system, which makes it easy for corporations to avoid paying taxes in poor countries and easy also for officials of such countries secretly to transfer embezzled funds into private bank accounts abroad.

Cohen holds that the distinction between global and domestic factors is "not very helpful and probably misleading" (p. 21) and supports this claim with the question whether the 10,000 private voluntary labor codes that various firms have supposedly adopted are part of the global order (Cohen, p. 19).[14] While that distinction is indeed (as we will see) unneeded in the context of Cohen's own moral diagnosis of the global poverty problem, it has some importance within my elaboration of the Strong Thesis which holds that, insofar as global poverty is causally traceable to the design of global institutional factors, we citizens of affluent countries are actively responsible for it. We are not merely (passively) doing too little to help and assist the poor, but we are – through the foreign policies of our governments and especially through their active shaping of the design of global institutional arrangements – actively harming them, or so I hold. Still, what I really need here is not a precise distinction between global and domestic causal factors, or between factors that are and are not part of the global order, but rather a workable distinction between causal factors that are shaped, controlled, and imposed by our countries and governments in our name and those that are not. According to the prevailing moral view that, other things being equal, negative duties take priority over positive ones, we bear a weightier moral responsibility for mitigating the contributions that the TRIPS Agreement makes to poverty, for example, than for mitigating the contributions made by the high altitude of the Andes.

So what about those 10,000 private voluntary labor codes? On my view, they are not part of the global order. Instead, they are an effect of an important element of its present design, namely of the fact that, while the WTO rules contain very elaborate prescriptions about how member states must protect intellectual property, for example, they contain no prescriptions about how they must protect workers. To the contrary, the WTO rules protect the mistreatment of workers by imposing tight constraints on discrimination by states against foreign-made products that were manufactured under oppressive working conditions. Through these constraints, the WTO rules put downward pressure on labor standards in poor countries which, to attract foreign investment, must outbid one another by offering ever cheaper and more abusable workforces.[15]

Third, negative duties. Cohen dismisses as mere "theological distractions" my claims that we are harming the global poor in violation of negative duties. He suggests instead that, if reforms of global rules could prevent as much death and suffering as I suppose, then our failure to adopt such reforms should be called "barbaric" and "a moral disgrace" (pp. 28–9). I see no reason to retract my claims that (1) global institutional arrangements are severely unjust if they, relative to a reasonably possible alternative, foreseeably produce large excesses of poverty and poverty-related suffering and deaths and that (2) the imposition of such a severely unjust design harms those who avoidably suffer the effects of poverty as a result. Moreover, these claims are not only true, but also more likely to be effective. Inviting people, in positive-duty style, to help overcome a moral disgrace is unlikely to work. As discussed in *WPHR*, citizens of wealthy countries have (deliberately or unconsciously) developed highly effective ways of organizing their lives to make physically distant misery mentally distant as well. The vast majority of them ignore positive-duty arguments and contribute nothing or very little to charities that fight chronic poverty abroad. The conduct of these people will not be changed by lamenting the mere failure to change the rules in order to "help" the global poor, especially when this lament is combined with Cohen's watered-down Conventional Thesis, which is compatible with the view that supranational institutional changes would probably not help the poor very much anyway. Confronting these people with negative duties and the Strong Thesis, by contrast, may well have a much greater positive impact on many. They do not (at least consciously) recognize that representatives of their affluent countries routinely and deliberately shape and take advantage of global rules to maximize the benefit to their compatriots at the expense of causing severe and widespread global poverty. To be sure, many such citizens may find a way to rationalize themselves out of their responsibility for this fact as well. There is no guarantee of success. But this is no reason not to try.

The appeal to negative duties has further advantages in regard to tackling the assurance problems many reforms must overcome. Consider, for example, the fact that most governments allow their banks to accept large deposits from officials in poor countries even when the bankers know that the funds have been embezzled. It is urgent to end this golden opportunity for embezzlers. This can be achieved only if many countries tighten their banking laws. And this in turn may require sanctioning countries that continue to permit their banks to accept such deposits. But so long as such permissiveness is not seen as a negative-duty violation (as harming the people whose money is stolen), there will be little support for sanctions – at least in the Anglophone countries, where the reluctance to sanction positive-duty violations is widespread. Far from being a theological distraction, my demonstrations that practices we uphold are unjust and harming the global poor may be important for achieving the needed reforms.

Fourth, poverty eradication. Cohen and I agree that there are many factors that contribute to sustaining the global poverty problem and that the attribution of causal or moral responsibility among them is not a constant-sum game. My thesis is that the global order is one such factor and that modifying this one factor would be sufficient to reduce the problem by at least half. My interest in this thesis is forward looking: I want to argue, and thereby stimulate support in the affluent countries, for reforms in the global order that would reduce the global poverty problem. But the potential for such reforms can usefully be explored, as Cohen suggests, by looking backward upon the period since 1980 with the question whether the global order could have been shaped differently during this period in such a way that the global poverty problem would now be at most half of what it actually is.

Fifth, synergies. In thinking about this question we should, as Cohen does in an exemplary way, consider both direct and indirect effects of global institutional design decisions. The spread of high prices for advanced medicines in the poor countries is a direct effect of the TRIPS Agreement, just as the huge outflow of embezzled money from poor to affluent countries is a direct effect of there being no transparent monitoring or control of such flows. The high incidence of corrupt and oppressive government, especially in resource-rich countries, is an indirect effect of rules of recognition, accepted worldwide, that allow even the most illegitimate rulers to confer legally valid property rights in "their" country's natural resources. These pernicious elements of the existing global institutional order could have been shaped differently and could yet be reformed.

In addition to considering both direct and indirect effects, we should also consider the effects of several reforms in combination. Two good reforms may work poorly in combination – or they may achieve vastly more against poverty than the sum of what each would achieve alone. In light of these clarifications, we can specify the Strong Thesis as claiming that there is at least one alternative design of the global order, or one combination of reforms, that, had it been in place for the last 30 years, would, through direct and indirect effects, have reduced the global poverty problem to less than half its present dimensions. I contend that there is at least one such combination of reforms, and one that would have entailed at most minor reductions in the incomes of the affluent.

Sixth, evidence. I find Cohen's chapter hard to read on this score. Some parts suggest that he finds it evident beyond a reasonable doubt that the Strong Thesis is false. Other passages suggest that he believes the Strong Thesis is defeated if it has not been proven beyond a reasonable doubt. Of course, these two views are consistent: they offer different but complementary grounds on which he can set the Strong

Thesis aside. Disagreeing with both views, let me describe how I see the evidentiary situation.

The available evidence does not allow a conclusive verdict about the Strong Thesis, but *the preponderance of existing evidence favors the Strong Thesis over its denial.* By showing this, *WPHR* meant to serve two practical aims. One is to elicit additional evidence regarding the Strong Thesis. If Western citizens and decision makers find themselves compelled to conclude that it is more likely than not that we are actively responsible for more than half of the millions of poverty deaths each year, then they will be more ready to study the impact of their global institutional design decisions upon the global poverty problem. As it is, social scientists studying poverty in the so-called developing world are paying much more attention to local factors (which can plausibly be presented as being either the responsibility of people in the affected countries or else no one's responsibility) than to global factors like the ones I have been highlighting. I have written about why we should be suspicious of this research bias (*WPHR* 2–13) and should not confuse absence of evidence with evidence for absence of our responsibility for world poverty. Insofar as the paucity of evidence about the Strong Thesis is due to its being dismissed by those (e.g., the World Bank) who might produce more evidence, this paucity cannot be a good reason in favor of such a dismissal.

One practical aim of my work was then to stimulate more serious social-science research into the impact of global institutional design decisions upon the massive persistence of severe poverty. Such research would be of great practical importance if it were fed into the decisions themselves. What I want to support, then, is a kind of mainstreaming: an evidence-based assessment by relatively disinterested parties of the likely impact on the global poor of any global institutional design decisions before they are made. Sorely lacking today, such assessments would obviously have to be checked and refined by examining closely, *ex post*, what impact such decisions actually had.

My second practical aim was strongly to motivate citizens and policy makers of wealthy countries to lend their political support to global institutional reforms and to compensate for their share of responsibility for the very substantial contribution that global institutional arrangements make to the persistence of severe poverty. Like the first, this second practical aim requires showing no more than that the preponderance of evidence favors the Strong Thesis.[16] For, in the world as it is, the proper response to our epistemically imperfect situation is not to withhold judgment on the Strong Thesis until a more conclusive case can be made for it. Rather, if it can be shown that the preponderance of evidence favors the thesis, the proper response of conscientious citizens of wealthy countries would be to act as if it were true; for the consequences of underestimating the harm we do to the global poor are far graver for them than the consequences of over-estimation would be for us.[17] In certain scientific contexts, it may well be appropriate to reject hypotheses that have no more than a prepon-derance of evidence in their favor. In practical contexts like the one at hand, such rejection would be gravely immoral. It would be gravely immoral, for instance, to continue operating a lead smelter when there is merely a preponderance of evidence for its emissions causing serious mental retardation among the children of the nearby village.[18] By sug-gesting that we should withhold judgment on (or even deny) the Strong Thesis in the absence of more conclusive empirical evidence, Cohen ignores and under-appreciates the fundamentally practical orientation of my work.

1.3 Does the preponderance of evidence favor the Strong Thesis?

The six preliminaries covered in Section 1.2 have clarified the meaning of the Strong Thesis and the claim of harm to the poor and have indi-cated how it ought to be assessed. Let us now discuss whether the preponderance of evidence favors it.

Playing the role of the defender of the Strong Thesis, I have devoted much work to outlining reforms of the current global order and, where possible, have given rough estimates of the gains that the world's poor would reap from specific reforms. It is striking that Cohen, who so forcefully denies the Strong Thesis and claims that I have not made an adequate case for it, ignores or at best pays little attention to some of the most prominent reforms I have proposed and the evidence I and others have offered concerning their likely impact. I reiterate some of this evidence in the following section.

The effects of some other reform proposals are admittedly harder to predict due to a lack of research – as when these proposals are new and/or not yet taken seriously by the influential agencies or agents who might initiate a serious study. But, contrary to what Cohen seems to assume, evidence for the impact of specific reform proposals can be supplemented by other considerations in support for the Strong Thesis. Thus, in addition to reiterating evidence for the proposals I have put forth thus far, I will also draw on evidence about the relatively minuscule size of the distributional shift that would be necessary to halve world poverty, about the vast power the leaders of the affluent states wield over the global order, and about how doggedly and effectively they are using this power to advance the interests of powerful national and international lobbies at the expense of the global poor.

Regarding the impact of specific reforms, we can begin with existing trade barriers, which we have some evidence about. In both editions of *WPHR*, I cited one of several thorough UNCTAD studies, which states in its overview section:

> There is strong evidence that in many product markets that are pro-tected in the North, producers in developing countries have a competi-tive advantage or are able to acquire one. The potential for large overall export gains is underscored by this year's *Report*. It is estimated that an extra $700 billion of annual export earnings could be achieved in a rela-tively short time in a number of low-technology and resource-based industries. Agricultural exports could add considerably to this figure. All-in-all, the increase in annual foreign-exchange earnings could be at least four times the annual private foreign capital inflow in the 1990s. Moreover, unlike a large part of such flows, the resources would be devoted to productive activities, with beneficial effects on employment.[19]

Criticizing me for failing to meet the highest standards of social scientific evidence, Cohen ignores the book-length UNCTAD report I cite and its figure of $700 billion per annum (which does not even include lost agricultural exports). He writes that

> a complete elimination of all trade barriers in agriculture and manufac-tures would produce a $22 billion gain for developing countries [foot-note omitted]. The resulting dent in extreme poverty would likely be pretty small because most of the direct benefit would not be captured by the extremely poor, or even by the poorest countries, but, for example, by Brazilian cotton exporters and Argentine beef exporters (p. 27).

In light of my divergent figure and the significant bearing this divergence has on the credibility of Strong Thesis, one might expect Cohen to say a little more about why he takes as conclusive this undocumented $22 billion figure from an unpublished PowerPoint presentation.[20]

Cohen is right to insist that what matters here are not the additional export revenues poor countries would earn, but the resulting net income gains for their populations and especially for the poor. This question, too, has been the object of various serious studies that Cohen ignores. I have cited De Córdoba and Vanzetti, who calculate annual welfare gains of $135.3 billion for the less developed countries.[21] I have cited Cline, who calculates $86.51 billion[22] and, if the dynamic effect on productivity growth is included, $203 billion[23] associated with a poverty reduction somewhere in the vicinity of 500 million people.[24] And I have cited the World Bank, which had earlier estimated a poverty reduction of 320 million people.[25] All these findings are grossly inconsistent with Cohen's claim that protectionist barriers cost poor countries only around $22 billion in export revenues. In this case, at least, Cohen's failure to find evidence in support of the Strong Thesis is due not to any absence of evidence, but to his failure to engage with the evidence that is already available.[26]

While the dismantling of protectionist trade barriers gets some attention, Cohen's essay does not even mention various other proposed reforms, about which I and/or others have written extensively elsewhere, that would have a significant impact on world poverty.

One is the reform of global rules governing resource extraction. What is notable about the current rules is that they fail to include any mechanism – such as the Global Resources Dividend (GRD) – that could sustainably fund global public goods relevant to the realization of human rights: including goods important to public health, education, environmental protection, disaster management, arms control, peacekeeping, refugee protection, and the control of human trafficking, small arms trading, and illicit financial flows.[27] The omission of such a mechanism from a global institutional design thoughtfully engineered by wealthy states and endorsed by poor-country elites is certainly no accident. Indeed, wealthy countries such as the United States have aggressively pursued modifications of international agreements and adjudicatory procedures on resource extraction that have had precisely the opposite effect than would the GRD, effectively enabling a minority of the world's population – citizens of affluent countries and the elites of the less developed ones – to appropriate the world's natural wealth on mutually agreeable terms while excluding the majority of humankind from its benefits.[28] If there were a GRD in place, designed sustainably to divert about $300 billion annually of the economic value of natural resource extraction and pollution, then severe poverty (as well as resource depletion and environmental damage) could easily be much reduced.

Another reform proposal that goes virtually unmentioned in Cohen's essay concerns the international patent regime for medicines. Along with experts from a wide range of disciplines, I have proposed the

Health Impact Fund (HIF) as a necessary complement.[29] The HIF aspires not only to make existing new medicines more affordable and available to poor patients, but also to provide incentives for pharmaceutical companies to conduct more research on the many diseases that disproportionately afflict the poor. Fundable from just 2 percent of what the GRD would raise, the HIF would lead to dramatic mortality and morbidity reductions among the global poor by stimulating the development and active promotion of new medicines against heretofore neglected diseases that sicken and kill millions of poor people each year.

The dollar figures mentioned above certainly seem considerable – but are they large enough relative to the disputed 50 percent reduction in global poverty? To get a better grasp of this question, we should consider what the world would be like if the global poverty problem had evolved in a more benign way since 1980 by shrinking to less than half its present extent. In one sense, this is obvious: we can just divide by 2 all the poverty statistics given at the beginning of section 1.2 above. But what would it mean in economic terms? How large is the aggregate shortfall of the world's poor people from a minimally adequate income that would allow them to maintain "a standard of living adequate for the health and well-being of himself and of his family, including food, clothing, housing and medical care" (Universal Declaration of Human Rights, Article 25)?

The surprise here is that this shortfall is tiny – despite the unimaginable catastrophe of a billion people chronically undernourished. The World Bank, whose data on the poverty problem Cohen invokes, reports that 1,377 million people were in 2005 living below its currently favored international poverty line (IPL) of $1.25 per person per day at 2005 purchasing power parities (PPP) – and 30% below this IPL, on average. Their total shortfall amounted to 0.33% of the 2005 global GDP at PPP,[30] which, at currency exchange rates, was equivalent to about 0.17% of world income (sum of all GDPs) or $76 billion or 0.28% of global household income.[31] So a denial of the Strong Thesis comes to this: there is *no way* that global institutional design decisions during 1980–2005 could – without substantial reductions in the incomes of the affluent – have been made in a more poverty-avoiding way so as to effect, over this entire 25-year period, a 0.14% ($1/700$) cumulative difference to the global distribution of household income in favor of the poor (dealing them a $38-billion instead of a $76-billion aggregate shortfall from the World Bank's IPL).[32] Is this credible: that institutional mechanisms (such as the HIF), carefully designed to alleviate poverty and funded at $300 billion per annum and combined with an

Table 8.1: The aggregate global poverty gap for three different international poverty lines

IPL in 2005 int'l dollars per person per day	Poor People in 2005		Aggregate Shortfall from the IPL		
	Number in millions	Average shortfall from the IPL	in percent of 2005 gross world income	in percent of 2005 global household income	in billions of dollars p.a.
			at 2005 PPPs	at current (2005) exchange rates	
$1.25	1,377	30%	0.33%	0.17%	0.28%	$76
$2.00	2,562	40%	1.28%	0.66%	1.1%	$296
$2.50	3,085	45%	2.2%	1.13%	1.9%	$507

end to rich-country protectionism (yielding, as we saw, annual income gains of $86.51–203 billion for people in the less developed countries), and with multiplier effects operating over so long a period, would not have made a $38-billion difference to the annual income of humanity's bottom fifth?[33] Even if we limit the discussion to just these two reforms – the GRD and the lifting of protectionist barriers – it is not my "strong" thesis that is daring here, I submit, but its denial.

The denial only becomes more daring once we look at how shares of global household income have actually evolved in the relevant period. Using household income per capita to divide the world's population into 20 equal groups ("ventiles"), this is the evolution of relative shares.[34]

Table 8.2: The distribution of global household income and its evolution in the globalization period

Ventile	1988	1993	1998	2002	% Change
Bottom Ventile	0.139%	0.091%	0.076%	0.109%	−21.4%
Second Ventile	0.198%	0.136%	0.142%	0.150%	−24.4%
Third Ventile	0.239%	0.167%	0.180%	0.187%	−21.8%
Fourth Ventile	0.275%	0.196%	0.215%	0.222%	−19.2%
Fifth Ventile	0.304%	0.230%	0.253%	0.254%	−16.3%
Sixth Ventile	0.364%	0.266%	0.301%	0.297%	−18.4%
Seventh Ventile	0.389%	0.304%	0.349%	0.342%	−12.0%
Eighth Ventile	0.462%	0.360%	0.424%	0.398%	−13.8%
Ninth Ventile	0.523%	0.432%	0.506%	0.467%	−10.7%
Tenth Ventile	0.632%	0.508%	0.584%	0.552%	−12.6%
Eleventh Ventile	0.736%	0.604%	0.701%	0.663%	−9.9%
Twelfth Ventile	0.953%	0.773%	0.888%	0.810%	−14.9%
Thirteenth Ventile	1.210%	0.995%	1.112%	0.994%	−17.9%
Fourteenth Ventile	1.692%	1.285%	1.467%	1.306%	−22.8%
Fifteenth Ventile	2.383%	1.845%	1.982%	1.666%	−30.1%
Sixteenth Ventile	3.673%	3.076%	3.227%	2.481%	−32.4%
Seventeenth Ventile	7.317%	6.566%	6.504%	5.344%	−27.0%
Eighteenth Ventile	13.844%	13.696%	13.223%	12.678%	−8.4%
Nineteenth Ventile	21.797%	22.610%	22.335%	22.280%	+2.2%
Top Ventile	42.872%	45.860%	45.532%	48.799%	+13.8%

The data show that there has been a very substantial increase in inequality, with the top eight percentiles gaining and all the rest of world population losing ground. The share of the bottom 40% of humankind has been reduced to below 2% of global household income, and that of the bottom half to below 3%. At the other end of the distribution, the 6% of global household income that the top ventile newly acquired in just 14 years is *42 times* the 0.14% of global household income that would have been needed to cut in half the aggregate shortfall of those living in extreme poverty (i.e., below the $1.25 IPL). This shortfall would also have been cut by more than half if the global poor had merely maintained their relative share, that is, if the global poor had merely participated proportionately in global economic growth. As it is, they saw their relative position reduced by a staggering 20% in just 14 years.

While global economic inequality has increased relentlessly over the last two centuries, there has been an important shift in the last twenty years or so: with fast growth in China and India, what drives the trend is no longer increasing international inequality (among countries' per capita gross national incomes or GNIs) but rapidly increasing economic inequality within countries. The WIDER database on the subject lists 5,313 surveys for 159 countries and areas. Available data for 111 of these jurisdictions are spotty or show no clear trend. In Brazil, France, Mauritania, and Sierra Leone, income inequality appears to be clearly lower this decade than in the 1980s – in the remaining 44 jurisdictions, clearly higher.[35] The United States is a case in point. In the 1980–2007 period, the income share of the bottom half declined from 17.68% to 12.26%.[36] In roughly the same period (1978–2007), the income share of the top one percent rose from 8.95% to 23.50% (2.6-fold); that of the top tenth percent from 2.65% to 12.28% (4.6-fold); and that of the top hundredth percent from 0.86% to 6.04% (7-fold).[37] The top hundredth percent – some 14,000 tax returns – now have nearly half as much income as the bottom half (150 million) of the US population and about two thirds as much as the bottom half (3,400 million) of the world's population. There has been a similarly dramatic rise in inequality in China, where the bottom decile lost about half its relative share over a fourteen-year period.[38] While Chinese per capita GNI increased by an amazing 236%, the bottom decile gained only 75% during the period.

How have the world's rich elites achieved such stunning gains in their income shares – how, for example, did that top 0.01% of US taxpayers raise its share of global household income from 0.25% to 1.93% in the very period on which Cohen focuses our attention? Is this huge gain due to a sudden dramatic upsurge in the amount of hard work done by this elite? Or is this dramatic ascendancy of US financial wizards, corporate executives, and rentiers perhaps related to globalization – specifically to the fact that the world has come to be dominated by an increasingly dense and influential global system of rules that they are best positioned to shape in their own favor and to take advantage of?

I favor the latter, commonsense explanation. As those global rules and structures have acquired an ever more profound influence on the distribution of the entire global product, their design has come to be heavily contested. But only a few agents have the power and influence to partake in this contest, namely those corporations and individuals in a position effectively to lobby the more powerful governments that are shaping these rules with little democratic oversight. Being able to use the US government to exert their influence on the design of global institutional arrangements allowed the US business and banking elite to extract ever more value from economic activity at home and abroad, including the poor countries: from private investments both licit and illicit, from cheap labor employed and natural resources extracted in poor countries, from the sale of new seeds and medicines whose exorbitant prices can now be protected by patents everywhere, from protected monopoly markups on software and entertainment products, and from government subsidies and other favors obtained through inducements or threats to move investment capital elsewhere.

How does Cohen want to explain the fabulous gain to the US super-rich and the concomitant drop in the already minuscule share of income of the global poor? Did it have nothing to do with the wealthy states' new power to impose exorbitant markups, also in the less developed countries, on advanced medicines and seeds – nor with the ca. $1,000 billion loss these latter countries suffer each year from corruption and tax avoidance?[39] Does Cohen want to say that the outsized rewards to the super-rich were necessary to elicit their dedicated efforts (which greatly benefited themselves and stuck the rest of us with the bill for the Global Financial Crisis)? By asserting that there is "no reason to accept" the Strong Thesis, this is what Cohen commits himself to: the immense and rapidly increasing inequality between rich and poor plus the vast power wealthy countries exert over an increasingly dense and extensive global order plus their proven success in using this power to benefit their corporations – all this does not provide *any* reason for believing that there was *some* way of designing this global order differently so that those at the top would have done a little less well and the bottom fifth's share (which actually dropped 0.183% just between 1988 and 2002) of global household income would have dropped by 0.14% less in the period since 1980.

This would be a spectacular claim indeed, especially when combined with the evidence provided above for the impact of more specific reforms. And it remains spectacular even in the face of Cohen's celebration of the supposedly great successes against poverty in China and India: "Over that period [since 1980], under the actual global rules, extreme poverty in China and India declined by hundreds of millions. Under what alternative rules and policies would it have declined further?" (p. 33). I have long argued that the World Bank figures Cohen here invokes do not offer an accurate portrait of the evolution of poverty worldwide. The main reasons are the Bank's focus on money alone and its reliance on consumer price indices and purchasing power parities that, weighting the prices of commodities in proportion to their share in national and international consumption expenditure, marginalize the prices of those basic necessities that poor people most urgently need.[40]

But let us just put this critique aside and take the Bank's figures at face value. What we find is that the Bank is indeed reporting a huge reduction in extreme poverty for China: from 835.1 million in 1981 to 207.7 million in 2005. In India, however, there is actually a reported increase over the same period: from 420.5 to 455.8 million – and likewise for the rest of the world: from 640.6 to 713.2 million. Even if no greater reduction of extreme poverty were possible in China,[41] it is *pace* Cohen not at all inconceivable that global institutional reform could have led to lower extreme poverty elsewhere, so that the number of extremely poor outside China – instead of rising 10 percent from 1,061.1 to 1,169 million – would have fallen 55 percent over the relevant 24-year period to 480 million. Had this happened, the total number of extremely poor in 2005 would have been less than half of what it actually was.[42]

Of course, the World Bank's poverty line of $1.25 per person per day is absurdly low. Just imagine covering all your needs for food, clothing, shelter, essential medical care, water and other basic utilities and for an entire year on what can be bought in the US today for $500![43] The Bank also reports figures for a more adequate poverty line of $2.50 per person per day. These figures display a starkly worse trend: the number of poor in India rose between 1981 and 2005 from 650.3 to 938.0 million – about 85 percent of the Indian population. Overall, the reported number of poor outside China increased by 40 percent, from 1,744.1 to 2,439.1 million. Had this number instead fallen by half in this 24-year period, then the number of poor world-wide would now be under half of what it actually is, even if we accept that the reduction in the number of poor in China from 987.5 to 645.6 million could not have been improved upon through any combination of global institutional reforms.[44]

But there is also no reason to follow Cohen's supposition here. Even if national reforms had led (or could have led) to major reductions in the incidence of poverty in every country, this would not constitute evidence against the possibility that global institutional reforms since 1980 could have achieved a further 50% reduction in the poverty rate. Consider this analogy. Your physician claims that exercise will cut your risk of a heart attack in half. Your nutritionist asserts that switching to a heart-healthy diet will reduce this risk by 80%. Even if the nutritionist is right and, following her advice, you have reduced your risk to 20% of what it was, this does not in any way undermine your physician's claim which, newly specified, is this: had you not merely switched your diet but also begun a regular exercise program, then your risk of a heart attack would now be not 20% but only 10% of what it was before.

Let us take stock. In our assessment of the Strong Thesis, we have reviewed evidence about the significant impact that specific reforms would have on the net income of the global poor, about the relatively small size of the distributional shift that would be needed to halve the aggregate poverty gap, and about how single-mindedly and effectively affluent states are using the vast power they wield over the global order to advance the interests of their corporations and citizens, even at the expense of greatly aggravating world poverty. Taken together, this evidence is easily enough to support two key conclusions. (1) The current design of global institutional arrangements, with all the myriad privileges wealthy states have inserted for themselves and their corpo- rations at the expense of the poor, ranks far below feasible alternative designs in terms of poverty avoidance. (2) The elimination of some or all of these privileges would have lessened the shift in the global income distribution against the poor sufficiently to allow global economic growth over the 30-year period (1980–2010) on which Cohen has focused to reduce the aggregate poverty gap to less than half of what it now actually is. With these conclusions supported by a clear prepon- derance of evidence, it would be highly irresponsible for citizens and policy makers from wealthy countries (without further detailed inves- tigation) to refuse to adjust their conduct in light of the Strong Thesis. Accepting this thesis is not comfortable. But millions of lives depend on how we individually and collectively decide to respond.

2 Response to Tan

While Cohen queries the empirical evidence for the Strong Thesis, Kok-Chor Tan's critique takes aim at a part of the moral framework. Specifically, Tan targets my emphasis on institutions, casting his critique not as an "outright refutation" but as an "invitation to clarify" two elements of my moral framework (p. 48). This is an invitation I happily accept. The two elements in question are (1) my proposal that human rights violations be understood in an institutional sense as instances of official disrespect; and (2) that the global institutional order harms the poor even on an understanding of harming that invokes exclusively negative duties. Regarding the first element, Tan argues that my proposed understanding of human rights implausibly limits the class of human rights violations to those cases in which the victims and perpetrators are members of the same social order. Regarding the second element, he claims that, by forgoing appeal to positive duties, I am unable to reach the conclusion that Tan and I share, namely, that the global order harms the poor.

In this response I take these two points in reverse order. Section 2.1 shows how wealthy countries and their citizens do indeed harm the global poor by violating their negative rights. Section 2.2 shows how my view does not implausibly limit the moral assessment of institutional schemes to insiders.

2.1 Global institutions, negative rights, and harm

How are the affluent countries and their citizens wrongfully *harming* the global poor? Tan well understands my view that the affluent countries are harming the poor by designing and imposing global institutional arrangements under which – foreseeably and avoidably – many cannot meet their basic needs. But Tan believes that I lack the resources to support my call for global institutional reforms: "we can morally demand this of the rich only if the rich have a standing duty of justice to put in place institutions of a certain kind. Absent this antecedent positive duty of justice, it is not clear how the rich are letting the poor down by not imposing on the poor one particular arrangement over another" (p. 60). Tan is wondering how the affluent can be "unjustly harming the poor when the former opt not to support an alternative arrangement that is more advantageous to the poor when the only duty there is at the outset is the negative duty of forbearance" (p. 61).

Tan's problem arises from the argument in *WPHR* being based exclusively on negative duties, duties not to harm. But his challenge is not the usual one, which can be put simply as follows:

1 contributing to institutional reform is doing something (positive);
2 negative duties require only that one abstain from harming others; therefore
3 negative duties cannot require contributions to institutional reform.

In response to this challenge (as formulated by Rowan Cruft), I had pointed out that negative duties may well require positive actions as when, for example, the duty not to break one's promises requires that one repay a debt one had incurred (*EIA* 68–9). And Tan sees how this response extends to institutional reforms as well. He writes that when people undertake to "establish new institutional mechanisms and safe-guards to counteract or mitigate the harms that existing features of the institutional order could inflict," then their efforts "require positive actions and, because they are steps to correct injustices, they are duties of justice. Yet they derive fundamentally from the uncontroversial moral principle that persons have the duty of justice not to inflict harm on another" (p. 47). So Tan agrees with me that we are not permitted to contribute to the imposition of an unjust institutional order, and one way we can avoid such contribution is by reforming this order.

If this is not Tan's challenge, then what is? Tan writes that "even if the present global order is *disadvantaging* the global poor, it remains to be shown that it is *unjustly harming* them" (p. 60; emphasis in text). Tan is right that my account must overcome a gap of this kind, but his formulation does not quite capture the core of my argumentative strategy. My institutional argument is not formulated

> in terms of an independently specified notion of harm. Rather, it relates the concepts of *harm* and *justice* in the opposite way, conceiving harm in terms of an independently specified conception of social justice: we are *harming* the global poor if and insofar as we collaborate in imposing an *unjust* global institutional order upon them. And this institutional order is definitely unjust if and insofar as it foreseeably perpetuates large-scale human rights deficits that would be reasonably avoidable through feasible institutional modifications. (*EIA* 4–5)

My question about social institutions is then not whether they are harmful, or harming certain people, but rather whether they are unjust. Insofar as institutional arrangements are unjust, those who contribute to their design or imposition are harming the people who are being treated unjustly by these institutional arrangements – in particular those who are "worse off than anyone would be if the design of the global order were just" (*EIA* 55). The harm I am focusing on is then the specific harm of contributing to the imposition of unjust institutional arrangements.[45]

For Tan's challenge to engage my argument, it would then need to be reformulated. To conclude that we are wrongfully harming the global poor by contributing to the imposition of the existing global institutional order, my argument must show not merely that it is disadvantaging the global poor (i.e., producing more poverty than would exist under some alternative institutional design) but that it is *unjustly* disadvantaging them. Only if the existing global order is unjust can our mere contribution to its imposition count as wrongful harming.

Because the specific harm I allege consists in contributing to the design or imposition of an unjust institutional order, particular judgments about such harm are dependent upon judgments about the justice of particular institutional arrangements. In order to decide whether some agents' contributing to the design or imposition of some institutional order is harming other people, we must first determine whether the institutional order in question is unjust. Because my claim that we are harming the global poor depends in this way on an account of social justice, Tan is entirely right to observe that "what counts as harm is not just a factual question but also a philosophical one" (p. 60). The relevant philosophical question here concerns the criterion of social justice that is to be used for deciding whether social institutions, and particularly existing global institutional arrangements, are unjust.

Depending on how this philosophical question is answered, we might end up with a more or less narrow or expansive notion of harm. In my response to Satz, I illustrated this point by entertaining an outlandishly expansive account (*EIA* 75–6): if social justice requires that any social system be so organized that fresh flowers are delivered to all its members every morning free of charge, then we count as harming our fellow citizens when we contribute to the design or imposition of a social order under which some of them are not getting such free fresh flowers delivered each day. My account of harm commits me to this inference. But it does not, of course, commit me to the absurd consequent, because I can (and happily do) reject the absurd antecedent.

The exercise shows how I would respond to what Tan writes in his conclusion, namely that "Pogge's approach, focusing on harm and the responsibility to repair harms done or being done, does not seem to have the resources to support global egalitarianism" (p. 62). As my long-standing debate with Rawls demonstrates,[46] I am in fact committed to global egalitarianism, that is, to the view that the global institutional order can be unjust merely on account of engendering excessive (and self-reinforcing) socioeconomic inequalities.[47] When we conjoin this view with my account of harm, we reach the conclusion that affluent people who contribute to the design or imposition of a global institutional order that foreseeably and avoidably gives rise to excessive socioeconomic inequalities are thereby harming those at the bottom of these inequalities. To be sure, this conclusion does not follow from my account of institutional harming alone (which by itself, as we have seen, is quite inconclusive). It follows from this account of harm *plus* a specific account of social justice: only if foreseeably and avoidably producing certain large socioeconomic inequalities renders a global institutional order unjust can contributing to its design or imposition be an instance of harming.[48]

In *WPHR*, I deliberately set aside my commitments to positive duties and to global egalitarianism. I have done this, of course, to reach those who reject these commitments – to derive important conclusions from minimal and widely shared premises.[49] Thus, forswearing any appeal to positive duties, *WPHR* rests its case entirely on negative duties: duties not to harm. And forswearing any appeal to global institutional egalitarianism, *WPHR* rests its case entirely on this very thin criterion of social injustice: an institutional order is unjust if it foreseeably produces a substantial and reasonably avoidable human rights deficit.[50]

However, by forswearing appeal to certain premises, *WPHR* is not thereby denying these premises. Not understanding this point, Tan sees me as endorsing the libertarian denial of positive duties: "Pogge's approach may placate the libertarian, but it will alienate most typical defenders of human rights" (p. 54). My objective was not to "placate" libertarians (and the much larger number of those with libertarian sympathies), but to convert them – to show them that conclusions they may initially resist can be derived from plausible premises about negative duties. Thus, to justify any further resistance, they need to argue against those *specific* negative duties, and can't get away with simply refusing to countenance any enforceable positive duties. And my arguments to this effect need not be at all disturbing to typical defenders of human rights because, by making these arguments, I am not denying positive duties. I am merely foregoing appeal to them. All this is, I think, fairly clear in *WPHR*. I am not, as Tan has it, "beginning from" or "endorsing" or "granting" or "conceding" the libertarian tenet (pp. 47, 60–1, 64n.8). I am merely *not denying* it. The only passage in which I refer to the libertarian tenet says that my view "can go well beyond minimalist libertarianism without denying its central tenet: that human rights entail only negative duties" (*WPHR* 72). And analogously for my forswearing appeal to any criterion of social justice stronger than human rights: "Human rights thus furnish a necessary, not a sufficient, condition of social justice: that some institutional design realizes human rights insofar as is reasonably possible may not guarantee that it is just" (*WPHR* 25).

In sections 4 and 5 of his critique, Tan questions whether I can, without asserting positive duties, support a moral obligation on the affluent to work for institutional reform in favor of the poor. In response, I have appealed to two propositions, namely (1) any institutional order that foreseeably gives rise to a substantial and reasonably avoidable human rights deficit is unjust; and (2) by contributing to the design or imposition of such an unjust institutional order, affluent people are violating a negative duty and, in particular, are harming those whom this order renders worse off than anyone would be if this order were just. These propositions could be disputed – and defended. But Tan has not disputed them, and so I won't defend them here. If these two propositions are sound, then they show what Tan had questioned: that negative duties alone can give affluent people a moral reason to work for the reform of human-rights violating social institutions.

Let me concede that affluent people can escape this moral reason by ceasing to contribute to the design or imposition of unjust social institutions. They might do this by emigrating to a poor country, by living as hermits in an affluent country,[51] or by fully compensating for their fair share of the avoidable human rights deficit through efforts that protect some of the victims of injustice. In these ways affluent people may be able to comply with their negative duty without working toward institutional reform. These possibilities underscore the importance of Tan's insistence that we also have positive duties to promote just social institutions. I certainly agree that we do. But since they are less widely accepted than negative duties and also widely thought to be less stringent, the *WPHR* argument does not appeal to such positive duties.

2.2 Human rights as official disrespect

Sections 2 and 3 of Tan's critique concern my understanding of human rights and, in particular, my proposal that "[w]e should conceive human rights primarily as claims on coercive social institutions and

secondarily as claims against those who uphold such institutions"
(*WPHR* 50–1). Tan misses the important point that this is a purely
terminological proposal: "I am merely asking what the assertion of a
particular human right should reasonably be taken to mean" (*WPHR*
65). I made this proposal to capture the widespread sense that

> human-rights violations, to count as such, must be in some sense official,
> and that human rights thus protect persons only against violations from
> certain sources. Human rights can be violated by governments, cer-
> tainly, and by government agencies and officials, by the general staff of
> an army at war, and probably also by the leaders of a guerrilla move-
> ment or of a large corporation – but not by a petty criminal or by a
> violent husband. (*WPHR* 63–4)

This passage is making a linguistic point about how the concept of
human rights is generally understood, and not a substantive point
about the relative severity of various crimes. Tan gets this badly wrong
by supposing that my proposal loses the universality of human rights,
imposes no constraints on how participants in an institutional scheme
may treat those they regard as outsiders, and assesses any conduct that
violates no human rights as morally permissible or at least less wrong.
The next three paragraphs discuss these three points in order.

My terminological proposal preserves the universality of human
rights. It understands the assertion of a human right to some good X
as tantamount to affirming that all human agents have a moral duty
not to contribute to imposing institutional arrangements under which,
foreseeably and avoidably, some human beings lack secure access to
X. Those who are not contributing to imposing institutional arrangements upon me are then trivially not violating my human rights. Those
who are so contributing must, on pains of violating human rights, live
up to their moral obligation to see to it that all those relevantly affected
by the institutional arrangements they uphold have, insofar as this is
reasonably possible, secure access to the objects of all their human
rights. So our human rights-based *obligations* are indeed limited in
scope to those relevantly affected by institutional arrangements we
contribute to upholding. But our human rights-based *duties* are
universal.[52]

Tan sees my terminological proposal as undermining the common
condemnation of genocide and colonialism, which are generally
regarded as paradigmatic human rights violations: "it is a common
strategy for tyrants to declare their specially targeted victims as social
outcasts or nonmembers to justify their mistreatment" (p. 53):

historically, the most remarkable atrocities were committed by states against persons regarded to be unfit for membership, that is, against persons who are seen not as members of the common social order. When a regime carries out genocide, it seeks not to impose a social order on the targeted people, but to eliminate it from membership in any social order. On other occasions, as in colonialism, atrocities were indeed committed against persons who fell outside the colonizers' social order. (p. 50)

This charge involves three mistakes. First, the fact that the Nazis *declared* or *regarded* Jews to stand outside the German social order has no relevance under my proposal. What matters is that the design of this order foreseeably caused reasonably avoidable massive human rights deficits for Jews. Second, those relevantly affected by the design and imposition of an institutional scheme need not be "members" of this scheme. Thus I write that "social institutions may have a significant impact on present non-participants. The political and economic institutions of the US, for example . . . greatly affect the lives of many persons who are neither citizens nor residents of this country. We should allow, then, that the justice of an institutional order may in part depend on its treatment of outsiders" (*WPHR* 38). And I offer "an army at war" (*WPHR* 63) as one of my paradigm examples for when human rights constraints apply. An army is a collective agent organized by a structure of rules, and these rules may foreseeably and avoidably render insecure the objects of human rights of foreigners. The Japanese army's orgy of rape, torture, and murder in the occupied territories, for instance, is clearly traceable to how this army was governed. And the horrendous crimes of colonialism, as well, were (quite deliberately) organized and facilitated through a host of rules and regulations.[53]

The third mistake is the most fundamental. My terminological proposal of an institutional understanding of human rights was not based on a distinction among those who get hurt (e.g., human rights are at stake only when insiders get hurt, never when outsiders get hurt). Rather, this proposal was based on a distinction among types of *iudicanda* (from Latin, meaning "things to be judged"). We might sort objects of moral assessment into four main types: agents, the conduct of agents, social rules, and states of affairs (see *WPHR* 77, 100). This distinction is often flagged terminologically by using different moral terms: assessing agents in terms of moral excellence or virtue and vice, for example, conduct as right or wrong, social rules as just or unjust, and states of affairs as better or worse. Observing that the language of human rights is typically applied to moral failings that are in some sense official, my idea was then to capture this fact by confining the language of human rights to the domain of social rules and institutional arrangements. According to this proposal, a critique in terms of human rights thus is always, in the first instance, criticizing social institutions – and then criticizing only indirectly the conduct of agents who contribute to the design or imposition of human rights violating institutional arrangements.[54] On this terminological proposal, whenever we criticize agents or their conduct on human rights grounds, we are setting forth a very specific criticism: namely that these agents are contributing to the design or imposition of institutional arrangements under which human beings foreseeably suffer greater insecurity of access to the objects of their human rights than would be reasonably avoidable through some feasible alternative design of those institutional arrangements.

On the institutional understanding, the language of human rights applies, in the first instance, to social institutions. But the responsibility for ensuring that social institutions realize human rights falls of course upon human agents, both individual and collective. This responsibility has a negative and a positive component: human agents must not contribute to the design or imposition of social institutions whose design foreseeably produces a reasonably avoidable human rights deficit; and they should also help make more human-rights compliant any other institutional arrangements in whose design or imposition they are not involved. Because *WPHR* forewent any appeal to positive duties, it focused exclusively on the former of these responsibilities, without affirming or denying the latter.

Not having understood my terminological proposal, Tan is in good company – the proposal has been widely misunderstood. I have obviously not made it clear enough. But there is a further, even more serious failing in that I formulated the proposal too strongly. Crucial for my argument was the idea that agents can violate human rights by contributing to the design or imposition of institutional arrangements that foreseeably cause avoidable human rights deficits. This idea is essential for a plausible assignment of responsibility for many human rights deficits in the modern era, which are among the largest of human history. But I did not need, and should not have argued for, the rejection of the interactional understanding of human rights. There was no need to deny that agents can violate human rights in ways other than through their contributions to designing or upholding institutional arrangements. I have already apologized for this mistake in my response to Cruft, and so can simply reproduce this apology here:

At the core of my book is the view that the human rights of others impose upon us a negative duty "not to cooperate in the imposition of a coercive institutional order that avoidably leaves human rights unfulfilled without making reasonable efforts to aid its victims and to promote institutional reform" (p. 170; see also pp. 70, 144 [*WPHR*, 1st edn]). The human rights of others may impose further duties upon us, positive or negative ones, but my argument is meant to avoid any commitment, one way or the other, with regard to such duties.

It goes against this ecumenical spirit, and therefore was a mistake of mine, to have written: "In proposing this institutional understanding, I reject its interactional alternatives: I deny, for instance, that postulating that persons have a human right to X is tantamount to asserting that some or all individual and collective human agents have a moral duty – in addition to any legal duties they may have in their society – not to deny X to others or to deprive them of X" (p. 65 [*WPHR*, 1st edn]). This mistake may have helped to mislead Cruft, and I apologize for it. I stand by my defense of an institutional understanding of human rights. But I do not want to deny (or assert) that human rights also impose positive or negative interactional duties. Taking a position on this matter is unnecessary for the book's argument and hence best avoided. (*EIA* 65–6)

In the second edition of *WPHR*, I have accordingly reformulated the last-quoted *WPHR* passage as follows: "In proposing this institutional understanding, I need not deny that postulating ..." (*WPHR* 71). I can still affirm that, on my institutional understanding, "human rights give you claims not against all other human beings, but specifically against those who impose a coercive institutional order upon you" (*WPHR* 73). But I would now add that I am not denying an interactional understanding of human rights according to which you have claims against all other human agents that they not act so as to deprive you of the object of one of your human rights.

3 Response to Chandhoke

The central thrust of Neera Chandhoke's critique seems to be that my account of duties toward the global poor is too limited. Like Rowan Cruft and Kok-Chor Tan, she insists there are positive duties to help the global poor. As I explained, *WPHR* disregards positive duties not because I deny their existence but because I wanted to reach those who deny them. So I can happily agree with Chandhoke that there is more to our duties toward the global poor than *WPHR* acknowledges.

Chandhoke's discussion of negative and positive duties raises two further points worth discussing. Taken together, they lead her to the stinging conclusion that I "seem to be concerned more about the negative duties of the citizens of wealthy countries than about the human rights of the global poor" (p. 81). I will try to show how my concern with the negative duties of the affluent arises from my concern for realizing the human rights of the global poor, clarifying the problem of the burden of proof (3.1) and the problems I see with following Chandhoke's recommendation.

3.1 Do negative-duty claims have a high burden of proof?

On Chandhoke's understanding, negative duties apply only where a harmful effect can be conclusively proven. And she believes – the increasingly dense and influential system of global rules notwithstanding – that negative duties will then apply only in "very special circumstances" (p. 78). This is so because in our highly complex world many causal factors are interacting, and it is not possible to disentangle the various causes of particular deprivations:

> [I]n many cases of severe poverty . . . it cannot be conclusively established that poverty is the result of decisions of Western-dominated global institutions. Therefore, these cases do not invoke even negative duties. Take the case of poverty-stricken Mali. . . . it cannot be definitively established that the unjust global order is directly responsible for infant mortality in Mali. Global institutional mandates that discriminate against Mali might well form one, but not necessarily the determining, factor in explaining infant mortality. (p. 72)

Elsewhere, she writes that my "concern constricts the scope of negative duties only to cases where clear causality can be proved. In cases where causality cannot be established, millions of people will continue to live lives of extreme deprivation" (p. 81).

There is nothing in *WPHR* to support Chandhoke's reading. It does not say that for a negative duty to come into play, it must be *conclusively established* that some humanly controlled causal factor is *directly responsible* for some harm, and is *the determining factor*. Many of the causal factors I discuss operate quite indirectly. By upholding the four (resource, borrowing, treaty, and arms) privileges, for example, the affluent states are harming poor populations indirectly by enabling and incentivizing coups, civil wars, and oppressive government. And by imposing the requirements of the TRIPS Agreement, the affluent states are also harming the poor indirectly by inducing their governments to suppress the trade in generic versions of advanced medicines. Chandhoke's account of *WPHR* is thus incorrect.

Chandhoke may nonetheless be right to fear that "in cases where causality cannot be established, millions of people will continue to live lives of extreme deprivation." This is so because many affluent people are inclined to ignore or deny my claim that they are contributing to the persistence of world poverty. The General Introduction to *WPHR* anticipated such reactions, and actual responses to the book are full of ingenious (and sometimes indignant) attempts to show that we are either not harming the poor or else doing so on a much smaller scale than I had alleged. These denials echo all the points Chandhoke makes: it is said that I have not provided conclusive proof, that global institutional factors are at most a minor contributor to the persistence of severe poverty, that responsibility must be assigned to local oppressors who, incentives notwithstanding, have it in their power to govern well, and so on. The human capacity for haggling down the extent of one's responsibilities is limitless, and much enhanced, as Rousseau shrewdly observed, by philosophical training.[55] So Chandhoke may well be right on this point: most of the affluent will continue to force millions into deprivation, even if they read *WPHR* cover to cover.

So understood, Chandhoke's point is one I take very seriously. It is of course hard to believe that any piece of writing could stop global poverty. The effect of positive-duty arguments, made by Peter Singer, Henry Shue, Peter Unger, and others, has also been greatly diminished by rationalizations and haggling – though one must hope they have mitigated world poverty to some extent. Anticipating such denial and resistance, I do seek arguments and reform proposals that contribute as much as possible toward ending what I see as the largest crime of human history. And I have worked out negative-duty arguments precisely because I thought they would have more of an impact than adding yet another positive-duty argument to an already well-stocked arsenal. By forswearing appeal to positive duties, I hoped to stimulate some rethinking among those who had already concluded that they have no stringent positive duties toward the global poor.

Chandhoke mischaracterizes my negative-duty argument by suggesting that it has very limited application in the real world. She has good cause to worry that its impact in affluent countries will be limited. I care about half-hearted responses to my argument and recognize its motivational shortcomings. But I do not acknowledge as a further fault that it provides a foothold for such half-hearted responses.

For illustration, imagine this scenario. You are a well-heeled citizen of a rich country working on a project your firm is completing in India in partnership with a provincial government. When speeding along a rural road, you see a child playing on your lane and a bus approaching on the other. Unable to stop in time, you hurt the girl badly. Having substantially exceeded the speed limit, you bear some responsibility for the accident. You could drive the child to the hospital, insist she receive the best available treatment, and guarantee all expenses. But, with your good connections to the provincial power structure, you also have various safe options to do substantially less than this. In fact, you could probably talk your way out of the whole thing without paying a penny. What ought you to do?

If you are like many affluent people, you will instinctively rationalize and haggle. With no unforeseeable and illicit obstacles on the road, your speed was really not unreasonable. The child had no business being on the road, and, had she been properly supervised, this accident would probably not have happened. It is even possible that the child's parents had their daughter play in the street intentionally in order to profit from an unsuspecting driver, perhaps to fund benefits for their male children – generosity in response to an accident like this would only encourage such behavior in the future. The girl was also not well taken care of more generally. She was not sufficiently educated about the traffic she might encounter on this road and thus not prepared for a fast passenger car mixed in with the occasional buses and animal-drawn carts. In addition, not being well fed, she was also sluggish: slow in understanding what was happening and in responding to your desperate honking. Moreover, her body's responsiveness to medical treatment is clearly diminished by her undernourished state and her consequently weak immune system. The cost of treating her is further inflated by the fact that the local hospital lacks a competent surgeon – one would have to fly in a surgeon or medevac the child to the provincial teaching hospital. Another culpable factor is that your car was available for rent without liability insurance – the only requirement was insurance for damage to the car. If Indian officialdom cared about their people, they should make liability insurance mandatory!

Looking at all these causal factors contributing to the harm or to the cost of mitigating it – all unrelated to yourself – it can surely not be conclusively established that you are *the determining factor* causing this accident and associated costs. It cannot even be conclusively established that your driving was unsafe: had everything else been right, your driving would very likely have caused no harm at all. It would thus be ridiculous to expect you to pay the entire bill for the girl's hospitalization. Nonetheless, you were involved in the unfortunate event and so, as a kind gesture, you offer the parents $200. Ten thousand rupees, that must be a huge amount for them and, given their considerable fault in the mishap, they should be glad for your generosity.

If you are a morally decent person, you will respond differently.[56] Your first thought will be that the little girl may die or be traumatized, scarred or disabled by the accident. You will also think of the parents who are likely to be terrified with worry about her life, permanent disfigurement or disability, and about the debts they may have to incur for medical bills and trips to the hospital. Realizing that all you have at stake is a few months' salary, you will resolve any uncertainty about causal and moral responsibilities in favor of the child and, secondarily, in favor of the parents. You will be far more willing to risk spending more than is really necessary than to increase the risk of disability or death to the child or of financial ruin to her family. If there is even a small chance that something you can do now will reduce the harm the girl will have suffered from this accident, you will do it without hesitation. And although, given your local connections, you need fear no repercussions from doing less, you will think of your efforts not as discretionary acts of kindness or generosity, but as a duty strictly owed.

WPHR appeals to the sense of moral decency in the latter *you*. Obviously, any causal explanation of child deaths due to deprivation, in India or other developing countries, is highly complex and fraught with uncertainties. Even at the macro-level, it cannot be conclusively established, for example, what percentage of Malawian child deaths would be avoided through global institutional reforms (e.g., through an end to WTO-tolerated Western subsidies of sugar and cotton which are obstructing Malawian exports of these same commodities). I understand that corruption in the Malawian elite and in the local aid establishment is also contributing to the deprivation of Malawian children. I understand that some readers are not especially privileged themselves compared to their friends, neighbors, and compatriots and feel that they have little say in the design of global institutions and can ill afford to help alleviate their effects. In short, I understand that my argument leaves plenty of space for the former *you* to rationalize and to haggle, and then to refuse to do anything ahead of receiving a full accounting that conclusively establishes precisely how much of the global poverty problem is due to global institutional arrangements and conclusively establishes also the exact share of this harm that can be assigned to *you*.

I certainly want to work to provide as good evidence as I can in response to such demands. But I also hope to awaken that other moral *you* who, noting the huge disparity in vulnerabilities between yourself and children growing up in dire poverty, will conclude that it is much worse to risk doing less than you owe, and then being responsible for the suffering and deaths of children, than to risk doing more than you strictly owe as compensation, and thus giving a little extra help, beyond the call of negative duty, to people much worse off than yourself.

3.2 Are positive-duty accounts unproblematic?

In a flawed comparison, Chandhoke compares the power of the positive-duty approach in a hypothetical ideal world of moral agents with the power of the negative-duty approach in our actual world whose inhabitants are highly prone to rationalizations and haggling even when they have little at stake. The preceding section has shown how the appeal to negative duties can be effective in a world of conscientious moral agents by providing them with substantive and stringent moral reasons that apply far beyond "very special circumstances." The present section will show that, applied to the actual world of not-so-moral agents, the positive-duty approach is rather less promising than Chandhoke believes.

For Chandhoke, the positive-duty argument is straightforward: Human beings have various human rights. These include socioeconomic human rights, which remain widely unfulfilled. Insofar as this human rights deficit is humanly avoidable, it constitutes a human rights violation: "the human rights of 3.6 billion people that have been granted by Article 25 of the UDHR have been left unfulfilled, and thus violated. For the failure to enable the realization of the good that the right is a right to can be justifiably seen as a violation of the right" (p. 74).

To move from the concept of a human right to those of a human rights violation and violator, we must be able to determine who, when human rights avoidably remain unfulfilled, is to count as violating these rights – or, to put it more constructively, who is obligated to fulfill these human rights on pains of being a violator of them. Chandhoke's answer: "those agents who are in a position to ensure the realization of a right" (p. 76).

But what does this mean? Take Toby Ord, for example, who has recently pledged to give to effective human rights organizations 10 percent of his annual salary up to £20,000 plus everything above this level – easily over half his lifetime income. Ord and the members of his organization Giving What We Can[57] will alleviate, but not end, the current massive human rights deficit. Ord could live on £17,000 (US $27,000) annually and thereby give an additional £1,000 for the fulfillment of as yet unfulfilled human rights (thereby saving over 20,000 years of healthy life over his lifetime, according to the calculator on the Giving What We Can website). Is Ord violating human rights by not literally giving all he can? If so, then nearly all human beings would fall into at least one of these two (possibly overlapping) groups: those whose human rights are violated and those who are violating the human rights of the former.

I assume Chandhoke would want to avoid this conclusion. But then the question arises: in a world in which human rights are massively underfulfilled, what do those who have more than they need to fulfill the human rights of themselves and their families need to do to escape the label *human rights violator*? How much from each of us is enough? How much will ever be enough?

Of course, the positive-duty approach has produced answers to this question.[58] But as none of these answers has gained widespread acceptance, affluent people, prone to rationalizations and haggling, continue to find ways to persuade themselves that they are doing no less than they need to do to escape being human rights violators. This is the world we live in: human rights are massively underfulfilled and virtually all persons in a position to reduce this underfulfillment believe that they need do no more than they are already doing in order to avoid being human rights violators.

In the real world, then, the appeal to positive duties is by no means an easy, straightforward answer to the problem of global poverty. Such appeals have been made, with rigor and eloquence, for a long time[59] – while the number of undernourished people is reaching ever new records and the economic cost of eradicating world poverty is becoming ever more minuscule relative to world income. I support positive duties and am glad that good people continue to appeal to them with some success. But this success is surely not impressive enough to make a different approach not worth trying, given the vast number of people who remain in dire need.

To be sure, the negative-duty approach does not appear to have transformative effects so far. But it is reaching new audiences and may be playing some role in the increases we have seen since Seattle (1999) in tangible antipoverty measures, especially in health care.[60] Moreover, this approach has one important advantage over the positive-duty approach. While Chandhoke offers no criterion for deciding who is and who is not a human rights violator on account of doing less than they can toward fulfilling human rights, the negative-duty approach sets clear limits to each person's obligations: affluent persons must compensate for their share of the harm they together produce. And while this cannot be computed precisely, it can be calculated reasonably closely (*EIA* 79–80) – though this calculation depends on the particular conception of global justice adopted (see above, p. 194). To fulfill our negative duties, each affluent person need only do enough to ensure that, if all other affluent persons followed suit, the global poor would be no worse off than the poor under a just global order would be. On a minimalist conception of global justice, which requires only that global institutional arrangements realize human rights insofar as this is reasonably possible, affluent people do not have to do very much to fulfill their negative duties. But most affluent people are refusing to do even this much. As a consequence, the remaining minority continues to labor under substantial positive duties to help fulfill human rights.

3.3 Is WPHR Western-centric?

Having responded to Chandhoke's main critique, I will now comment briefly on her suggestions that *WPHR* is Western-centric. This suggestion is made at four points. First, she writes that "Pogge pays but lip service to the long shadow cast by the history of an appropriative colonialism" (p. 73). My discussion of colonialism, slavery, and genocidal conquests is (1) the centerpiece of my response to the libertarian assertion that today's affluent populations have a valid claim to their vastly disproportionate wealth and income, (2) central to my elaboration of the negative duty not to profit from wrongs and injustices at the expense of their victims (see *WPHR* 203–10 and *EIA* 69–74), and (3) one key support of the Global Resources Dividend proposal: "we must not uphold extreme inequality in social starting positions when the allocation of these positions depends upon historical processes in which moral principles and legal rules were massively violated. A morally deeply tarnished history should not be allowed to result in *radical* inequality" (*WPHR* 209). This criticism is therefore unwarranted.

Second, misreading my discussion of the Rwandan genocide, Chandhoke attributes to me the view that "citizens of the Western world were only 'bearably' responsible for the thousands of dead in Rwanda for two reasons. The people who caused these deaths were not remotely connected to the West, and the West did not profit"

(p. 73). I was, in fact, *attributing* this view to most citizens of the affluent states. My own view – elaborated in an essay[61] – is that these states
contributed greatly to the genocide and this not merely through the
past colonial exploits of Belgium and France. The US and UK contributed very directly to the genocide by successfully preventing
UNAMIR – the UN peacekeeping force stationed in Rwanda to
oversee implementation of the Arusha Accords – from doing its job.
They achieved this end through the complicity of Kofi Annan who, as
head of the UN Department of Peacekeeping Operations, was the
direct superior of General Roméo Dallaire, the commander of
UNAMIR. Annan sent several telegrams forbidding Dallaire to take
actions that were well within his mission parameters to prevent the
genocide. Later, after the genocide had begun with a daily death toll
around 10,000, the US and UK successfully lobbied for a UN Security
Council resolution (912 on April 21, 1994) that *reduced* UNAMIR's
troop strength by 89 percent.

Third, Chandhoke suspects that I reject the thesis of some dependency theorists "that the erstwhile colonized world can develop only
if world capitalism is either smashed or radically transformed because
intrinsic to capitalism is the exploitation of labor and raw materials
found in the Third World" (p. 70). She is right (cf. *WPHR* 299, n. 265).
I think minor modifications of the global economic and political order
would suffice to eradicate most present human rights deficits – though
such reforms would also need to be protected from revision by curbing
the opportunities of affluent corporations and individuals to buy legislative outcomes at both national and supranational levels. Much
greater changes are probably necessary to reach and maintain an equitable global distribution. This more ambitious goal is not my focus
and cannot be attained without realizing human rights first.

Fourth, Chandhoke asks why I make the achievement of global
justice the exclusive business of people in the affluent countries:

> Are we, who live and work in the developing world, fated to remain
> consumers of acts, whether these are acts of harm or of duty, performed
> by the West? Do those of us who live in India have any kind of duty
> towards the poor in other countries? And if we do not, do we lack status
> as moral beings who count? (p. 80)

I am not making the achievement of global justice the exclusive
business of people in the affluent countries. For instance, my proposals
for the reform of the resource and borrowing privileges (discussed in
chapter 6 of *WPHR* and in my "Response to Wenar" below) requires

efforts by conscientious citizens and politicians of resource-rich but economically poor countries to put foreign creditors officially on notice that debts incurred by illegitimate rulers will not be repaid by future democratic governments.

By addressing affluent people everywhere, *WPHR* gives no support to the view – popular among poor-country elites – that underdevelopment is the responsibility and task of the wealthy countries alone. Affluent citizens in poor countries should think about their own responsibilities to use what powers they have within imperfect political processes to achieve a more just society.[62]

The global poor should also play a role in the realization of their human rights, but their capacity to do so is severely diminished by the harms inflicted on them. This is why I have been working on a number of institutional reforms which could empower them. If I mostly address the world's affluent, it is not because I see the poor as passive subjects rather than as agents, but because I don't take myself to have any standing to advise them. I do have such standing vis-à-vis citizens of the affluent countries, which derives from the moral values they profess and massively violate. With respect to the poor, I want them to have more time and money and power so that they can effectively defend their own interests as they conceive of them. Chandhoke may feel more comfortable speaking for them than I do, but ideally they would speak for themselves.

4 Response to Ci

4.1 The institutional view and commonsense morality

Like Christopher Wellman,[63] Charles Mills and Leif Wenar, Jiwei Ci belongs to a minority of critics who have approached my work with the thought that it *might* be fundamentally right, might provide important insights into why severe poverty manages to persist on a massive scale and how changes in the thinking of the affluent could greatly contribute to overcoming this problem. I am grateful to Ci for his scholarly care and great efforts to reach an accurate and comprehensive understanding of *WPHR*.

Unlike Tan, Ci agrees with my institutional understanding of human rights and finds it compelling. He endorses my reliance on widely held views about negative duties, combined with the institutional approach, to generate the conclusion that citizens of wealthy countries have stringent duties to reform unjust global institutions and to compensate for their share of the harm these institutions inflict on the global poor. But Ci is also concerned that this conclusion, though justified, "represents a big leap from the way in which the notion of negative duties is typically comprehended." Thus, he wonders whether acceptance of my conclusion requires "a greater transformation in commonsense moral thinking and motivation than [I seem] fully to anticipate" (p. 85).

I find much to agree with in Ci's analysis, and accept the challenge to think carefully about how my work is meant to contribute to the goal of eradicating poverty. Such reflection must begin with a diagnosis. I see the massive persistence of severe poverty as a byproduct of a historical trend toward ever greater human-made harms being produced with ever less sense of wrongdoing – a trend that comes

> about through the uncoordinated activities of many influential players – each seeking its own advantage, learning from its setbacks, processing new information, and strategically adjusting itself to compelling moral norms by seeking to find and to exploit moral loopholes and other methods of morality avoidance. An invisible hand, rather less benign than the one acclaimed by Adam Smith, ensures that the world, driven by these self-seeking efforts, equilibrates toward a mode of organization that gives the strong as much as possible while still allowing them to be in compliance with their moral norms. Such a process gravitates toward the worst of all possible worlds to which the strong can morally reconcile themselves. (*WPHR* 6)

Disturbing this reconciliation by analysis of our contributions to the imposition of extremely harmful global institutional arrangements, I seek to encourage readers in affluent countries[64] (1) to initiate and support reforms of global institutions that cause widespread and severe poverty, and (2) to compensate for their share of responsibility for this harm by supporting effective poverty-fighting organizations. Giving the first goal its due weight and seeing how it reinforces and complements the second can help address the problem Ci draws to our attention.

4.2 Explaining the inaction of citizens of wealthy countries

Focusing on the second goal in isolation, I agree with Ci that simply arguing that citizens of wealthy countries are morally implicated in harming the global poor may not make much headway on the global poverty problem. This problem, however, may be due to causes other than those Ci focuses on. Ci is pessimistic on the grounds that, even if I am right that it is a widespread moral belief among the affluent that harming is worse than failing to help, there is also widespread skepticism among the same crowd to my applying this distinction to institutional as well as interactional harms.

I have a somewhat different diagnosis of how affluent citizens manage to remain unmoved by my arguments. This diagnosis puts center stage not the institutional character of my explanation of the persistence of severe poverty, but the (related) distance and apparent uncertainty of the relation between cause and effect. Most of today's affluent citizens in the West have no problem agreeing that the institutional regimes of France in the 1780s, of the Soviet Union around 1930, or of China around 1960 were grievously unjust and in fact massively violated the human rights of many of those upon whom they were imposed. And they have no problem holding those who partook in designing and imposing these unjust institutional arrangements – the French monarchs, Stalin, and Mao – morally responsible for the massive violations of human rights they engendered. If they do not assign to themselves any responsibility for the considerably greater harms that global institutional arrangements are producing today, the reason cannot be, then, that they reject wholesale duties to refrain from imposing institutional harm.[65] Most, I think, take cover behind a cloud of uncertainties as is so beautifully displayed in Josh Cohen's essay. These are uncertainties about how institutional reforms would be conceived and implemented, about unintended side effects they might have, about what overall difference they would make to the incidence and severity of poverty worldwide, about one's own contribution to upholding the status quo, and about what one can personally do to make a difference. Once a few such uncertainties are elaborately set forth, one is tempted to throw up one's arms and declare that "[s]ocial science is not that easy" (p. 25) and may find it ridiculous to attach any responsibility for world poverty to any particular affluent individual in New York, Tokyo, Frankfurt, or Palo Alto. The distance between one's own conduct and malnutrition in Haiti, violence in the Congo, or trafficking of teenage girls from Nepal is just too great. One's exact contribution to the massive global human rights deficit cannot be demonstrated, and one is therefore entitled to presume that it is zero.[66]

People think and rationalize in many different ways, and I don't want to suggest that the diagnosis I have offered fits all cases of those who remain unconvinced. But it fits better with my experience of pressing people on this around the world than Ci's diagnosis, which could be seen as one element in this wider account. My diagnosis invokes the apparent causal (and geographical) remoteness between the people responsible for world poverty and those whose lives are threatened and blighted by it. This sense of distance is heightened in a sense by the fact that my causal explanation passes through complex global institutional arrangements. But the ease with which we can see ourselves as geographically, causally, and morally distant from the global poor can also be overcome by a better understanding of the institutions that connect us with them.[67]

The way affluent people close themselves off from my arguments are then not very different from the ways in which they close themselves off from the positive-duty argument Peter Singer pioneered some 40 years ago.[68] The global poor are *emotionally* distant: most of them live far away and one knows almost none of them personally and is not engaged by statistics that document deprivations in the millions.[69] The global poor are *causally* distant: it is wholly unknown and unknowable what net impact (if any) my donating or demonstrating – co-dependent on the conduct of a few billion other human agents – is going to have on the lives of poor people in distant lands. And the global poor are also *morally* distant: one is sorry that they are having a hard time, but one does not think that one owes their problems any attention or concern.

It is on this last front, especially, that I hope to be able to add something through my appeal to negative duties. Many believe that one has much stronger moral reasons to help neighbors in distress than to help total strangers who live very far from one's own home and with whom one is sharing no bonds of language, culture, religion, or nationality. But few would endorse a similar gradient for our duties not to harm: the moral reasons to refrain from drunk driving do not become much weaker when we are briefly working in India or holidaying in Indonesia. They remain strong when those one is putting in jeopardy are not neighbors or compatriots but people with a different language, culture, religion, latitude, or nationality. The factors that are widely thought greatly to weaken ordinary duties of mutual aid are not widely recognized as making much of a difference to the stringency of our ordinary duties not to harm.

4.3 The importance of institutional reform

Even if, as I concede is unlikely, most citizens of affluent countries were to be convinced by my arguments and make some compensatory donations to poverty relief, this may not make much of a lasting dent in the global poverty problem because the underlying causes of global poverty – unjust institutions – would remain. Increased rates of donation to charities and NGOs dedicated to poverty eradication, if sustained over time, may shield a larger fraction of the global poor from the devastating effects of unjust institutions. Institutional reform, by contrast, could reduce or eradicate the problem at the root, greatly reducing the need for continuous mitigation efforts.

If my work makes some contribution to the struggle against world poverty, then it might do so in three main ways: (1) by showing that, as relatively privileged people, we have far more stringent responsibilities with regard to this problem than most of us had realized; (2) by foregrounding global institutional reform as the preferred strategy for overcoming the problem; and (3) by developing specific global institutional reform proposals on which we might concentrate our political energies.

Given the state of the world, there are many possible institutional reforms that would reduce human rights deficits. This fact contributes to the problem by making it harder to gather political support behind a particular reform proposal. Corporations manage to overcome their differences for the sake of effecting institutional change through a united lobbying effort, as in the case of the TRIPS Agreement. Those working for greater justice in global institutional design have been far less successful at uniting their efforts. Such much-needed unity requires collaboration and organization – it cannot be achieved by good arguments alone. But arguments can help, in particular arguments that limit the range of promising reform options.

To be suitable as a focal point of political efforts, a proposed reform should satisfy five conditions. First, it should have clear *moral appeal* to ordinary citizens of affluent countries, for instance by palpably embodying the idea that all human lives are of equal value. Second, it should also have *prudential appeal* to at least a substantial proportion of our policy makers, public officials, and corporate leaders. This means that a proposed institutional reform must be shown to be both *feasible* (once implemented, it must be able to generate its own support among those with the power to uphold or erode it) and *realistic* (it must be able to garner support from key stakeholders under existing institutions toward its implementation).[70] Third, an institutional reform should be *scalable* so that its inauguration is more easily achieved and also for the sake of keeping small any unexpected problems (a crucial source of learning in an institutional design exercise). Fourth, such a reform should *enhance the relative strength of those with an interest in further reforms* – primarily the poorer half of humanity. Finally, such a reform should also be able to serve as an *exemplar* that can be replicated in other parts of the global institutional architecture.

The proposed Health Impact Fund (HIF) is conceived with these desiderata in mind. Financed by a partnership of affluent and less developed countries, the HIF would give pharmaceutical innovators the option to register any new product, which would then be sold worldwide at manufacturing cost and be rewarded on the basis of its worldwide health impact during its first ten years. Through this straightforward mechanism, the HIF would provide access to new medicines that would otherwise be greatly marked up, stimulate innovators to promote the optimal use of their registered products, and incentivize the development of new medicines for heretofore neglected diseases. These three improvements would combine to yield massive health gains especially among the world's poor.[71]

The HIF would require long-term funding commitments to incentivize new pharmaceutical research efforts. Reaching the $6 billion level contemplated for the inaugural years will be difficult but not impossible. Here it is helpful that the HIF would broaden the profit opportunities and greatly improve the public image of the pharmaceutical industry while also ensuring a flow of important but inexpensive medicines that would save money for patients, insurers, national health systems, international agencies, and NGOs. The HIF is morally appealing because it values the health gains of all human beings equally and improves especially the (presently appalling) health situation of the global poor. It is also scalable, by enlarging the annual reward pools, and replicable, for example in the domain of green technology innovations.[72]

The HIF would render the existing global order substantially more just and would also be a promising start for an institutional reform program that would eradicate severe poverty. Achieving the HIF reform would require a serious effort by perhaps ten thousand citizens of affluent countries and influential people from the less developed countries. Those who do not wish to continue to be merely contributors to an oppressive global order can mitigate the harm global institutional arrangements continuously produce by supporting the HIF. Others may find another reform proposal more promising. But we need to bet on a limited number of such reforms and join our efforts to bring about *one* real example of a successful reform of the global order that manifestly reduces the massive human rights deficits this order is contributing to.

Successful implementation of one such reform could reduce not only poverty but the stubbornness of wealthy citizens' moral views to which Ci draws our attention. Once politicians and the general public can see vividly – through a successful structural reform – the heavy influence global institutional arrangements exert on global poverty and disease, the idea that they are responsible for severe poverty can gain a more secure footing in their moral thinking. This would help consolidate this reform, generate political support for further reforms and increase citizens' willingness to compensate for their contribution to world poverty.[73] I share Ci's concern about the possibility of persuading enough citizens in the affluent countries, but I am encouraged by the thought that once we accomplish just one reform successfully, further improvements would come so much more easily.

5 Response to Kelly and McPherson

Erin Kelly and Lionel McPherson write that they are concerned not with my "claims about causes of and solutions to global poverty" but rather with my "philosophical views" (p. 103). Although they share my conviction that the elimination of global poverty is a morally urgent priority, they aim to separate this concern from what they see as the implicit "cosmopolitan egalitarianism" running through my work – including *World Poverty and Human Rights*, which explicitly disavows reliance on such a view. Claiming that the moral urgency of eliminating poverty can be accounted for without endorsing egalitarian commitments, Kelly and McPherson advocate their own theory, which they call "cosmopolitan cooperationism." In this response I focus mainly on their interpretation and critique of my view before concluding with a few words on how this view relates to their proposed alternative.

5.1 Three distinct questions

Kelly and McPherson's critique is marred by a failure to keep distinct three questions I have discussed in my work to date:

(1) What is the most plausible full conception of (global) justice, whose realization would result in a fully just global order?
(2) What full conception of global justice coheres best with Rawls's conception of domestic justice?

(3) What is the most plausible core criterion of basic justice: one that
is widely sharable among diverse cultures and whose realization
would result in a minimally just global order?

Plainly, the answers to these three questions can be different. In my
view, they *are* different, and keeping the three questions in order clears
up much of what Kelly and McPherson seem to find puzzling and
inconsistent in my work. The following passages from their essay are
representative:

> Emphasizing a duty to eradicate global poverty is not enough . . . to
> substantiate the inconsistency line of argument that Pogge runs against
> Rawls. (p. 105)

> [W]e will argue forthrightly that commitments to eradicating global
> poverty and to global fair trade, which are targets of modest principles
> of global justice, do not imply a commitment to egalitarianism.
> (p. 105)

> Pogge seems sympathetic to two strategies for advancing the cosmopoli-
> tan egalitarian mode of criticism, despite his disavowal of controversial
> moral foundations. The first strategy is to argue that societies should
> have a fair opportunity for economic growth, where the criteria for fair
> opportunity should be decided by an agreement that representatives of
> all persons would reach when situated behind a global veil of ignorance.
> (p. 107)

The *first passage* exemplifies a conflation of my views on (2) and (3):
my argument that Rawls's domestic and international theories are
incompatible with one another is quite distinct from my efforts to
formulate a core criterion of basic justice that can be endorsed by a
wide range of fuller moral outlooks and positions (including Rawls's
non-egalitarian Law of Peoples).[74]

To the extent that the *second passage* intends to contrast Kelly and
McPherson's view with mine, it exemplifies a confusion of (1) and (3):
I quite agree that my commitment to egalitarianism is not implied by
my defense of a core criterion of basic justice that is focused on the
elimination of foreseeable and avoidable human rights deficits. Indeed,
if it were implied, then this would render pointless my answer to (3);
for those who reject egalitarianism would then also reject my minimal
conception of justice, defeating my ecumenical aim.

Finally, the *third passage* confuses (1) with both (2) and (3): My
commitment to egalitarianism does not threaten my "disavowal of

controversial moral foundations," because this commitment is not part of my core criterion of basic justice. And the claim that Kelly and McPherson attribute to me – that "societies should have a fair opportunity for economic growth, where the criteria for fair opportunity should be decided by an agreement that representatives of all persons would reach when situated behind a global veil of ignorance" (p. 107) – is not a claim that I rely upon but similar to one that I argue follows from assumptions that Rawls and Rawlsians endorse.[75]

While these passages demonstrate a conflation of the three questions, the first two passages at least correctly imply that my chief concern is to answer the third question: What is the most plausible core criterion of basic justice that would be widely sharable across cultures and could point the way to a minimally just global order that would not give rise to large foreseeable and avoidable human rights deficits? Given the depth and extent of global poverty today, which constitutes and entails massive deficits in the fulfillment of social and economic as well as civil and political human rights, this is the question that most urgently demands our moral attention. Let me therefore focus on the criticisms put forth by Kelly and McPherson that bear on this question, and on the core criterion of basic justice I have proposed in response to it. Doing so gives me a chance to address once more some of the most common misunderstandings of *WPHR*. With this aim in mind, I consider in turn Kelly and McPherson's doubts about the minimalism of my conception of justice, their attempt to defend Rawls against the criticisms I raise in the book, and their proposed "cosmopolitan cooperationism."

5.2 The minimalism of WPHR

Kelly and McPherson raise questions about whether my minimal conception of justice is really as minimal as I claim it to be. Specifically, they write that "the notion of human rights that Pogge relies on to identify harms is more expansive than commonly recognized prohibitions and bears a strong relation to his earlier, more explicit egalitarian commitments" (p. 104). The only evidence they cite for this claim is chapter 5 of *WPHR*, which supposedly reveals that I am "drawn to a Lockean account of economic justice, which begins from the idea that persons have equal moral claims on natural resources" (p. 104).

Clearing up two interrelated mistakes involved in this characterization can help clarify the conception of justice presented in *WPHR* and the way in which it is minimal. First, *pace* Kelly and McPherson's suggestion, I am not myself "drawn to a Lockean account of economic justice," nor is such an account part of my minimal conception of justice. My brief discussion of Locke was meant to provide a "less controversial argument" for the conclusion that the global order harms the poor – an argument that "avoid[s] the controversial appeal to *relative* harms, involving comparisons across alternative economic orders, by appealing instead to a more robust noninstitutional baseline" (*WPHR* 142–3). This does not imply that I reject a relative notion of harm, which I write is "not beyond defense" (*WPHR* 142). Rather, in seeking diverse ways of supporting my criterion, I also invoke premises that are at home in a more conservative Lockean view. My core criterion of basic justice is, then, neutral between the Lockean view and more cosmopolitan views. The aim is to show that many can endorse my criterion while remaining faithful to their own philosophical commitments.[76]

This brings us to the second mistake: Kelly and McPherson falsely imply that the Lockean conception of economic justice is itself egalitarian in a way that makes it ill-suited for my ecumenical aims. Locke's conception is egalitarian only in the anodyne sense that "in a preinstitutional state of nature, persons have equal moral claims on all natural resources" (*WPHR* 143). No serious view holds otherwise. But beyond this unexciting premise, it is far from egalitarian.[77] Thus, although Locke's conception does affirm certain noncomparative entitlements, it does not disfavor inequality as such and even subjects voting rights to a property qualification.

The Lockean argument brings out the way *WPHR*'s conception of justice is minimal. In both its premises and its demands for institutional reform, this conception avoids taking a stand that contradicts mainstream moral views, including noncosmopolitan views that I would otherwise take exception to.

5.3 The contrast between WPHR and The Law of Peoples

As noted, my claims about what conception of global justice Rawls should support, given the express commitments of his domestic theory, are distinct from my efforts in *WPHR* to formulate a core criterion of basic justice. Here Kelly and McPherson may have been misled by my bringing Rawls's theory into my argument at various points. Let me then explain how my minimal conception relates to Rawls's *Law of Peoples*.

As already suggested, Kelly and McPherson are incorrect in their claim that, in contrast to Rawls, the moral universalism of *WPHR* is committed to the idea that "fairness would require an equal distribution of social and economic benefits, except when there is a morally compelling rationale for departures from equality" (p. 109). The chapter they cite is committed to no such view. Far from advocating worldwide distributive equality, it invokes a widely held basic moral universalism (*WPHR* 98) in order to criticize citizens of affluent countries for incoherently endorsing two minimal justice requirements within any country while rejecting them on the global level: "The first minimal requirement is that, at least within the limits of what justice allows, social rules should be liable to peaceful change by any large majority of those on whom they are imposed. . . . The second minimal requirement is that avoidable life-threatening poverty must be avoided" (*WPHR* 102). Even Rawls could support these requirements, and neither of them comes close to the "default view of fairness" Kelly and McPherson ascribe to *WPHR*.[78]

For all their skepticism of moral universalism, Kelly and McPherson write:

> A humanitarian duty of assistance recognizes the moral arbitrariness, on some level, of national boundaries with regard to the basic needs of persons. Active concern for basic needs would seem to represent a moral minimum in the domestic and global spheres of justice. Discounting the moral significance of national boundaries – that is, regarding basic needs – emphasizes that a humanitarian duty of assistance is directly responsive to persons. (p. 114)

To be sure, Kelly and McPherson's "moral minimum" addresses a question that is different from my own: their minimum concerns the needs of others it would be wrong to ignore even if they are foreigners, whereas mine concerns the threshold conditions institutional rules must meet for it to be permissible to impose them on others. While neither is stronger or weaker than the other as a matter of logic alone, it is hard to imagine someone accepting Kelly and McPherson's while rejecting mine: If, as they recognize, it's wrong not to help fulfill basic needs abroad if one can easily do so, then it is surely no less wrong to impose global institutional arrangements that foreseeably cause large basic needs deficits that another design of those same global institutions could reasonably avoid at little cost to ourselves.

Rawls believes that our responsibilities with regard to world poverty boil down to a duty of assistance and that the persistence of severe poverty is due solely to domestic causes:

> the causes of the wealth of a people and the forms it takes lie in their political culture and in the religious, philosophical and moral traditions that support the basic structure of their political and social institutions, as well as in the industriousness and cooperative talents of its members, all supported by their political virtues.[79]

WPHR, by contrast, sees most severe poverty as traceable to unjust supranational institutional arrangements that cause severe poverty either directly or indirectly by helping to support and perpetuate oppression, corruption, and violent conflict in poor countries. Speaking from the standpoint of my minimal conception of justice, I do not dispute Rawls's (poorly defended) rejection of any egalitarian principle of global distributive justice, but I do dispute his empirical explanation of severe poverty and his view that a mere duty of assistance, without reforms of the global institutional order, provides a sufficient response to world poverty.[80] These two flaws render Rawls's international theory unpromising as a basis for addressing questions of basic justice and institutional reform.

5.4 Cosmopolitan cooperationism

Let me close with a few words about how Kelly and McPherson's addition to Rawls's theory – their so-called cosmopolitan cooperationism (see their discussion on p. 113) – intersects with my minimal conception. To the extent that their proposal goes beyond the mere duty of assistance and begins to address some of the systemic injustices of present global institutional arrangements (especially the international trade regime), it is a welcome step toward addressing the root causes of severe poverty.

Without analyzing their proposals in detail, I would emphasize that such proposals should meet two tests: they must be *feasible*, generating their own support among the more influential stakeholders as they would exist under the reformed regime; and they must be *realistic*, garnering within the current regime sufficient support for implementation (see note 70). Needless to say, the cosmopolitan cooperationist view is compatible with my minimal conception of justice, and so, as with conceptions of human rights based on positive duties, I see no reason to reject it, especially as the "duty of just engagement" adds a concern with reciprocity in global economic relations that was lacking in Rawls's *Law of Peoples*.

6 Response to Wenar

Before responding to Leif Wenar's doubts about my proposals to reform the resource privilege, I should note that it is very gratifying to find in his essay two related points of agreement. First, we both understand that what is commonly called the "resource curse" is not some unaccountable destiny – like poor soil or proximity to a fault line – but a human-made disaster caused by the resource privilege: the worldwide legal recognition of those who have power in a country as entitled to confer legally valid ownership rights in this country's natural resources to foreign buyers. Second, we both seek to use this understanding toward practical, political ends. We seek ways of reforming the resource privilege so as to curb its fuelling violent political conflicts, oppressive national regimes, and rampant corruption in the less developed countries.

The main targets of Wenar's essay are my proposed reforms to the resource privilege: the constitutional amendment and Democracy Panel. And his main worries are practical: whether implementation of the reforms is politically feasible and whether they would be effective in mitigating the resource curse and in improving the prospects for democracy in resource-rich poor countries. As an alternative to my democracy-based reforms, he proposes his own set of reforms based on the concept of property rights. Prior to this main critique, Wenar also expresses some differences in his understanding of the responsibility of wealthy countries and their citizens in the *imposition* of the privilege. As this part of his essay is tangential to his main critique, I will comment on it only briefly before concentrating the remainder of my reply on comparing our respective proposals for reforming the resource privilege.

6.1 Imposition without collaboration

Wenar is skeptical about my claim that the affluent countries and their citizens collectively impose the resource and borrowing privileges, because he takes this claim to presuppose a denial of anarchy in international relations:

> According to Pogge, the citizens and governments of the rich countries
> (perhaps in concert with the leaders of poor countries) impose the major
> structural rules of the global economic order like the two international
> privileges, meaning that in some sense these actors have coercive control
> over setting and enforcing these rules. According to mainstream inter-
> national relations theory, there is no agent that has such coercive control
> – any more than there is such an agent in classic state of nature theories.
> (p. 131)

In fact, however, collective imposition is compatible with anarchy
in international relations. In calling the imposition of the resource and
borrowing privileges *collective*, I am not implying that this imposition
is *collaborative*, as though there were some international agency or
treaty mechanism that officially accorded rulers of less developed
countries resource and borrowing privileges that affluent countries are
then required to enforce. The worldwide practice of legal recognition
I critique is not one that the affluent countries collaborate to impose
upon themselves or one another. There is no need for collaboration in
this sense because the practice serves the interests of each affluent
country by enabling it to secure a steady supply of cheap resources for
its firms and population. The practice persists, then, through the
willing participation of the affluent countries, amplified by eager
support from the ruling elites of the poorer countries. Imposition
comes into view only when we examine what this treasured practice
does to the rest of humankind, to the typical citizens of poor countries.
They are coercively deprived of control over their natural resources
and rarely benefit from the revenues generated by their sale. They
are victimized by rulers who fund their violent oppression and
embezzlement by selling the people's resources and burdening them
with debt. They are raped and killed by the millions in violent struggles
for power that are incentivized by the prospect of capturing some
country's resource and borrowing privileges (and fuelled by arms sales
from richer countries). And they suffer the disastrous environmental
harms caused by the rush to maximize revenues from natural-resource
sales.

Wenar organizes his constructive critique of my proposed reform
of the resource privilege according to four separate components: the
grounding value problem, the criterial problem, the authoritative
notice problem, and the enforcement problem. In discussing Wenar's
objections, I will pay special attention to how his approach differs
from mine in each of these dimensions. I then conclude by considering
some additional issues he raises regarding my proposal.

6.2 The grounding value and criterion
for resource ownership and transfer

Wenar defines the *grounding value* problem by reference to the question: "to which values should reformers appeal to distinguish among the regimes currently offering resources on the international market?" (p. 134). He then characterizes us as differing on the question of grounding value, with me proposing democracy for this role while he proposes property rights instead:

> the value of enforcing property rights is a value that no corporation or rich government can credibly deny [footnote omitted]. The [Wenar's] proposal presents itself as a demand that the major players in the global market correct large-scale violations of property rights. Such a demand is considerably less contestable than a demand to boost democracy in resource-rich countries. (p. 137)

The opposition Wenar constructs here mischaracterizes both my position and his own. My grounding value is not democracy but human rights. I oppose the resource privilege because it promotes violence, oppression, and poverty, thereby contributing substantially to massive human rights deficits in poor countries with large natural-resource endowments. Moreover, my critique and proposed reform turn more fundamentally on property rights than on democracy: I argue that a realistic path toward greater fulfillment of human rights would aim for an international understanding that a country's resources belong to its people and that their sale must therefore be (directly or indirectly) authorized by them. A democratically elected government can be presumed to have such authorization, to be selling national resources with their owners' consent. National-resource sales by a junta reigning in the wake of a military coup cannot reasonably be presumed to be so authorized. When we purchase such resources, we are, as Wenar quotes me as writing, involved in "dispossessing the local population and the rest of humankind" (p. 132).[81]

The property rights of a country's people in its national resources may well be the grounding value of Wenar's own account. His commitment to such property rights appears to be fundamental (grounded in natural law, perhaps) rather than grounded instrumentally in human rights. Still, he mischaracterizes his position by suggesting that it can find *sufficient* grounding in property rights. In fact, the principle that a country's resources belong to its people does not enable a distinction between legitimate and illegitimate sales. So Wenar needs something further, some analogue to my broadly democratic authorization, to make this distinction. He proposes something less demanding for this role: *possible* consent.[82]

How are we to judge, according to Wenar, whether a people could have consented to a sale of its resources? In response, he reverts to his official grounding value: our ordinary understanding and practice of property rights:

> For an owner to be able to authorize sales, the owner must at least: (1) be able to find out about the sales; (2) be able to stop the sales without incurring severe costs; and (3) not be subject to extreme manipulation by the seller. If these minimal conditions do not obtain, neither the assent nor the silence of the owner can possibly authorize any sale of that owner's property. (p. 141)

Through the expression "at least" Wenar indicates that he thinks of these demands as necessary conditions. So understood, they are credible – few would dispute that meeting these three conditions is necessary for valid sales. But if Wenar's appeal to our ordinary understanding and practice of property rights is supposed to help him against those who, like me, have proposed a more demanding criterion, then he needs to show that the three conditions he has listed are *sufficient* for valid sales. Wenar does not make this claim, and few of his readers would, I suspect, agree with it. Would you agree that another person's sale of your car or land, and pocketing of the proceeds, is valid so long as merely you (1) were able to find out about the sale, (2) were able to stop the sale without incurring severe costs, and (3) were not subject to extreme manipulation by the seller? I would be surprised. Of course, the one additional element whose presence, in conjunction with the others, *would* legitimate the sale of your car or land is that you (4) actually authorized the sale. What this shows is that Wenar's three conditions cannot possibly serve as an explication of the notion of consent itself, not even in the limited sphere of property sales. Rather they are, at best, necessary conditions for a sale's legitimacy. So what Wenar needs as a supplement to his account in the context of a people and its resources is something corresponding to condition (4): authorization. And this, I would think, requires some sort of democratic exercise.

Let us examine Wenar's problem more closely by observing how he uses his points about ordinary property rights to construct his criterion for the validity of international resource sales. He demands that citizens must have at least minimal civil liberties and political rights. There must be, that is, at least some absolutely minimal press freedom if citizens are to have access to information about what resource deals the regime is making. The regime must not be so deeply opaque that it is impossible for the people to find out what happens to the revenues from resource sales. Citizens must be able to pass information about the regime to each other without fear of surveillance and arrest. The regime must put some effective political mechanisms in place through which the people can express their unhappiness about resource sales: at least a non-elected consultative legislature that advises the regime, or at the very least occasions on which individuals or civic groups can present petitions. There must also be a minimally adequate rule of law, ensuring that citizens who wish to protest resource sales publicly and peacefully may do so without fear of cruel judicial punishment, disappearance, serious injury, or death. (pp. 141–2)

Wenar again expressly ("at least") characterizes as merely *necessary* conditions the demands he is here making on a national regime in order for it to be regarded as capable of effecting valid governmental resources sales. I agree, of course, with Wenar and against the status quo, that meeting these demands should be considered necessary for valid governmental transfers of ownership rights in national resources. But to support his case against those who, like I, favor a more demanding standard, Wenar would need to show that the conditions he formulates are *sufficient* for valid sales.

To see the difficulty, suppose Wenar's rules – or rather their proposed proxy: Freedom House ratings – were recognized and observed worldwide, so that any regime not meeting the minimal conditions just quoted would really not be able to receive money in exchange for resources of the country it rules. In such a world, de facto governments would have powerful incentives to satisfy the conditions Wenar lays down. And this would, of course, be a very good thing. But one might worry that these conditions are too easily satisfied. A non-elected consultative legislature could just be another bunch of army officers sharing the spoils (as was the case in Suharto's Indonesia). Letting people know what resource deals their rulers have struck, and allowing people, on occasion, to present a protesting petition – all this is surely not enough to recognize the people's property rights in their country's resources.

It turns out, then, that I am a truer champion of property rights than Wenar is. His proposal would vindicate merely three preconditions of secure property rights – that national resources not be sold without the knowledge of the population owning them, nor with severe

pressure or extreme manipulation being brought to bear on this population – while mine would vindicate the fourth by requiring that such
sales actually be authorized by the owner. My requirement of broadly
democratic authorization is not an alternative to, but an essential
component of, the vindication of the property rights of national
populations.

Wenar might respond that, even if actual authorization (in some
form) is a further necessary condition for the legitimacy of national
resource sales, the vindication of conditions (1)–(3) is the best we can
hope to accomplish in our world of resource-hungry consumers, profit-
hungry corporations, and venal politicians. He might add that, by
asking for more, we would likely end up with nothing. This is a sensible
response. Wenar's proposal may well be a crucial political step to take
now toward modifying the existing legal regime and practice. But, even
then, I would still want to preserve the thought that what would count
as legally legitimate under his international rules could still be morally
illegitimate, even within the property-rights framework. Companies
purchasing national resources from authoritarian regimes that publi-
cize their sales and permit petitions, such companies may still be –
morally speaking – accepting stolen property, even if their legal title
will prevail in the courts. And while Wenar's proposal and his work
toward its adoption are truly admirable, we should endorse this proposal with an eye to possibly tightening it later to the point where
governments need some genuine consent from their people in order to
effect legally valid transfers of ownership rights in national resources.
Yes, this may not currently be feasible. But it does not follow that
there is nothing wrong with some "relatively decent" rulers enriching
themselves by selling national resources without the people's consent.[83]

Was I really venturing far beyond the bounds of feasibility by
demanding broadly democratic authorization as a condition for valid
resource sales? Perhaps. But there is an important nuance to be added,
which renders my proposal, in another respect, less demanding than
Wenar's. I was not advocating that resource-importing countries
should impose such a constraint upon themselves unilaterally. Rather,
the chapter on the four privileges (*WPHR*, ch. 6) is written entirely
from the perspective of a "fledgling democracy," asking what its political leaders can do to make a return to authoritarian rule less likely.
By curtailing the revenues future authoritarian rulers can realize from
resource sales, one can reduce the staying power of such rulers as well
as the incentives for potential predators to take power in the first place.
I proposed passage of a constitutional amendment[84] that declared
invalid future resource sales effected without some specified demo-

cratic authorization. A proper discussion of the realism of my proposal turns then on whether it is feasible to stop or reduce international resource sales that lack democratic authorization (not generally, but) specifically from countries that have adopted such a constitutional amendment.

I was not defending, then, the broader demand that we affluent import foreign natural resources only if their sale has been authorized in some broadly democratic way, but the narrower demand that we respect and honor another country's democratically adopted constitutional amendment that declares invalid any natural resource sales that do not meet certain broadly democratic authorization conditions specified in that amendment. This narrower demand, confined to countries with such a constitutional amendment, is more likely to be honored by affluent countries – or so I argued. But, as Wenar cites (pp. 135–6), I also expressed serious doubts that it would do much to discourage future resource purchases that lack the authorization required by the constitutional amendment.

6.3 The authoritative notice problem

Wenar defines the *authoritative notice* problem by reference to the question: "what is the decisive public indication that the criterion used is or is not satisfied?" (p. 134). He then criticizes my proposed Democracy Panel on the ground that it is vulnerable to regulatory capture. This would indeed be the case if the membership of the Democracy Panel were to be determined by the member states of the United Nations, as Wenar presumes. My proposal was, however, that states would democratically adopt the constitutional amendment and would then themselves select and authorize trusted experts to determine authoritatively, in real time, whether the country is (still) democratically governed or not. So my thought was to require democratic authorization by a country's people on both levels. On the first level, sales of national resources are valid if and only if the government transacting the sale is democratically authorized by the people. On the meta-level, a declaration that some government is not democratically authorized by the people it rules and therefore unable to sell national resources in their name – such a declaration is valid if and only if its source is democratically authorized by this country's people. They could authorize the UN to make this decision on their behalf. But I did not suggest this for exactly the reason Wenar provides: the danger of regulatory capture.[85] I suggested instead that the people (or, more plausibly, their elected representatives) should appoint a group of suitable individuals whose loyalty, integrity, and knowledge of their country's constitution they have reason to trust and should authorize a majority of this group to issue an authoritative declaration that the government's resource sales are not, from now on, to be considered authorized by the people. This group of trusted individuals, living outside the country and perhaps convening under UN auspices when the need arises, is my paradigm of a Democracy Panel in the one-country case.

If several countries pass constitutional amendments of the kind I proposed, then it might make sense for them to collaborate. Rather than set up a Democracy Panel for each country, they would then set up a Democracy Panel for several countries – for instance, a Democracy Panel that judges in real time the democratic credentials of the governments of six Latin American countries that have all passed similar constitutional amendments. In this scenario as well, it would be the six participating countries (not outsiders!) that would decide together the composition of the Democracy Panel. A joint Democracy Panel of this sort (monitoring six countries) would save on money and labor, and it might also acquire a certain international standing that would allow it to pronounce, with some authority, on the democratic legitimacy of other Latin American countries (outside the six). But there is also the danger of a loss in reliability. For example, democracy may be eroded in one of the six countries, but a majority on the Democracy Panel may continue to certify this country as sufficiently democratic because they feel greater loyalty to some of the other countries and do not want to cut off those other countries' important resource purchases from the lapsed state. If a country judges this sort of scenario to be a real danger, then it may want to decline participation in a joint Democracy Panel and instead appoint a Democracy Panel for the monitoring of its own constitutional amendment only.

We see here how the findings of Democracy Panels are authoritative also in a second sense: they are authorized by the people whose national resources are at stake. Such authorization strengthens the appeal to property rights: when a Democracy Panel rescinds a government's authority to sell national resources, it is acting pursuant to, and conveying, the owners' own instructions.[86] Foreign corporations, governments, and courts would find such authorized rescissions harder to ignore. Freedom House ratings, on which Wenar wants foreigners to rely, could gain the same advantage if a national population properly authorized reliance on them.

6.4 The enforcement problem

The final problem Wenar discusses concerns enforcement: "what institutions could possibly be powerful enough to enforce a judgment that trade in resources with some regime should stop?" (p. 134). His main criticism on this front seems to be that governments such as the United States would be reluctant to enforce Democracy Panel rulings. Here non-enforcement against other states is not to be lamented: it is both unrealistic and undesirable that the US navy should challenge Chinese merchant ships transporting minerals from a no-longer-democratic Argentina to the port of Shanghai. But domestic legal deference to Democracy Panel rulings is desirable. Such deference would involve not so much *enforcement* as *non-enforcement*: US courts should not enforce, when these are under legal challenge, purported ownership rights that importers acquired from illegitimate governments. Such challenges might be made likely if the constitutional amendment requires future governments to challenge – in international fora as well as in the national courts of importing countries – any resource sales effected by any of its predecessors that had been officially declared undemocratic by the country's authorized Democracy Panel. The prospect of such legal challenges is meant to deter potential buyers and thereby to reduce the resource revenues undemocratic rulers can earn by lowering both sales volumes and unit prices.

The desired effect is enhanced by the prospect of even earlier legal action, while the authoritarian government is still in power. Imagine the following scenario. During a period of democratic rule, Nigeria passes a constitutional amendment that explicitly bars future undemocratic rulers of itself from selling Nigerian natural resources. Later, a group of army officers seizes power in Nigeria by force. These officers manage to find an oil company willing to pay them large amounts of money in exchange for oil the officers allow this company to extract in Nigeria. Has the company acquired legally valid ownership rights in the oil it is extracting? We can easily imagine such a claim to be challenged in national courts, for instance in the United States. If such a challenge is successful, it would deprive the company of the option to call upon the courts to defend its possession of the Nigerian oil and its successor products. It would put potential buyers of such products on notice that they are buying stolen property – conduct that, when engaged in knowingly, is a criminal offense in most jurisdictions.

Can national courts, in the US for instance, be brought to accede to such challenges? I think this is achievable, if there is sufficient popular support as well as (consequent) support from the US State Department. In any case, Wenar's proposal and mine, and indeed any other reform proposed for the endorsement of the US government, here face the same hurdle. We need to convince the American public that the US should not recognize ownership rights in resources that were acquired from states with a low Freedom House score (Wenar) or states whose Democracy Panel has declared the de facto government illegitimate (my proposal). I don't know which task is easier. But my proposal is bound to be useful insofar as it is certainly easier to get national courts not to recognize ownership rights when these were acquired from sellers who not merely have a low Freedom House score but also have been officially declared unauthorized through a proper ruling by a Democracy Panel that the people themselves had democratically empowered pursuant to a democratically adopted constitutional amendment. Moreover, I would think that my proposal more reliably tracks what matters morally: that national resources be sold only with the free and informed consent of their owners. To that extent, it might be more appealing, and therefore politically more feasible, than Wenar's alternative which, I hasten to add, much deserves further elaboration and reflection.

6.5 Remaining issues

There are two further problems Wenar raises regarding my proposal. First, he points out that my constitutional amendment proposal will not help populations currently ruled by undemocratic governments. He writes: "any solution that turns on a democratically passed amendment can only help in those countries that have already achieved democratic governance – so not Equatorial Guinea, for example, which has never been democratic" (p. 136). This is correct. My proposal aims to reduce a serious problem for fledgling democracies which often relapse for the specific reason that their resource richness attracts predators, generating instability, coup attempts, and undemocratic rule as a result of the resource privilege. It does not apply to countries without the requisite constitutional amendment and is, in this respect, less demanding than Wenar's. I see this as reason to continue elaborating both proposals also as possible complements to one another.

Next, Wenar expresses his concern that the constitutional amendment, if passed, would generate antidemocratic incentives among both affluent states and potential dictators:

Consider the incentives of rich-country leaders whose corporations are buying oil from a poor-country despot who seized power after Pogge's amendment was democratically passed. These rich-country leaders know that, if democratic governance returns to the poor country, their corporations will face accusations of misappropriation of foreign goods. These leaders will then have significant political incentives to assure that democratic governance does not return to the poor country. And potential authoritarians, aware of these future incentives to entrench them, will be more likely to attempt to destabilize the democracy in the first place. So the proposal would generate significant incentives that point in a counterproductive (antidemocratic) direction. (p. 136)

The problem that Wenar points to becomes less serious when the proposed constitutional amendment is seen to work in tandem with the proposed Democracy Panel. This panel would de-authorize in real time an illegitimate government's resources sales. Accusations of misappropriation would thus not have to await a return to democracy. In the court of public opinion, at least, corporations buying resources from (and lending money to) a relapsed former democracy would immediately face accusations that they are stealing resources and propping up an illegitimate regime. Other governments would then face the choice of whether to support their companies continuing business as usual or to honor the will of the people who – after a coup or gradual erosion – are no longer governed according to the broadly democratic principles they had laid down for themselves.

7 Response to Mills

7.1 The importance of non-ideal theory

I find much to agree with in Charles Mills's forceful approach to questions of global justice and his critical assessment of my own view. A central point of agreement is our shared judgment that an overly narrow focus on so-called ideal theory can be counterproductive and distorting, and that more focused attention on the most urgent moral problems facing the world today is more likely to provide solid guidance and to gain wide agreement. This has been a central feature of my treatment of questions of justice all along: "Those for whom the practical social task is primary . . . would not begin with the foundations upon which a whole edifice of moral knowledge is to be erected. Instead, they would start from concrete moral issues actually in dispute and then extend their moral reflection as far afield as is necessary to reach agreement."[87]

Despite our common focus on addressing existing injustice instead of detailing what a perfectly just world would look like, we nonetheless set forth different frameworks for understanding injustice. The conception of (minimal) justice I propose claims that in order for an institutional scheme to be just, it must not foreseeably and avoidably produce massive human rights deficits. The present design of the global institutional order is therefore unjust insofar as it foreseeably produces massive human rights deficits that far exceed what some feasible alternative designs of this order would produce. Whether this design meets the standard of minimal justice can be assessed independent of how it came about.

The aim of Mills's essay is to supplement my view with two components that he believes are consistent with the spirit of our common project and further strengthen my overall position. Mills proposes conceiving of non-ideal theory as (1) centrally concerned with rectificatory justice, and (2) specifically with the rectification of racial and gender injustice. I address these two concerns in turn, explaining the sense in which I agree and disagree with the concerns Mills proposed to move center stage.

7.2 Rectificatory justice

Rectificatory or corrective justice focuses on protecting present victims of injustice. There are three variants, according to whether the *site of injustice* is taken to lie in the past or in the present and, if in the present, according to whether the *aim of rectificatory justice* is to reform this site of injustice or else to neutralize or mitigate its harmful effects. The word "site" here, made familiar by Jerry Cohen,[88] refers to the highlighted *iudicandum*, the entity under moral assessment. Among these morally assessable entities are human agents, their conduct, social rules/institutions, and states of the world.

While Mills's discussion covers all three variants of rectificatory justice and touches upon *iudicanda* of all four types, my own work is focused primarily on present, ongoing institutional arrangements, especially those at supranational levels. I diagnose the present design of these institutional arrangements as severely unjust and attempt to work toward feasible reforms. Insofar as such reform efforts fail politically, I am also concerned to work out what obligations the more advantaged persons have to neutralize or mitigate the effects of ongoing unjust social institutions pursuant to our negative duties not to contribute to their imposition and not to benefit from their injustice. In this context, I have used the word "compensation": we must compensate those harmed by the injustice of an institutional order according to our contribution to its design or imposition and according to the benefit we derive from its injustice. In the space of *iudicanda*, my work then is primarily on social institutions and secondarily on human conduct insofar as it upholds or reforms such social institutions or mitigates their effects. It discusses primarily the second variant of rectificatory justice (institutional reform) and derivatively the third (compensation).

This focus on reforming existing institutional arrangements is present also in Mills's work, for instance in the following passage: "For non-ideal theory, the thought-experiment would become the working out by free and equal persons of what measures of rectificatory justice would be required to dismantle a basic structure *already* organized around unfair principles that deny freedom and equality to the majority, and bring into existence socially subordinated subpersons identified as 'women' and 'nonwhites'" (p. 160; emphasis in text).

This passage understands rectificatory justice as demanding the repair of institutions that are presently unjust. But Mills also focuses much of his essay on historical wrongs, such as colonialism and slavery, and our responsibilities to neutralize and mitigate their present effects. A minor foray aside,[89] this has not been a central concern of my work. Let me explain why.

The unjust effects historical wrongs continue to wreak in the present can be loosely classified as either personal or statistical. The former are effects on specific present individuals, as when one person's present opportunities are enhanced by the fact that her parents amassed a fortune by collaborating in a military coup or another person's opportunities are restricted by the fact that, after the military junta murdered his parents, he grew up poor and without an education. Statistical effects are exemplified by an extremely uneven wealth distribution or by massive racial disparities in education that have evolved historically through the workings of unjust economic institutions (feudalism) or racial discrimination and slavery.

Mills's interest is clearly in statistical or systematic unjust effects of historical wrongs. I share this concern, but not under the same description. Massive racial disparities in education can and must be eradicated, regardless of their past and present social causes. Because any past social causes can no longer be altered, this eradication can be achieved only by adjusting *present* social institutions, practices, and conduct. Insofar as these remain unadjusted and avoidably perpetuate the disparity, they are unjust. Fighting this injustice of present social institutions, practices, and conduct strikes me as the right approach because it constructively focuses on what needs to be done here and now and also avoids notoriously controversial – and, I believe, unnecessary – claims about how various populations would be faring today if certain historical wrongs had not occurred.[90] These claims are unnecessary because, if a present social order avoidably perpetuates massive (and therefore evidently nonrandom) race-based disparities, then it is unjust even if it is color blind and regardless of the extent to which the social causes of the disparity lie in the past (e.g., historical crimes) or in the present (e.g., racist discrimination).

I am here restating my long-standing view that – contrary to what economists call the anonymity condition – the heavy concentration of deprivations and disadvantages upon certain groups (people with dark skin, females, etc.) heightens the injustice of present institutional arrangements.[91] If such arrangements are unjust when they give rise to avoidable human rights deficits that are randomly distributed across all socially salient groups, then they are even more unjust when they give rise to equivalent human rights deficits that are concentrated upon people with dark skin, females, or gays, say, or on members of specific ethnic, linguistic, or religious groups. This is so even when the institutional arrangements under assessment are "intrinsically" impartial (sex-neutral, color blind, etc.). To illustrate: If a society's institutional order is unjust when its citizens are at high risk of serious assault because of an understaffed and poorly organized national police force, then such an order is even more unjust when the same prevalence of serious assaults is mainly suffered by females as a result of the police turning a blind eye to domestic violence. And a national institutional order that avoidably inflicts severe poverty on 15 percent of the country's population is rendered even more unjust by the fact that one or more socially salient groups are heavily overrepresented among the poor. And this is so regardless of what social causes may underlie the correlation. Insofar as it arises from historical wrongs (such as slavery that gave whites a huge head start in a competitive society), present institutions are flawed by allowing "[a] morally deeply tarnished history . . . to result in *radical* inequality" (*WPHR* 209). Insofar as the correlation derives from present racist attitudes and practices, present institutions are flawed insofar as they avoidably fail to erase and to counterbalance these forces. Present social institutions must be shaped in light of historical wrongs and prevailing biases: must be designed, insofar as this is possible, so as to phase out the latter and to mitigate the impact of both.

Nonetheless, *WPHR* does incorporate backward-looking arguments at least in a defensive way. Those with libertarian sympathies sometimes claim that inequalities and group disparities – no matter how extreme – are unobjectionable if they arose recursively through chains of voluntary transactions under some appropriate market rules. In response, I adopt an economical way to sideline such claims by pointing out that its antecedent is plainly false: actual historical rules and transactions both massively violated any credible normative standards and therefore cannot confer legitimacy on the present global distribution. More broadly, I then argue that a history pervaded by such monumental crimes should not be allowed to give rise to radical inequalities (*WPHR* 209–10). This argument seeks not to mitigate the effects that specific crimes had on specific present persons or groups, but rather to strengthen the case for eradicating all extreme disadvantages in starting position.

Simplifying slightly, the central requirement of social justice, on my minimal conception of it, is that social institutions be designed so that human rights deficits are avoided insofar as this is reasonably possible. The justice of social institutions largely depends then on their actual effects: on the extent to which one design, compared to its feasible alternatives, causes those affected by these institutions to have secure access to the objects of their human rights. But what the effects of this one factor are depends in turn on many other factors – such as, for example, the natural environment, the distribution of income and wealth, available technologies, prevailing practices and conventions, as well as the dominant religions and culture, including any prevalent biases against certain groups defined by their gender, ethnicity, skin color, language, religion, or lifestyle. To be just, institutional arrangements must be adapted to these other factors: must be designed to reduce prevalent biases and prejudices as well as to mitigate their effects, for instance, or be designed to counteract historically accumulated radical inequalities that leave the civil, political, social, economic, and cultural human rights of marginalized groups in jeopardy. Though the central requirement of justice, as I understand it, does not refer to race or gender – here my understanding is, I believe, in line with Mills's point "*that gender and race are themselves artifacts of an unjust basic structure*" (p. 156; emphasis in text) – this central requirement does in this world focus our moral attention overwhelmingly upon those who are suffering the effects of past and present racist and sexist wrongs – because they are the ones among whom today's vast human rights deficits are massively (almost exclusively) concentrated (*WPHR* 223). By fulfilling human rights, the institutional reforms I consider morally most pressing would rectify what Mills sees as the effects of great historical wrongs.

7.3 Race and gender

Race and gender have in common that many of the most horrendous historical wrongs are associated with them. But they differ in how these wrongs affect the present. The social starting position of most persons is conditioned by the social position of two parents who are of opposite sex but fall into the same race classification. This may make it easier for appropriate social institutions to wash out gender-based injustice than race-based injustice. A girl's prospects of being born into a household that can meet her basic needs are no worse than a boy's prospects – though it is, of course, highly likely that she will not in fact receive as much social support as she would receive if she were a boy. By contrast, the households into which dark-skinned children are born are on average vastly more disadvantaged in terms of country and socioeconomic class than the households into which white children are born. This huge statistical handicap, which for half of all dark-skinned children comes on top of a gender disadvantage, is further compounded by the fact that the interests of those in socially inferior positions tend to receive less respect and sympathy from persons in their social environment, tend to be marginalized in national legislative and policy-making processes, and are likely to live in countries whose international bargaining power is negligible.

By highlighting this difference, I am not suggesting that race disparities are somehow more serious or more urgent justice concerns than gender disparities. Rather, I seek to stress that we must understand how specific disadvantages are transmitted from one generation to the next in order to understand how we can best fight them in the present. In the case of gender, the main obstacles are culturally entrenched practices and attitudes as well as social institutions that are still discriminatory at least in impact. A highly promising path toward eradicating these obstacles is institutional reform. Feminists have achieved substantial progress in the last 50 years in reforming social institutions in many jurisdictions. In some countries, such as Norway, the end of gender disparity is clearly in sight and within reach, and they provide highly instructive models of reform that may be adaptable to other societies. But in most countries substantial and mutually reinforcing gender disparities persist in multiple dimensions. Far more research should be done on how increasingly influential supranational institutional arrangements are, and might be, affecting gender disparity. Even if these international rules and practices are formally sex-neutral, different sex-neutral formulations of them may differ substantially in their impact on gender disparities. This is so because the effects of international rules and practices are co-determined by other causal factors, such as national institutions and cultural practices and attitudes as well as biological sex differences. We need to learn much more about how present globalization is affecting gender disparities and about the feasible global institutional reforms that would improve these effects.[92]

Race disparities tend to be larger because they accumulate over generations. We can see this intranationally – in the United States, for example, where men earn about 25 percent more than women on average,[93] while whites earn about 60 percent more than blacks.[94] Looking globally, the effect is hugely compounded by the high correlation of race with nationality and nationality with income. To get a sense of the latter relationship, consider that per capita income in the Euro zone is about *36 times* that in sub-Saharan Africa.[95] This huge inequality affects females and males equally and thus has no impact on global gender disparity. But since the two regions are nearly all-white and all-black, respectively, the geographical inequality essentially *is* a racial disparity. Solid statistics are hard to come by, but we can assume that, globally, the income ratio between households that white children are born into and households that black children are born into is somewhere in this vicinity, above 30 to 1. It would take substantial shifts in the distribution of global income to reach a world in which the existing correlation of skin color and life chances is erased – or else a very long time: even if from now on the change in per capita income in sub-Saharan Africa were to best that in the Euro zone by one full percentage point each year, it would take more than 360 years to reach parity.[96] This period is similar to the time it took for this huge inequality to be built up over centuries of brutal colonialism, slavery, and genocidal warfare.

Mills is right to put before us this huge race-based disparity as a large, stunning mark of our world which we all sort of know and yet rarely fully realize. He is right that this disparity was built up with immense brutality that was largely ignored and occasionally justified by liberal thinkers. (Mills mentions Locke, Hume, Kant, Hegel, Mill, and de Tocqueville, p. 168.) He is right that the present generation of liberal thinkers and affluent whites makes things far too easy for themselves when they set aside race and racism as yesterday's problem: we don't think of ourselves as racists and we surely don't believe that we inherit our forefathers' sins – yet we also feel deeply entitled to inherit the spoils of these racist crimes, our 36:1 birth advantage.[97] Mills is right that overcoming this huge race-based disparity is central to the struggle for justice in the present world, and he rightly conceives this struggle as envisioning a world in which race would not even exist as a socially relevant concept.

It is my hypothesis that we citizens of affluent countries can most effectively work for such a world by focusing on those who are most disadvantaged by the injustice of present global institutional arrangements. These are the ca. 3 billion human beings – most of them women and girls with dark skin – who are too poor to be able securely to meet their basic needs. Yes, such severe poverty has always existed. But, as we learned from the two tables above (pp. 186 and 187), global per capita income has grown so far as to render this sort of poverty entirely avoidable at only slight opportunity cost to the world's affluent. Severe poverty nonetheless persists on such a massive scale because we in the affluent countries, through global institutional arrangements we impose, have managed to reduce the poorest 40 percent of humankind to less than 2 percent of global household income. Our foremost goal must be to achieve global institutional design changes that would realize the human rights of the global poor. Reaching this goal would still leave us far from a just world in which racial disparities and hence race itself have disappeared; but it is a crucial first step on the way toward it and would substantially reduce race-based and also gender-based disparities.

In working on this foremost goal, my greatest inspiration is the antislavery movement in the nineteenth century (*EIA* 81–3). Its members knew that the slaves shipped in chains to the Americas were black, and they defended the rights of these slaves by presenting them as human beings, as brothers and sisters. We know that those kept in poverty today are overwhelmingly dark-skinned and we can defend their rights by appeal to their humanity. As a few thousand of an earlier generation organized themselves to abolish slavery, so we can – and must – organize ourselves to abolish poverty.

Notes

*In writing these responses, I have been greatly helped by critical comments and suggestions received from Paula Casal, Alison Jaggar, Tienmu Ma, Nori

Spauwen, Kit Wellman, Leif Wenar, Andrew Williams, and a lively audience in Seyla Benhabib's Political Theory Workshop. The reply took longer than expected, and I thank my critics for their patience.

1 I am using in-text references to refer to passages in this same book. Additional in-text references beginning with "*WPHR*" refer to Thomas Pogge, *World Poverty and Human Rights: Cosmopolitan Responsibilities and Reforms*, second rev. edn (Cambridge: Polity, 2008). And in-text references beginning with "*EIA*" refer to the Symposium on *WPHR* published in *Ethics and International Affairs* 19(1) (2005): 1–83. This symposium contained a brief introduction by me (*EIA* 1–7), critical comments on the book by Mathias Risse (*EIA* 9–18), Alan Patten (*EIA* 19–27), Rowan Cruft (*EIA* 29–37), Norbert Anwander (*EIA* 39–45) and Debra Satz (*EIA* 47–54), as well as my reply to these comments (*EIA* 55–83).

2 The undefined expression "moral injuries" is interesting. I presume a slave-holder suffers no moral injury if his slaves are set free without compensation to him. If this is right, I could support the Strong Thesis by pointing to global institutional reforms that would entail more-than-slight reductions in the incomes of the affluent, so long as these reductions constitute no moral injury. I will not explore this opportunity here and focus instead on the "Strong Thesis" as Cohen formulates it.

3 See *WPHR* 16–18, 28, 55–6, 145–7.

4 FAO, "1.02 Billion People Hungry," news release June 19, 2009, www.fao.org/news/story/en/item/20568/icode/ (accessed April 5, 2010). The FAO notes that it is for the first time in all of human history that the number of chronically undernourished people has broken above the one-billion mark.

5 WHO and UNICEF, *Progress on Drinking Water and Sanitation: Special Focus on Sanitation* (New York and Geneva: UNICEF and WHO, 2008), p. 30. Also available at www.who.int/water_sanitation_health/monitoring/jmp2008.pdf.

6 Ibid., p. 7.

7 Fogarty International Center for Advanced Study in the Health Sciences. "Strategic Plan: Fiscal Years 2000–2003." Bethesda, MD: National Institutes of Health, n.d., www.fic.nih.gov/about/plan/exec_summary.htm (accessed April 5, 2010).

8 UN-Habitat, *The Challenge of Slums: Global Report on Human Settlements 2003* (London: Earthscan, 2003), p. vi.

9 UN-Habitat, "Urban Energy," n.d., www.unhabitat.org/content.asp?cid=2884&catid=356&typeid=24&subMenuId=0 (accessed April 5, 2010).

10 UNESCO Institute for Statistics, *International Literary Statistics: A Review of Concepts, Methodology, and Current Data* (Montreal: UNESCO UIS, 2008), 9. Also available at www.uis.unesco.org/template/pdf/Literacy/LiteracyReport2008.pdf.

11 See ILO, *The End of Child Labour: Within Reach* (Geneva: International Labor Office, 2006), p. 6.

12 This is the World Bank's official poverty line, most recently redefined in terms of daily consumption whose local cost has the same purchasing power as $1.25 had in the US in 2005. See Shaohua Chen and Martin Ravallion, "The Developing World Is Poorer than We Thought, but no Less Successful in the Fight against Poverty," World Bank Policy Research Working Paper WPS 4703 (2008), p. 44. Available at econ.worldbank.org/docsearch (accessed April 5, 2010). Relative to a more adequate poverty line twice as high ($2.50 per day in 2005 international dollars), the Bank reports that nearly half the world's population, 3,085 million people, were poor in 2005, with average consumption levels 45 percent below this line (ibid., p. 45).

13 World Health Organization, *Global Burden of Disease: 2004 Update* (Geneva: WHO, 2008), pp. 54–9, table A1. Also available at www.who.int/healthinfo/global_burden_disease/2004_report_update/en/index.html.

14 In view of Cohen's stern upholding of rigorous standards of social scientific inquiry, it is amusing to trace the sources he cites in his paper. In this case the evidence for all those many private voluntary codes comes from a private communication from Gap Clothing Company's Senior Vice President for Social Responsibility (p. 42, n. 3). This is hearsay, and from a rather dubious source: a clothing company infamous for its use of sweatshops.

15 See Christian Barry and Sanjay Reddy, *International Trade and Labor Standards: A Proposal for Linkage* (New York: Columbia University Press, 2008).

16 By contrast, the Conventional Thesis is compatible with holding that the global order bears little responsibility for causing severe and widespread poverty and that reforms of this order would make little difference to its incidence. It is therefore inadequate for this second practical aim.

17 See Christian Barry, "Applying the Contribution Principle," in Christian Barry and Thomas Pogge (eds), *Global Institutions and Responsibilities: Achieving Global Justice* (Malden, MA: Blackwell, 2006), pp. 291–3.

18 This point is discussed further below in the section "Do negative-duty claims have a high burden of proof?"

19 UNCTAD, *Trade and Development Report: Fragile Recovery and Risks* (New York: UN Publications 1999), IX. Also available at www.unctad.org/en/docs/tdr1999_en.pdf.

20 See note 16 in Cohen's essay and www2.lse.ac.uk/publicEvents/sampletext/ppt/20051118-Rodrik.ppt (accessed April 5, 2010), which appears to be the presentation (by Dani Rodrik) that Cohen has in mind. After his reliance on The Gap (see note 14 above), this is another example of the disturbingly common practice of considering only the sources that support what one wants to believe.

21 Santiago Fernandez de Córdoba and David Vanzetti, "Now What? Searching for a Solution to the WTO Industrial Tariff Negotiations," in Sam Laird and Santiago Fernandez de Córdoba (eds), *Coping with Trade*

Reforms: A Developing-Country Perspective on the WTO Industrial Tariff Negotiations (Basingstoke: Palgrave Macmillan, 2006), p. 28, table 12.

22 William R. Cline, *Trade Policy and Global Poverty* (Washington, DC: Center for Global Development, 2004), p. 180, table 4.1.

23 Ibid., p. 255, stated in 1997 dollars.

24 Ibid., p. 252, table 5.3, as slightly revised in a subsequent "Technical Correction to the First Printing."

25 World Bank, *Global Economic Prospects 2002* (Washington, DC: World Bank, 2002), pp. 168–78. The number of poor here referred to is the number of those living on less than $2.15 per person per day at 1993 purchasing power parities (PPPs). The Bank estimated this number at about 2.7 billion during the relevant period. According to these estimates, then, removal of trade barriers would have reduced the incidence of poverty by about 11–19% – a rather substantial dent relative to the 50% reduction here under discussion. See my *Politics as Usual: What Lies behind the Pro-Poor Rhetoric* (Cambridge: Polity Press, 2010), p. 20.

26 As cited at *WPHR* 20 (17 in the 2002 edition), the widely publicized and frequently cited UNCTAD Report is referred to in "White Man's Shame," *The Economist*, September 25, 1999: 89.

27 The Global Resources Dividend, described in *WPHR*, ch. 8, is probably my best-known and most discussed proposal for global institutional reform. It is not discussed in Cohen's essay.

28 One example, concerning seabed mining and the 1982 UN Convention on the Law of the Sea, is discussed at *WPHR* 131–2.

29 For a book-length discussion of the proposal and much additional material about it, see the project website at www.healthimpactfund.org.

30 Figures based on Chen and Ravallion, "The Developing World Is Poorer," pp. 27 and 42–6. The table is reproduced from and further explained in my *Politics as Usual*, p. 70.

31 Also, this $76 billion shortfall that the whole world must overcome is less than one tenth of the military budget of the US alone, and also less than one tenth of the $787 billion the US alone spent on economic stimulus during the 2009 economic crisis.

32 Cohen relies on these World Bank statistics in talking about the extent and evolution of poverty in East Asia, China, India, Nigeria, Pakistan. I have grave doubts about the method underlying these figures (see *Politics as Usual*, chs 3–4). For one thing, I believe that the Bank's poverty line is much too low. Let me note then that, even if we raised the Bank's international poverty line from $1.25 to $2.00 per person per day at 2005 PPP, the poverty gap would still amount to only $296 billion or 0.66% of world income at currency exchange rates. For 2005, the Bank reports 2.56 billion people living – by 40% on average – below this higher poverty line (Chen and Ravallion, "The Developing World Is Poorer," pp. 27 and 42–6).

33 As alluded to here, the impact that GRD spending and the lifting of protectionist barriers would have on poverty rates would be magnified by

multiplier effects. By having and spending more income, poor people increase the incomes of other poor people. And by spending more on food, health care and education, poor people and their children become more productive, and therefore potentially better paid, members of the workforce in future years. Reinforced by such multiplier effects, a regular flow of $300 billion annually into poverty eradication efforts could over time easily have halved the deficit of the $2.50-poor, which in 2005 stood at $507 billion.

34 Data kindly supplied by Branko Milanovic of the World Bank. The four years listed are the only ones for which comprehensive data are currently available.

35 See UNU-WIDER (United Nations University-World Institute for Development Economics Research), *World Income Inequality Database*, version 2.0c, May 2008. www.wider.unu.edu/research/Database/en_GB/database (accessed April 5, 2010).

36 The Tax Foundation, "Fiscal Facts," July 30, 2009, table 5, www.taxfoundation.org/publications/show/250.html (accessed April 5, 2010).

37 Emmanuel Saez and Thomas Piketty, "Income Inequality in the United States, 1913–1998," *Quarterly Journal of Economics* 118 (2003): 1–39, as updated in "Tables and Figures Updated to 2007 in Excel Format," August 2009. Available at elsa.berkeley.edu/~saez/ (accessed April 5, 2010), table A3. Ibid., table 1 decomposes the 16% average per capita household income growth during the last US economic expansion (2002–7), showing that the top 1% enjoyed real growth of 61.8% while the remaining 99% of the population had 6.7% growth. The top 1% captured 65% of the economy's real per capita growth. In the preceding expansion under Clinton (1993–2000), the top percentile had captured 45% of the real per capita growth of the US economy.

38 Dropping from a 3.08% income share in 1990 to 1.60% in 2004. The World Bank has recently withdrawn its 1990–2004 data about household inequality in China, now providing only data for 2005 which show much lower inequality (the bottom decile at 2.4%). This is apparently due to methodological revisions including an inflation of all rural incomes by 37%. If the Bank will introduce such revisions for other countries, it will soon be able to report much lower intranational inequality. This revision should be resisted. It is absurd to consider two persons economic equals when one of them cannot afford to live in the city (and must perhaps commute a long distance to her place of work) while the other, with 37% more income, can afford to live in the city.

39 See Dev Kar and Devon Cartwright Smith, *Illicit Financial Flows from Developing Countries 2002–2006* (Washington, DC: Global Financial Integrity, 2008), p. iv. These outflows are about 10 times larger than all official development assistance (80 times larger than assistance for basic social services), much of which illicitly flows right back into secret private bank accounts in the global North. These outflows also dwarf the global poverty gap which, even relative to the World Bank's highest poverty line

of $2.50 per person per day (2005 international dollars), amounted to only $507 billion in 2005.

40 For example, when the prices of basic foodstuffs double, the consumer price index may register only a small rise – because basic foodstuffs are only a small portion of individual household expenditure and because other commodities, such as consumer electronics, may be falling in price. Similarly, when the World Bank ascribes much higher purchasing power to the currencies of poor countries than their exchange rate would suggest, it is in each and every case overstating the purchasing power of these currencies relative to food. It is the very low prices of services, especially, that drive up the calculated purchasing power of poor-country currencies. Food is cheaper in poor countries, to be sure, but not as much cheaper as PPPs would suggest. In fact, the PPPs the Bank relies on in its poverty measurement exercise are on average about 50% higher than the corresponding PPPs for "food and non-alcoholic beverages" (see *Politics as Usual*, n. 127).

41 I contest this, of course. The GRD would certainly have accelerated poverty reduction in China.

42 All data from Chen and Ravallion, "The Developing World is Poorer," p. 44.

43 To make this thought-experiment realistic, you must imagine away various potentially life-saving amenities that a resident of the United States can access without money – such as 24-hour emergency room access, public rest rooms, and clean tap water. Such amenities are unavailable or charged for in the world's impoverished areas.

44 All data from Chen and Ravallion, "The Developing World is Poorer," p. 45.

45 Tan tends to de-emphasize or ignore altogether the fact that the rich are not only *failing to bring about* a global order that allows the poor to meet their basic needs, but also *imposing* a global order that does not. Thus he writes, describing my view: "[The global poor] are being unjustly harmed by the rich because it is the choice of the rich not to bring into effect the social arrangement that would be kinder to the poor" (p. 58). He further asks: "is Pogge entitled to say that the poor are being harmed when they are deprived of a feasible arrangement under which they can have adequate access to basic goods?" (p. 58). But obviously what I am claiming is not, *pace* Tan, that the mere failure to bring about a global order favorable to the poor counts as harm – as though no institutional scheme currently existed and the rich were asked to devise one to eliminate severe poverty that they played no role in causing. It is not our *failure* to establish such a global order that I condemn as harm, but rather our continued *imposition* of a global order that engenders severe and widespread poverty. To be sure, I do try to show that a more poverty-avoiding design of the global order is possible and could be realized with only minor opportunity costs for the affluent countries. But the point of this effort is to show that the existing design is grievously unjust by showing that most existing

poverty is foreseeably avoidable through a different design. This is how we are harming the poor: not by merely failing to create a poverty-avoiding global order, but by actively designing and imposing an *unjust* global order, that is, an order known to produce huge human rights deficits that a different design of this order would avoid.

46 See especially "An Egalitarian Law of Peoples," *Philosophy and Public Affairs* 23 (1994): 195–224.

47 On this broad understanding, egalitarianism also includes prioritarian conceptions, which do not value equality as such but give greater weight to the interests of the worse-off.

48 I write "can" here because often the victims of an unjust institutional order are also contributing to its imposition. The US political system before 1860 was unjust on account of its explicit authorization of slavery. By supplying their labor, the slaves contributed to the imposition of this system. Yet, it is not plausible to conclude that the slaves (wrongfully) harmed one another by submitting to their coercive exploitation.

49 This point is discussed further in my response to Kelly and McPherson below.

50 The word "reasonably" is meant to acknowledge not merely the limits of human foresight, but also the possibility that the institutional reduction of human rights deficits might sometimes have high costs in terms of culture, say, or the natural environment. It is best to avoid the claim that human rights must never give way in such cases – certainly in our world, where human rights could be largely or fully realized through institutional reforms that would not entail such high costs.

51 By choosing one of these first two options, one avoids contributing further to the harm global institutional arrangements are inflicting but one does not compensate thereby for earlier such contributions.

52 Compare: I have obligations to keep promises only to those to whom I have made promises, but my duty to keep my promises is universal: I owe it to everyone to keep whatever promises I may have made to her or him. I discuss the distinction between duties and obligations in my response to Cruft (*EIA* 68–9).

53 I am not committed to saying that two human rights violations foreseeably and avoidably producing the same human rights deficits to the same extent are equally unjust. My view is compatible with holding that the causal pathway on which social institutions produce a human rights deficit is also relevant to their moral assessment: other things equal, deficits that are *officially mandated* or *legally authorized* are on my view more serious than ones that are *engendered*, though all three count as human rights violations in virtue of their being foreseeably and avoidably produced by social institutions. See *WPHR* 47.

54 In this way, my terminological proposal led me to the paradoxical-sounding conclusion that it is possible for one person's human right to physical integrity to be fulfilled, even though he falls victim to an assault, and

another person's human right to physical integrity to be unfulfilled, even though she is never actually assaulted (*WPHR* 44, 71). This is possible if the institutional order these two persons are living under affords sufficiently secure access to freedom from assault to white males, say, but does not afford sufficiently secure access to freedom from assault to women of color.

55　It is reason that engenders amour-propre, and it is reflection that strengthens it; reason shoves man back upon himself, and it is reason that separates him from everything that discomforts and afflicts him: it is philosophy that isolates him; it is through philosophy that he secretly says, in the face of some suffering person: perish if you will, I'm safe. Only dangers to the whole society trouble the tranquil sleep of the philosopher and raise him from his bed. One can with impunity cut the throat of his fellow human being right under his window; he need only put his hands over his ears and argue with himself a little in order to prevent nature, which revolts within him, from identifying him with the person being murdered.

(Jean-Jacques Rousseau, *Discours sur l'Origine et les Fondements de l'Inégalité parmi les Hommes*, http://pedagogie.ac-toulouse.fr/philosophie/textesdephilosophes.htm#rousseau, my translation)

56　The following remarks are informed by, and broadly in line with, Christian Barry, "Applying the Contribution Principle," in *Metaphilosophy* 36 (2005): 210–27.

57　See www.givingwhatwecan.org/ (accessed April 4, 2010).

58　One prominent such answer is provided by Peter Singer in his "What Should a Billionaire Give – and What Should You?," reprinted in Patricia Illingworth, Thomas Pogge, and Leif Wenar (eds), *Giving Well: The Ethics of Philanthropy* (Oxford: Oxford University Press, 2010), ch. 1.

59　The most famous example is Peter Singer's "Famine, Affluence, and Morality," *Philosophy and Public Affairs* 1 (1972): 229–43. This argument has been elaborated more recently by Peter Unger in *Living High and Letting Die: Our Illusion of Innocence* (Oxford: Oxford University Press, 1996). See my short review of the latter, "Take and Give," *Philosophy and Phenomenological Research* 59 (1999): 189–94.

60　See Paul Farmer, *Partner to the Poor: A Paul Farmer Reader* (Berkeley: University of California Press, 2010), esp. ch. 24. Development assistance for health rose at a 3.6 percent annual rate from 1990–99, then at a 7.5 percent annual rate from 1999–2007. See Institute for Health Metrics and Evaluation, *Financing Global Health 2009* (Seattle: IHME, 2009), pp. 20–1. Unadjusted for inflation, these annual rates are 6.4 and 10.5 percent, respectively.

61　Thomas Pogge, "Moralizing Humanitarian Intervention: Why Jurying Fails and How Law Can Work," in Terry Nardin and Melissa Williams (eds), *Humanitarian Intervention*, NOMOS, vol. 47 (New York: New York University Press, 2005), pp. 158–87. This essay is cited at *WPHR* 28.

62   It is true – as the defenders of the rich countries and of their globalization
      project point out – that most severe poverty would be avoided, despite the
      current unfair global order, if the national governments and elites of the
      poor countries were genuinely committed to "good governance" and poverty
      eradication. It is also true – as the defenders of governments and elites in
      the poor countries insist – that most severe poverty would be avoided,
      despite the corrupt and oppressive regimes holding sway in so many poor
      countries, if the global institutional order were designed to achieve this
      purpose. This mutual finger-pointing serves both sides well, convincing
      many affluent citizens in rich and poor countries that they and their govern-
      ment are innocent in the catastrophe of world poverty. But on reflection it
      is clear that, while each side is right in pointing at the other, neither is right
      in acquitting itself.

      (Thomas Pogge, "Severe Poverty as a Human Rights Violation," in
      Thomas Pogge (ed.), *Freedom from Poverty as a Human Right: Who Owes
      What to the Very Poor?* (Oxford: Oxford University Press, 2007), p. 46)
63   See Wellman's "Famine Relief: The Duties We Have to Others," in A. I.
      Cohen and C. H. Wellman (eds), *Contemporary Debates in Applied Ethics*
      (Malden, MA: Blackwell, 2005), pp. 313–25; "Responsibility: Personal,
      Collective, Corporate," in R. Goodin, P. Petitt, and T. Pogge, (eds), *A
      Companion to Contemporary Political Philosophy*, 2nd edn (Oxford: Black-
      well, 2007), pp. 736–44; "International Criminal Justice," ch. 6 in Andrew
      Altman and Christopher Wellman, *A Liberal Theory of International
      Justice* (Oxford: Oxford University Press, 2009); and his entry, "Thomas
      Pogge," in Deen K. Chatterjee (ed.), *Encyclopedia of Global Justice* (Berlin:
      Springer, forthcoming).
64   This readership is not altogether homogenous and includes not only ordi-
      nary citizens but also policy makers and public officials. This will later
      show the way to how Ci's worry might be resolved.
65   One might be tempted by another explanation here: wealthy citizens,
      especially in the US, seem to morally (and not just epistemically) discount
      to an excessive degree harms that are *engendered* by institutions, such as
      those engendered by the global order, even while they denounce *officially
      mandated* and *legally authorized* harms (cf. *WPHR* 47). It might be claimed
      that this is what explains why those autocrats are held responsible for the
      harms they caused while we exempt ourselves from responsibility for
      global poverty. I find this response unconvincing, however, as we judge
      the autocrats responsible not only for their officially mandated or legally
      authorized political repression (KGB executions and the Cultural Revolu-
      tion) but also for their economic policies which engendered widespread
      poverty.
66   For a more detailed discussion of this rationalization process, see section
      3.1 above.
67   As evidence of wealthy citizens' reluctance to accept the institutional view,
      Ci writes:

Given this moral common sense, it is easier to live with oneself for ignoring the injustice of the global economic arrangements imposed by one's government than for, say, not donating to a charity aimed at helping needy locals, for the former failure involves institutional (if negative) duties while the latter failure involves interactional (if positive) duties, and on the radar of moral common sense the first registers as a much smaller failure, if a failure at all. (p. 92)

But this example is indecisive between Ci's explanation, focusing on the reluctance to accept the institutional view, and the one I just provided, which emphasizes the distance effect. Indeed, Ci himself at times shows signs of agreeing that the institutional view retains its force in the context of extreme injustice here at issue:

We retain our ability to be upset by institutional injustice that is out of the ordinary, but most of the time we are less demanding of the ground rules of our society than of one another's personal conduct under such rules as happen to prevail, as long as these rules do not conflict with our seldom examined moral common sense. (p. 91)

Even if Ci is correct that, above some minimal threshold of justice, the interactional view dominates, this need not block acceptance of my argument because our global institutional arrangements plainly have not reached any such minimal justice threshold.

68 See Peter Singer, "Famine, Affluence, and Morality," *Philosophy and Public Affairs* 1 (1972): 229–43.

69 See here the extensive research done by Paul Slovic and his co-workers, for example, Paul Slovic: "Can International Law Stop Genocide When Our Moral Intuitions Fail Us?" (2009), available at: www.decisionresearch.org/research/genocide/darfur/ (accessed April 4, 2010). Tell an affluent audience a story about someone who started crying when she learned that the number of undernourished people had gone up by 20 million, and you are likely to get a chuckle.

70 See my "Human Rights and Global Health: A Research Program," in *Metaphilosophy* 36(1–2) (January 2005): 182–209 at 185.

71 See Aidan Hollis and Thomas Pogge, *The Health Impact Fund: Making New Medicines Accessible for All* (Oslo and New Haven: Incentives for Global Health, 2008). This book and many other discussions of the HIF proposal can be freely downloaded at www.healthimpactfund.org.

72 These are likewise underutilized due to patent-protected markups to the detriment of all. It would make sense to offer innovators the option to allow free use of their technology in exchange for rewards based on emissions averted.

73 This might seem like a far-fetched and uncertain story, but something like it seems to have happened in analogous domestic contexts as well: once

citizens of the US saw how the design of economic institutions could have such a powerful effect on unemployment and poverty rates during the Great Depression, they gradually became more inclined to hold themselves and their politicians responsible for the design of the national economic order and its effects on the distribution of income and wealth. See my *Politics as Usual*, pp. 15–17, for a fuller account.

74 The minimal conception of justice should be acceptable given Rawls's *philosophical* views, such as his rejection of a global principle of distributive justice (John Rawls, *The Law of Peoples*, Cambridge, MA: Harvard University Press, 1999, pp. 116–19), though it of course rejects some of his *empirical* commitments, such as his endorsement of explanatory nationalism, which I discuss further below.

75 See "The Incoherence between Rawls's Theories of Justice," in *Fordham Law Review* 72(5) (2004): 1739–59, at 1748.

76 That Kelly and McPherson misunderstand the basic shape of my argument here is surprising given that it parallels Rawls's attempt, which they seem to endorse (see Kelly and McPherson, p. 112), to make his principles of international justice acceptable not only to liberal but also to "decent" societies. Presumably Kelly and McPherson do not think Rawls's reaching out to nonliberal societies commits him to including nonliberal principles in his international theory of justice or to accepting such principles as part of his own views about domestic justice. Similarly, my attempt to show that my minimal criterion is acceptable to Lockean and other views does not commit me to including such views within my minimal conception of justice or to accepting them as my own.

77 It is worth noting, however, that Kelly and McPherson have an unusually broad view of what counts as an egalitarian view, sweeping not only the sufficientarian Lockean view but also the utilitarian Singer under that heading (in addition to the cited passage, see p. 104 and p. 105).

78 While I do not defend the default view of fairness in *World Poverty and Human Rights*, I do cite Rawls's theory as an example of how a failure to justify discrepancies between domestic and international theories of justice violates moral universalism (*WPHR* 110–14). But this does not appeal to the idea of a default view of fairness.

79 John Rawls: *The Law of Peoples* (Cambridge, MA: Harvard University Press, 1999), p. 108.

80 By calling the duty of assistance insufficient, I am not rejecting it. Indeed, I have commended Rawls's eventual inclusion of this duty in his international theory ("The Incoherence between Rawls's Theories of Justice," 1759), though I do not see how it could be adopted in his international original position, in which only the interests of liberal and decent peoples are represented, not those of burdened societies.

81 I make the further point that much government borrowing also involves wrongful dispossession, as illegitimate rulers borrow money in the name of "their" country, which the people of this country are then obliged to repay with much interest. See *WPHR* sections 4.9 and 6.3.

82 "The criterial question here is whether the political conditions in the country in question are good enough for it to be possible for the citizens of the country to agree to some regime selling off the country's natural resources" (p. 137); ". . . whether the citizens of a country could possibly consent to their resources being sold off" (p. 142).

83 "Democracy is too strong a value to ground a feasible proposal for reform of international institutions. By Pogge's criterion even the nondemocratic but relatively decent Kuwaiti government, for instance, could not legitimately sell its country's oil to foreigners" (p. 137). Seeing that nearly half of Kuwait's population is denied citizenship along with many basic civil, political, social, economic and cultural human rights, I am not convinced this is quite the definitive *reductio ad absurdum* Wenar takes it to be.

84 This might also be an ordinary law or other legal instrument, e.g., in a state without a written constitution.

85 "This agency should not be another government, or group of governments, as such judgments by governments would often be, and even more often be suspected or accused of being, influenced by self-serving political concerns or by political pressures and incentives" (*WPHR* 162).

86 During the apartheid era, the struggle for divestment gained considerable strength from the evident widespread support it enjoyed among South African blacks.

87 *Realizing Rawls* (Ithaca, NY: Cornell University Press, 1989), pp. 4–5. I have also been consistently critical of the tendency of political philosophers to assume in ideal theory the fantasy of a closed society, thereby ignoring the often dramatic impact of national institutional arrangements upon foreigners (ibid., 256–7). More recently:

> Should not our assessment of alternative feasible designs of the US economic order, say, also take account of its impact on foreigners, on much poorer persons (in Africa and Latin America, for instance)? Theorists typically ignore such questions by stipulating that there are no affected outsiders [footnote omitted]. But this stipulation renders their consensus hollow: The theorists' superficial agreement about a fictional state in which there are no affected outsiders conceals deep disagreements about the real world which would emerge if the stipulation were lifted.

("Can the Capability Approach be Justified?," *Philosophical Topics* 30(2) (2002): 167–228 at 169)

88 See G. A. Cohen: "Where the Action Is: On the Site of Distributive Justice," *Philosophy and Public Affairs* 26 (1997): 3–30.

89 See "Historical Wrongs: The Two Other Domains," in Lukas Meyer (ed.), *Justice in Time: Responding to Historical Injustice* (Baden-Baden: NOMOS, 2004), pp. 117–34.

90 Mathias Risse incorrectly takes me to be making such claims and works to cast doubt on them: "Most historians find colonial rule to have been

inadequate while it lasted, but that does not mean that its legacy, all things considered, continues to impose harm that outweighs technological advances in infrastructure, medicine, and other areas that it brought" (*EIA* 14).

91 This point is further explained at *WPHR* 49–50 and in my *John Rawls: His Life and Theory of Justice*, trans Michelle Kosch (New York: Oxford University Press, 2007), pp. 52–3.

92 As one small step in this direction, I have co-organized a research project aimed at developing new indices of poverty and gender equity. Funded by the Australian Research Council, Oxfam GB, and the International Women's Development Agency, and involving our editor Alison Jaggar as a team member, this project is conducting field work in six poor countries.

93 See www.bls.gov/cps/cpswom2008.pdf (accessed April 4, 2010).

94 See www.census.gov/prod/2009pubs/p60-236.pdf (accessed August 21, 2010), table 1, p. 6.

95 See the World Bank's *World Development Indicators* (*WDI*) website, available only to subscribers. We find there also that the difference in life expectancy between these two regions is 29 years. In the Euro zone, over 88% reach age 65, in sub-Saharan Africa fewer than 44% do. The reference to life expectancy may serve as a reminder that gender and race-based disparities exist in many dimensions – wealth, income, schooling, employment, political participation, personal security, health, life expectancy, self-respect, and others. In the text I focus largely on income, for comparison and illustration.

96 See the related discussion in my "The First UN Millennium Development Goal: A Cause for Celebration?," *Journal of Human Development* 5/3 (2004): 377–97 at 389.

97 Ibid.

Index

to free disposal of national
wealth, 130
human. *See* human rights
to life, 73
to natural resources, 2
negative, 53, 58, 63n5, 64n8,
80–81, 152, 192
to not be harmed, 46, 52
political, 15, 96, 141–44, 225
positive, 58
property. *See* property rights
to security, 63n5, 65n18
to social protection, 77
to subsistence, 58–59, 63n5,
65n18, 76–77
unequal, 156
Risse, Mathias, 41, 43n17, 239n1,
249n90
Rodrik, Dani, 43n16, 240n20
Roosevelt, Eleanor, 142
Rorty, Richard, 92
Rousseau, Jean-Jacques, 202,
245n55
rulers, 3–5, 39–40
authoritarian, 97, 129, 226
dictators, 143
illegitimate, 15, 180, 209,
248n81
oppressive, 5
Parable of the Bad Lords, 29–30
relatively decent, 226
of resource-rich countries, 225
undemocratic, 229
rules, global economic, 147. *See also*
global institutional order
and anarchy, 131, 222
as cause of poverty, 19–41, 175,
179
and dependency theory, 43n21
design of, 189
and differential growth, 32
and domestic institutions, 35–40,
44n30
and gender disparities, 237
and human rights, 184
imposition of, 7, 20

minor modifications to, 7, 19,
105
moral responsibility for, 7, 37, 46.
See also responsibility, moral
on natural resources, 132, 226
and Rawlsian justice, 112
reforms to, 6, 28, 127, 178
rules, social, 158, 198–99, 219, 232
Rwanda, 144
genocide, 71, 73, 125, 207–8

Said, Edward, 163
Salvatore, Ingrid, 41
Sample, Ruth, 161
sanctions, 8, 38, 40, 127, 179
sanitation, 177
Sartre, Jean-Paul, 163
Satz, Debra, 41, 43n17, 194, 239n1
Saudi Arabia, 38, 88, 117, 149n31
savings, 116
segregation, 158
self-determination, 117, 122n45, 130,
137
Shafter, Jonathan, 138–39, 149n22
shelter, 74, 177
Shiffrin, Seana, 41
Shklar, Judith, 92
Shue, Henry, 50, 56, 58–59, 62,
65n18, 202
Sierra Leone, 34, 36, 41, 188
Singapore, 20
Singer, Peter, 55, 58–59, 105–6, 202,
212, 245nn58–59, 248n77
slavery, 155–56, 158, 161, 163–64,
167, 169–70, 207, 233–34, 237,
239n2, 244n48
antislavery movement, 238
Slovic, Paul, 247n69
Smith, Adam, 210
Smith, Rogers, 168
social membership, 49–55, 63n5,
64n7, 192, 197–98
social memory, 17
social science, 7, 21–22, 25, 131,
176, 181, 183, 211, 240n14
social systems, 3, 49, 53, 156, 194